THE DIALECTIC OF DISCOVERY

FRENCH FORUM MONOGRAPHS

50

Editors R.C. LA CHARITÉ and V.A. LA CHARITÉ

THE DIALECTIC OF DISCOVERY

ESSAYS ON THE TEACHING AND INTERPRETATION OF LITERATURE PRESENTED TO LAWRENCE E. HARVEY

EDITED BY
JOHN D. LYONS
AND
NANCY J. VICKERS

FRENCH FORUM, PUBLISHERS
LEXINGTON, KENTUCKY

Library of Congress Catalog Card Number 83-81598

ISBN 0-917058-50-X

Printed in the United States of America

TABLE OF CONTENTS

ACKNOWLEDGMENTS

This volume is the result of the work and kindness of many people. David McLaughlin and Agnar Pytte, president and provost of Dartmouth College, provided both warm encouragement and a generous subvention. The Ramon Guthrie Fund of Dartmouth College covered incidental expenses. Suzanne Coonley handled correspondence and the coordination of manuscripts. The photograph of Lawrence Harvey is by Adrian Bouchard. Mario Specchio's article was translated by Michael Rafter and Carmine Iannaccone and Robert Garapon's article by the editors. The cover design is by Kate Emlen. This whole project has been sustained by the loving care of Sheila Shea Harvey.

J.D.L.
N.J.V.

FOREWORD

Lawrence E. Harvey is, without doubt, one of the preeminent scholars of his generation. His studies of Corneille, of the Renaissance love sonnet, and of the poetry of Samuel Beckett are fundamental for all future work in those fields. Yet, in addition to the sheer brilliance of his scholarship, his career offers the remarkable peculiarity of having been pursued entirely in an undergraduate institution, Dartmouth College.

Large universities with graduate schools are the environment in which the scholar of literature traditionally carries out research and influences the profession at large. Less often noted is the influence exerted on scholars by the institution in which they work. College scholars cannot count on having courses only or primarily in the genre, period, or critical problematic to which they are accustomed. Courses become the solicitation to scholarly discovery, discovery made not in spite of but frequently on account of the naiveté one faces, on account of the uncharted journey that one travels with students who are themselves bound they know not where.

It is in part because of this context that Lawrence E. Harvey's scholarship is unusual in its generic and chronological range—from 17th-century theater he moved to 16th-century poetry, and from there to Samuel Beckett, whose work he was among the first to study with intense scholarly curiosity. The theoretical character of Harvey's work also merits attention. While his approach has always been closely textual, it asks questions that go beyond the simple uncovering of textual structure and coherence towards the range of philosophical inquiry that appears, for instance, in his study of Corneille's *Polyeucte*. Theory in his books and articles is not the criticism of criticism which today frequently monopolizes theories of literature, but rather a reflection on the text itself and the possible models that can be derived from that text. By treating Louise Labé's work, for example, as a model corpus of Renaissance love sonnets, Harvey was able to make all his descriptions of her poems more than commentary or explication; at each step the way was opened towards general concepts that could be applied to other sonnet sequences. All generalizations in turn led back to Labé and enriched his reading of her poetry. The uniting of theory and practice fundamental to this form of criticism permits the scholar to move easily to the classroom and from the classroom. At every moment the critic as teacher must ask: Why should one read this work? Each text becomes a complex of intellectual problems so that the critic is never justified by the texts. Instead the texts justify themselves as readable in the hands of the skilled critic.

Out of this broad and constantly relived initiation into literature, an initiation that is experienced in sympathy with the most naive and fresh readers, come objects of study that are new and untraditional. Although Louise Labé and Samuel Beckett have now become major figures in the literary canon and thus in the university curriculum, when Harvey began his work on them they were either unknown or considered minor. Harvey's criticism, moreover, can be seen as preparing Americans to understand the philosophical orientation of current continental criticism. At the same time it applies to French literary works some of the disciplined formal analysis that was, in the 50's and 60's, not yet widespread in Europe. It is in recognition of his unique and far-reaching contribution that Lawrence E. Harvey's friends, colleagues and former students offer these essays on the teaching and interpretation of literature.

The first articles of this volume appropriately meditate on the role of the teacher as practitioner of literature and rhetoric. Colette Gaudin considers the question "Where are you speaking from?" Through her experience as a philosopher teaching literature, as a French woman teaching in an American university which was, at her arrival, predominantly male, she obtains a perspective on this "place" of the teacher's speaking. She finds, in contemporary French and American classrooms, that the university as institution has become unconscious of what it is doing, providing less ground on which to answer questions about teaching. The emphasis on specialization has destroyed the traditional role of the teacher as ethical example. Noting that "mai '68" was in part motivated by a nostalgia for a teacher-student collaboration in the renewal of society, she finds that unconsciousness is growing, not diminishing.

Neal Oxenhandler, in a fictionalized memoir, addresses the question of values in the classroom from a somewhat different perspective—that of the practice of literary criticism. He describes the privileged moments of Modernism and Existentialism as attempts to rescue the Humanist tradition, stretching back to the Middle Ages and the Renaissance, and he finds that both of these rescue missions failed. The Structuralists with their incapacity to examine their own epistemological basis and the critics of "disvalue" who engage in deconstruction make it even more difficult to link language with any system of values. Yet Oxenhandler gives reasons for qualified optimism in the adventure of the classroom dialectic.

The Renaissance classroom dealt with the concept of presence without deconstructive guilt but with a historical problem paralleling something that Oxenhandler discovered in contemporary students. In teaching Baudelaire to adolescents, he had asked, "Can students eighteen or nineteen years old project their lives forty years into the future?" The difficulty of making sense out of a text which has no direct connection with any experience of the reader is a recurrent problem in all literary teaching. For the Renaissance, this assumed even larger proportions because of the emphasis on translation as mediation between historically different cultures. The classroom became, as Glyn Norton demonstrates with an impressive documentation, the place where presence could be restored through a kind of projection known as *energeia* or *actio*. The triumph of *energeia* would result in the metaphorical dissolution of the classroom and of the written word through the sense of an immediate experience of the spoken word, the projection of the student-imitator into another life. Both Gaudin and Oxenhandler deal with the modern dissipation of *energeia*, a situation which Oxenhandler locates in the conscious attempt to reduce literature to its status as written artifact.

Elias Rivers' vision of teaching resoundingly defies such pessimistic conclusions. Although he evokes a historical evolution from pre-literate poetry to written literature, Rivers sees the classroom as an attempt to recapture the oral interpretive community, a community which is, he maintains, absent from the Western vernacular tradition. Essentially the classroom performance attempts to abolish the diachronic status of the textual tradition in a synchronic, vocal presence. Rivers' hope for the classroom community of interpretation embodies a Humanism penetrated with the energic and active principles of which Norton writes. The gap that it bridges is a historical one that grows when the experiences of the reader cannot correspond in time with those of the writer. It is perhaps more than coincidence that the two texts explicated by Rivers as examples of the necessary closing of gaps are from the 16th and early 17th centuries, from writers who had studied in a Renaissance classroom. After that period, other gaps appear in literature, ones based not on the separation of cultures in time but on the specialization of knowledge.

Hugh Davidson reminds us that this specialization is not only a modern problem, and he provides a lesson in the discipline which all of the preceding articles directly or indirectly invoke: rhetoric. This term, which since the Renaissance has fallen into disfavor and even scorn, is rehabilitated by Davidson as a "comprehensive attitude and discipline" with its own technicality and dignity. As shown by Voltaire's treatment of Newtonian natural philosophy, rhetoric works against the captivity of knowledge within specialization. This example of rhetoric in action reminds us of the civil and moral aspirations of that discipline. One can speculate on the relationship between the situation outlined by Gaudin and the historical episode described by Davidson. It appears that the contemporary institution of the university suffers from a lack of presence which it perpetuates —as one apparently can perpetuate an absence—by ignoring rhetoric or by pretending that it functions in isolation from other disciplines. An implicitly anti-rhetorical rhetoric thus penetrates the university, though clearly not the classrooms of the contributors, who are conscious of the way in which language shaped the community of speakers and readers.

Courtly literature tells a good deal about both literature and learning. In an essay on one of the *novelle* of Matteo Bandello, John Lyons considers the way a literary genre adapts itself to reflect the court. Like the university described by Gaudin, Bandello's court can accept all discussions except those that upset the functioning of the court itself. Bandello's tale can be read as a depiction of the open, almost transparent functioning of the court. But it can also be read as wittily undermining courtly appearances by showing that the most spontaneous and artless form of oral narration is based on studied imitation of books and that the most trusting and passive of courtiers has in fact found an artificial way of containing and hiding his mistrust.

The relation between discourse and the world in Bandello is characterized by a historical shift in attitudes towards reality. The three following articles all deal with the articulation of tradition and literary innovation. Stephen G. Nichols studies the formation of the troubadour canon. Paradoxically, according to Nichols, a later generation of poets constructed this canon by rejecting the works of their precursors. Robert Garapon and Mario Specchio each examine a twentieth-century author in his role as reader of a preceding textual tradition; each demonstrates how distant voices not only echo within present ones but indeed animate them.

The attempt to overcome a textual heritage is also at the center of Judd Hubert's essay. Hubert first underlines the dominant presence of both scholars and scholarly discourse (lectures, lessons, citations, and maxims) in Shakespeare's *Hamlet*; he then stresses that it is precisely the standard curriculum of the Renaissance classroom that must be forgotten before Shakespeare's protagonist can act. Indeed the student-prince promises as much to his father's ghostly apparition. The required action, of course, ultimately depends upon the manipulation of yet another pre-text—a text committed to memory by its players.

Writing, too, is a form of acting, of playing, and Richard Regosin, in turning to the "book and volume" of Montaigne's brain, once more suggests the necessity of clearing "the table of memory" before engaging in any dialectic of self-discovery as ambitious as that recorded in the *Essais*. The rhetoric dutifully learned and copied under the watchful eye of the Renaissance teacher must here be shed in order to free the mind, to allow the exchange between self and other (and other self), between interior and exterior worlds that constitutes truly educative experience. In Regosin's compelling analysis of Montaigne's shift in narrative perspective he reveals a process that erases certain memories and selectively pulls back others, that permits textual and personal experiment, that enables specifically autobiographical *recordation*—not only a recalling but a recording.

James Cox focuses on another personal record, one that literalizes a traditional autobiographical metaphor (life's journey) by relating the seemingly objective story of a voyage that Richard Henry Dana would later describe as "a parenthesis" in the sentence of his life. *Two Years Before the Mast* details Dana's experiences as a nineteen-year-old Harvard student who leaves the classroom for the sea, who sails from Boston around Cape Horn to California and back. Dana's voyage, a time of physical healing and emotional change, also shifts the perspective of the first-person narrator; it throws his previous experience into new focus through the learning processes of the narration itself. The implication of Dana's travels, and of his travel book, extend beyond the personal to the broadly cultural since a dialectic between East and West, between two Americas, between Europe and America is inscribed in them: "California is after all," writes Cox, "the place where European civilization, which has already conquered a primitive civilization, is about to be defeated once again by aggressive Yankee capitalism."

The American instinct for the newness of westering and its implied rejection of the oldness of the East concludes both Elizabeth Harvey's study of Thoreau's "Walking" and this volume. To return eastward to Europe is to retrace footsteps left imprinted in the works of art and literature that form a major part of America's cultural inheritance. To go westward is to forget and alter, once again to clear the "table of memory" in order to permit the creation of new worlds. Harvey demonstrates, however, that Thoreau's American vision would not erase that memory, that heritage, but rather decompose it; it would dissolve the imposing boundaries of the past into a richly fertile swamp, a nourishing literary ground from which new forms and a new identity could emerge.

Colette Gaudin underlined the experience of the European moving westward to America, Elizabeth Harvey that of the American gazing eastward to Europe, and these framing articles point to still other dialectics central to the experience of Lawrence E. Harvey. The essays here offered by those fortunate enough to know him as teacher and colleague bear witness to the extent of his influence both in their diversity and in their insistence on the profound importance of cultural interaction. It is, he has taught us, the responsibility of the teacher of language and literature to animate the classroom with the energies of that dialectic, to perpetuate the process of discovery.

LIST OF MAJOR PUBLICATIONS
BY LAWRENCE E. HARVEY

BOOKS

The Aesthetics of the Renaissance Love Sonnet: An Essay on the Sonnet in the Poetry of Louise Labé. Geneva: Droz, 1962.
Samuel Beckett: Poet and Critic. Princeton: Princeton Univ. Press, 1970.

ARTICLES

"The Denouement of *Mélite* and the Role of the Nourrice." *Modern Language Notes*, 71 (1956), 200-03.

"The Ironic Triumph of Rodolphe." *French Review*, 30 (1956-57), 121-25.

"The Noble and the Comic in Corneille's *La Veuve*." *Symposium*, 10 (1956), 291-95.

"The Cathedral Image in Zola's *La Terre*." *The Explicator*, 15, No. 8 (1957), 1-3.

"The Utopia of Blindness in Gide's *Symphonie pastorale*." *Modern Philology*, 55 (1957-58), 188-97.

"The Cycle Myth in *La Terre* of Zola." *Philological Quarterly*, 38 (1959), 89-95.

"Intellectualism in Corneille: The Symbolism of Proper Names in *La Suivante*." *Symposium*, 13 (1959), 290-93.

"A Poetic Envoi Considered as Art." *Modern Language Notes*, 74 (1959), 118-23.

"Art and the Existential in *En attendant Godot*." *PMLA*, 75 (1960), 137-46.

"Michaux's *Chant de mort*." *The Explicator*, 20, No. 1 (1961), 1-5.

"Corneille's *Horace*: A Study in Tragic and Artistic Ambivalence." In *Studies in Seventeenth-Century French Literature*. Ed. Jean-Jacques Demorest. Ithaca: Cornell Univ. Press, 1962, pp. 65-97.

"Samuel Beckett: Initiation du poète." *La Revue des Lettres Modernes*, No. 100 (1964), pp. 153-68.

"Samuel Beckett on Life, Art, and Criticism." *Modern Language Notes*, 80 (1965), 545-62.

"The Role of Emulation in Corneille's *Polyeucte*." *PMLA*, 82 (1967), 314-24.

"Art and Nothingness in *Antigone* and *Ondine*." *L'Esprit Créateur*, 9 (1969), 128-45.

"A Poet's Initiation." In *Samuel Beckett Now: Critical Approaches to His Novels, Poetry and Plays*. Ed. Melvin J. Friedman. Chicago and London: Univ. of Chicago Press, 1970, pp. 171-84.

REVIEWS

Rev. of *La poesía di Joachim Du Bellay*, by Guido Saba. *Modern Language Notes*, 78 (1963), 546-50.

Rev. of *Molière and the Comedy of Intellect*, by J.D. Hubert. *L'Esprit Créateur*, 3 (1963), 46-48.

Rev. of *Corneille: His Heroes and Their Worlds*, by Robert J. Nelson. *Modern Language Notes*, 82 (1967), 371-79.

Rev. of *Samuel Beckett. A Collection of Critical Essays*, ed. Martin Esslin. *Modern Language Journal*, 51 (1967), 500-03.

Colette Gaudin

The Teacher at the Crossroads

To be others, to be oneself. To use a shared
language, in the hope that it is one's own.
Catherine Clément

At the time of May '68, a new question was heard in the classrroms of
French universities, disconcerting more than one professor: "Where are
you speaking from?" Even if teachers must always be ready to explain
what they are talking about and to define *how* they are saying it, they can
scarcely reply directly or simply to someone who calls into question the
origin of their discourse. One possible reply would be, "I talk because *I*
know and because I am authorized to do so." Some professors tried this,
thus confirming in their students' eyes their image as "petty and threatened gods who feed on the students' passivity."[1] Another response would
be to answer with a question, since, after all, the fact that students are
listening also plays a part in the problem of pedagogical discourse. Jean-
François Lyotard attempted this approach at Vincennes several years after
May '68: "What are they here for? One day you posed the question seriously to the class. They told you that it was their business, not yours."[2]
Does this mean that the question "Where are you speaking from?" is pertinent only in an atmosphere of confrontation and that it simply disappears
when the peaceful division of labor separating knowing from not knowing
is reestablished? I think not, not only because there are echoes of this
question in the many current debates about teaching, but also because
this question evokes the three elements—speech, place and person—whose
interrelation has always marked the paradoxical place of the teacher.

It is not a question of conflating place and function (the latter has long been the object of contradictory value judgments within teaching), but rather of examining a particular *lieu de parole*. Since Foucault, this expression has come to mean a combination of procedures of selection and exclusion which conditions both the object of discourse and the image of the group to which one speaks. Today it is widely recognized not only that the teacher's discourse is shaped by the constraints of knowledge, but also that knowledge itself is formed and transmitted in institutional circuits which limit and particularize it while giving it the appearance of universality. We now possess the basic theoretical elements for a demystification of the "fictitious universalism" propagated by institutions of learning.[3] But these institutions, as places of discourse, are complex. In this article I would like to study how teachers situate and at the same time displace themselves in relation to the various forces which converge in the classroom.

The Teacher

I myself find it difficult to determine my present place other than by giving an account of where I have been. It might be enough to say that, although I am a French woman, I teach French language and literature in an American university. At one level it is very simple: "sent" by the Ministère de l'Education Nationale, I am part of what France still calls "the cultural mission." But my geographic displacement is coupled with a change of discipline, since I have moved from philosophy, which I taught for several years in France, to literature. Moreover, as a woman, I have followed an itinerary that resists simple description. I was trained to speak as a neuter witness of a universal culture—i.e., to say "we" with the philosophers. In the early sixties, when I found myself isolated in an American university environment which was exclusively masculine, there was no doubt as to my place. I represented something foreign but at the same time essential for cultural polyphony. My cultural exoticism hid and to a certain extent erased—for me as well as for others—the fact that I deviated from the accepted norm and gender of the school. As a result, I was blind to the fact that my status as a woman was only barely tolerated, and I assumed that the accommodation I experienced was a sign of the full professional acceptance to which I was accustomed. When other women were hired, I fortunately lost my status as an exception. The development of feminist thought, as well as changes in philosophy in general, led me gradually to think about my differences outside the framework of an abstract egalitarianism and to reconsider my whole professional position.

To say that I work inside one culture (American) by teaching the product of another (French) would give a static image of my position. It would ignore the dialogic practice of teaching, the evolving (dis)connection of these two cultures and the constant crisscrossing of difference. Sometimes students themselves will suggest this static image to me by expecting me to offer them an intuitive knowledge of French reality—as if I were for them what a Bororo tribesman is for an ethnographer. I must explain to them that my knowledge is as historically mediated as their own, that, moreover, I do not have a privileged or all-encompassing perspective merely by virtue of my distance from France. Such a situation is not unique to the uprooted intellectual. Is it not the situation of any teacher—perhaps more specifically in the humanities—to the extent that he or she must dispel, while occupying the place of the Master, the illusion of mastering meaning? When the heuristic procedures consist of pluralizing, deferring or distancing meaning, the journey ceases to be a metaphor of access to intellectual life, or, as Descartes described it, the outward sweep at the end of which one returns to the "chez soi" of thought. It becomes a voyage without limit or pole, similar to the image of "drifting"—the end of the true journey announced by Lévi-Strauss.[4]

Teaching, however, remains firmly associated with images of stability and continuity. Inasmuch as the teacher is seen as the guardian and transmitter of a tradition, the school can be "fantasized" as a protected and privileged space: ivory tower for the scholar, threshold to adult culture for the student. Although this representation is constantly threatened and contradicted from within and from without, it shows a surprising persistence. In analyzing both its inadequacies and its resilience, I would like to suggest that a more fitting image of the contemporary school is perhaps that of a "crossroads"—a place of encounter and momentary repose where two figures of knowledge and ignorance meet with the impossible desire to *know* each other's true origin and direction.

What Is Teaching?

Teaching as we generally understand it has several dimensions that intersect: institutional, intellectual and pedagogical.

It is widely acknowledged, at least in the Western world, that introducing young people to the values and techniques of a society should be an organized social effort. The "institution" is the visible manifestation of this social aim. In the United States this word is generally used to indicate the concrete reality and the organization of a particular school or university.

In France, however, the term is used in the singular with very different connotations. It conveys the long-standing idea of centralization which attaches each limb and organ to a single *body* (the teaching body, the body of magistrates, etc.). It is well known that the institution of French education is marked by its clerical origins as well as by Napoleon's paramilitary organization. American institutions, on the other hand—what we call *academia* at the university level—are less monolithic than their French counterparts and are linked more directly with cultural movements of the moment. Yet they also regulate what is said in the "free and open" classrooms through a network of selection, exclusion and control.[5]

It is essential not to view the institution, French or American, simply as a seat of power which exerts its force from a position outside the classroom inward to direct the scene of teaching. For the institution itself must be perceived as subject to other forces which are both exterior and interior to it (its educational policies, the socioeconomic status of the population, to name a few) and which work as a hidden mechanism governing the functioning and the efficacy of the institution. These forces may be compared to an unconscious which mediates the dynamics of knowledge within the classroom and whose presence is "repressed" by those wishing to maintain the illusion of a "teaching scene" independent of all political and economic constraints. It is, therefore, the institution itself that functions as an unconscious within the classroom. Its manifest role becomes purely organizational and exterior to knowledge; it consists in segmenting the entire educational system, establishing clear chronological and hierarchical distinctions. These distinctions are felt within the classroom and reflected in both the teacher's and the student's attitude towards knowledge. The notion of an independent culture is, thus, a fantasy. It is a fantasy, however, which arises periodically, whether it be in the form of "humanism," as it was denounced by Sartre and Foucault, or in the form of the transcendent "scientific community" imagined by Bachelard.[6]

Since antiquity, culture and society have been intimately linked. In his book *Histoire de l'éducation dans l'Antiquité*,[7] Henry Marrou illustrates this by relating the birth of the humanist tradition of teaching among the Greeks to their enterprise of colonization. He shows that *paideia*—too often translated simply as "pedagogy"—means not only "to educate," but also "to civilize." Humanist education for the Greeks was to a certain extent a method for assuring the cohesion of the Empire.[8]

I have not explicitly mentioned pedagogy. Yet the questions raised by classroom teaching must obviously enter into any discussion about the nature and transmission of culture. Ideally, pedagogy is linked to the structure of knowledge. Its methods of explanation and of exercise should be guided by the internal logic of each discipline (*l'ordre des raisons*). But pedagogy, like knowledge, is inseparable from the historicity of culture and from the policies and politics of the institution. For example, one could raise many preliminary questions related to teaching the grammar of a language. To what extent should one analyze rules? Should one use a synchronic or a diachronic perspective? What sample of the language should one consider the norm? Should one accept, as a linguistic given, that masculine pronouns, in certain cases, refer to both genders? And so forth.[9] Moreover, pedagogy is not just a technique for transmitting knowledge; it also has an interpersonal dimension represented by the relationship between teacher and pupil.

As the ethical pact which underlies education erodes, and as knowledge loses its unity, the influence of the teacher as a model and as a spiritual guide becomes problematic. And yet this ideal of the teacher's role reappears at a time and place where one would least expect it: as one of the demands of the students in May '68. For, while they disputed the position of authority assumed by specialists, the students also wanted their teachers to be more than mere "technicians of practical knowledge." In their appeals urging professors to join them against the institution, one perceives a yearning for culture as a "shared quest." Manifest in their revolutionary zeal is the paradoxical dream of restoring the position of the university as the guiding force of both intellectual and social transformation.

Michel de Certeau, who has analyzed at length the condition and the operation of the school in contemporary society, shows that the situation has evolved in a direction exactly contrary to what the students wanted. Schools no longer have a privileged position in the distribution of culture, and culture is no longer viewed as the center of orthodoxy: "Teaching wavers between two alternate poles: whether to turn strictly towards knowledge (which a good initiation into psychology will let you convey), or to enter with the students, through force or seduction, into a tug-of-war (thus reducing scientific discourse to some kind of metaphor)."[10]

The parallel between "force" and "seduction" is not so paradoxical as it might seem. In both there is an ellipsis of the process by which knowledge is acquired. The first oppresses knowledge under the authority of an institutional position. As for seduction, it has "no need for proof," as Jean Baudrillard says, for "everyone knows that charm operates within the immediate reverberation of signs—there is no intervening time, no time allowed first for the sign and then for its interpretation.... Charm is always something like annunciation and prophecy, the kind of discourse whose symbolic power comes neither from interpretation nor from belief."[11] Baudrillard criticizes Foucault's analysis of the effects of power inherent in

discourse and in knowledge by reproaching him for remaining too positiv-
istic in regard to power and for not risking the hypothesis that power is
always based on a simulation. "Since Machiavelli, political leaders have
always known, somehow, that the source of power is in the mastery of
a *simulated* space, that politics is not a real function or a real space."[12]
One might reinterpret the pedagogical arena in this perspective. It seems
as if, since knowledge and power are made impalpable by the very fact of
their diffusion, the school proposes an ideal theater where their conjunc-
tion can be reenacted. Hence, we have the attempts to fall back either on
that phantom of knowledge which we call "culture for its own sake"—with
the accompanying nostalgia for a strong power that alone can maintain
such a possibility—or on the seductive teaching styles capable of drawing
students towards this culture.

Perhaps we should stop trying to think of these three elements (the
content of teaching, the techniques of transmission, and their institutional
framework) as if they were a cohesive structure and as if changing one of
them would be sufficient to reform the process of education in its entirety.[13] As Derrida says, the ways (*trajets*) in which the political objectives
are transmitted within the school's apparatus are "not always 'representa-
ble' precisely because, by nature, they are not representative and because
they are not of the order of conscious manipulation and reflection."[14]
What does it mean, then, to be and to function in this place whose topol-
ogy escapes a global representation?

Where Are We Speaking?

Among the different components which constitute the general field we
call teaching, one constant emerges: discourse (*parole*).[15] Let us examine
this discourse as it functions in the environment circumscribed by the
school.

To teach: "to show how to do something."[16] This is the first definition
given by the dictionary, followed by "to give instructions to." These definitions reduce the role attributed to speech and emphasize the transmission
of a skill. Depending on the subjects taught, the teacher will, thus, be
expected to furnish either a model of performance or an explanatory discourse. But whether it be dancing, driving an automobile, or geometry,
showing and demonstrating are not often purely visual gestures. When the
subject taught is more purely linguistic, on the other hand, one could consider the teacher's speech as a model of performance like others: a model
of good French or of a good *explication de texte*; this amounts to making
language an instrument exemplifying a pre-established norm. Etymology

indicates that the Greek verb meaning "to show" (*deiknumi*) has the same Indo-European origin as Latin *dicere* and that the English words *teach* and *token* have a root in common with Latin *signum*. These remarks point to the double semiotic structure of the teacher's language: it is a sign of a sign, or a signifier to the second degree. In this respect, this language is no farther from its primary object—text, knowledge or technique—than in the language of any interpreter, be it a literary critic, judge or lawyer. Its specificity, however, lies in that it takes place in a school, a place of transmission and repetition.

Yet teachers are not necessarily "rehearsal managers" or drill instructors (*répétiteurs*).[17] As teachers, we know how to elicit student participation in the process of understanding and discovery. The school encourages us to do so, to provoke new questions and to explore new ways of thinking. But how far can one go? Who or what stops the momentum of a critical mind? As Derrida asks, is it not precisely the reproduction of self-criticism in philosophy which forms "the basic element of philosophic tradition and preservation?"[18] While the very texts which ground tradition are always capable of engendering critical thought, the moment this thought becomes a pedagogical exercise it is confined within the walls of the school. "No one discusses and no one plots against the school," says Alain.[19] In a way, it is true that we take the school for granted. But the acceptance or the absence of plotting is perhaps the most subtle ploy for neutralizing or naturalizing this imaginary space which is both protected and protective.

When the philosopher Jean Guitton was a prisoner in Germany in 1940, he immediately saw an opportunity to transform his captivity into a spiritual retreat. But it was in his capacity as a professor that he was able to profit from his enforced leisure, as he says in the preface to his book, *Regards sur la pensée française: Leçons de captivité*.[20] He places his work under the aegis of the famous passage in Descartes:

I was then in Germany, where I had gone because of these wars that are not yet finished; and, as I was returning to the army from the coronation of the emperor, the onset of winter left me in quarters where, not finding any entertaining conversation and fortunately having no cares or passions to bother me, I would stay all day shut up in a heated room, at perfect leisure to devote myself to my thoughts.[21]

Despite the apparent similarity of Guitton's and Descartes's situations, it is the difference of their undertakings which seems to me essential. They share neither the same moment of thought nor the same intention. Instead of a movement towards the *cogito*, Guitton's "lesson" features a return towards tradition based on a *cogito* already assured; his discourse is the exposition and the interpretation of a common heritage presented as a "tableau." Rather than illustrating a moment of philosophical meditation, this example offers us a model of the "ideal" classroom—a place where both teacher and student are captives, equally distant from the upheavals of contemporary history. Both reply, through the exercise of their individual liberty, to the gesture of the institution which invites them to forget the walls of the school as well as what is happening outside. By distinguishing Descartes and Guitton, I am not attempting to oppose the practice of philosophy to the teaching of philosophy, for the problematics of teaching is always inscribed in philosophy. I merely wanted to indicate how the school itself hides the problem and fosters the illusion that philosophizing and teaching are *naturally* the same thing.[22]

At the other extreme, the legendary figure of Socrates, which haunts teachers, offers the model of teaching without walls or bars. It is said that Socrates philosophized anywhere and with anyone. All places and all audiences were equally good for the exercise of a discourse that was itself its own foundation. Socrates represents the freedom of breaking into speech, of making truths arise, and such an act does not have to be enclosed in a definite place. As Jean-Luc Nancy said about the teaching of philosophy, "before the established right to categorize, there is the right, which was never established, to 'agorize,' to begin to speak in the public forum." And further, "the intention to speak is not only the intention to speak *about* (it is not even primarily this . . .), but also, necessarily, the intention to speak *to*."[23] Certainly the image of the public forum seems totally divorced from the reality of the classroom. But we can recognize that this image corresponds to a profound desire to speak out and, thus, to restore that dimension of teaching which precedes any institution.

Discourse as an act of speech, whether of the teacher or of the student, represents a chance for each to reenact the first moment of discovery. There is also a desire not to begin, but to enter right away into the pure openness of speech. Foucault speaks of this desire at the beginning of his inaugural lesson at the Collège de France, adding: "instead of being the person from whom this speech comes, I would be, as it unfolds, but a slender gap, the point of its possible disappearance."[24] No wish could be further from the reality of teaching. Foucault himself treats it with a haughty rhetorical irony. After all, he is giving a "lesson."

All these tensions reflect the drama of the teacher's presence as a physical part of the corps of teachers within a given space. Ambivalent attitudes towards the school as a place correspond to the ambiguity of the "order of discourse" which both permits and restricts speech. In May '68, for example, very few teachers accepted the fact that the police (the forces of law and order) had come to defend their freedom of speech. Indeed, it was the violation of the university's "extraterritoriality" that made many teachers join forces with the students. The students themselves wavered considerably when they tried to define the university as a space. Some of them demanded that the university's *autonomy* be assured as a guarantee of the freedom of thought "outside of the restrictions of time"; others called for permanent criticism of this "make-believe autonomy," always in danger of being recuperated by those in power; a third group of students, the most utopian, dreamed of a world in which school and society would be totally coextensive.[25]

School is, therefore, a place both difficult to define within its borders and difficult to relate to what is beyond those borders. One wonders, however, if there are no particular experiences that might permit us, in some way, to become conscious of these very limits and to define them.

How to Become a Teacher

To become a doctor, you study medicine; to become an engineer, you study engineering. There is no similar pattern for becoming a university teacher. One might study psychology or sociology, but this would merely be an addendum to the core of knowledge one acquires before passing it on to one's students. As the French say, one "enters teaching." It would be more accurate to say that one never leaves it. One only moves from one side of the desk to the other, revealing the illusory nature of this accepted division.

In the chapter of *Tristes Tropiques* entitled "How I Became an Anthropologist," Lévi-Strauss, who believes that anthropology is "one of the rare authentic vocations," describes how the ritual repetition of the classroom triggered in him a need to flee towards cultural and geographic difference. Since, for him, teaching is itself a flight from direct action towards the security of repetition, he finds a similarity between the anthropologist and the teacher, both of whom turn away from the immediate demands of their social group.

Besides disciplines that lead towards "specific" careers, continues Lévi-Strauss, there are the others, the arts and sciences, which lead only to teaching and to research:

The student who chooses them does not say good-bye to the world of childhood: on the contrary—he hopes to remain behind in it. Teaching is, after all, the only way in which grown-ups can stay on at school. Those who read letters or the sciences are characterized by resistance to the demands of the group. Like members, almost, of some monastic order they tend to turn more and more in upon themselves. . . . Teaching and research have nothing in common, as they see it, with apprenticeship to a profession. Their splendours reside, as do also their miseries, in their being a refuge, on the one hand, or a mission, on the other.[26]

However, *mission* and *refuge* are not in contradiction. After all, should not one have the assurance of a truth, of a symbolic *chez-soi*, to orient one's mission? The work of missionaries consists in opening up to others the circle that encloses the initiate. But missionaries must also be able to return to the mother-house to renew their spiritual forces in order to avoid being absorbed by the Other or becoming "strangers in their own land" (to borrow Descartes's own expression). In the same way, teachers come back to their books, to their research, within the periphery of their discipline, in order to distribute afterwards the fruit of their work. But this parable is too transparent.

On the one hand, recent shake-ups in philosophy have created uncertainty in the strategies used to disseminate truth. On the other hand, the university in France is no longer a place that nurtures future intellectuals; students see it, rather, as a breeding ground for the unemployed, and they look at times with envy or even resentment at their professors who enjoy a measure of security. Why, then, do they persist in taking "unproductive" courses in a place that has become, as one student said in 1978, the site of the "impossible rendezvous"?[27] This same student maintained, paradoxically, that he was still attached to the dream of a culture "that someday, miraculously, would assume some significance in the eyes of society." His dream is of a utopia or fantasy world and in this respect differs radically from the American theme of "relevance." But what this student says also constitutes a bitter denunciation of the inconsistent world the university has become. The student himself, in order to get some pleasure ("what I am doing is of no use; it's just for kicks"), must always look "elsewhere," "là où ça invente" ("where it's happening"), towards the great "marginal" authors not taught in school.

Part of the problem is that the boundaries separating the "inside" of the institution from the "outside" have become blurred and that those on the inside, those who continue to exercise the privilege of speech, do not necessarily notice this. It seems that the more the university turns in on itself, away from the outside world which makes it uneasy, the more it loses its inwardness. The university is not truly *in* society, because it only gives out worthless diplomas. Yet it has not succeeded in accepting its marginality.[28]

Whatever one does, school continues to divide an outside from an inside. The crisis of the university in its many forms revolves around the difficulty of connecting the scholastic and the social worlds. On both sides of the Atlantic, teachers react in two ways to this crisis: either defensively, by reworking certain aspects of traditional teaching practices, or aggressively, by rethinking their teaching practices in ways that go beyond the mere refinement of traditional pedagogical methods and curricula.

Much could be said about the defensive response to this threat of dislocation. One could analyze, for instance, the history of the teaching of philosophy in France as an example of the fate of a besieged discipline. (This history has many points in common with that of the "liberal arts" in the United States.) Once celebrated as the culminating moment of a secondary education, the teaching of philosophy shrank little by little, first as a consequence of the expansion of natural and social sciences and, more recently, under restrictive governmental decisions.[29] To the extent that the university constitutes a single body or corps (corporation), it defends itself like an organism. Various biological images have been used to describe the different reforms and adjustments made from within the institution. One hears of bringing in "new blood," of reinforcing the "healthy parts," of eliminating "dead cells," of avoiding "self-mutilation," etc. But there are also reactions that one could compare to the defense mechanism Freud calls displacement.[30] Sometimes, in trying to defend a traditional discipline against accusations of being "old-fashioned" or "dogmatic," professors unwittingly undermine the integrity of the very discipline they intended to preserve by shifting its focus towards subjects that are more stylish or intellectually more accessible. The eclecticism of philosophy in France and the first attempts at interdisciplinary studies often represented slippages of this order. As Althusser said, "philosophy created its own psychology, its own social sciences, in order to contemplate its own existence and its own dignity."[31] I agree that displacement and defense are at times necessary. But, since any defensive reaction always reproduces the logic of the opponent, its relation to its source must be analyzed. In the fifties, for instance, the displacement of the teaching of philosophy towards the social sciences could be interpreted as a "symptom" of the reluctance—or the inability?— of those in the field to reformulate truly philosophical questions in the light of new developments. In such a climate of insecurity, one essential aspect of the teaching project, namely, the reaffirmation of the discipline, is, thus, neglected.

Other reactions to the present crisis of the school in society have since emerged. Rather than being purely defensive, these responses indicate a desire to affirm the possibility of teaching within the present cultural context. Such transformations appear in attempts that are necessarily limited at the beginning, but that may have some chance to spread. In France, for example, some critics and philosophers are putting into practice what theory has already formulated about texts, namely, that they are not the containers of thought, but, according to Heidegger's expression, bearers of "unthought." Henri Meschonic thus defines the orientation of a "talmudic seminar" as opposed to an "authoritarian seminar":

My work is a theoretical quest, with what one knows in what one doesn't know. . . .
Right from the start [I want] to lead the 'beginner' into the historicity of contradictions, of strategies, of non-certainties. Not to make beginners secure, because to make
secure, to conciliate, is to sterilize the relationship to knowledge and to turn the students into non-selves. But to work towards recognizing orientations, to situate oneself
and to situate others.[32]

Recent developments in curricula in the United States, including such
programs as Women's Studies, Afro-American Studies and Native American
Studies, represent attempts to explore new orientations towards knowledge.
Women's Studies are an examplary case of a new field born in the margins
of the institution and attempting to make a place for itself within its confines. As it is a nascent discipline, teaching and research tend to be more
closely linked than in most other fields. What is said in the classroom (by
students as well as teachers) has an immediate effect on the direction and
content of research. At the same time, Women's Studies are marked by the
necessity to "situate oneself and to situate others," a necessity that incorporates both the theoretical and the concrete aspects of the question of
female otherness as it confronts the "sameness" defined and reified by the
institution and traditional culture. Finally, the interest of this example is
that Women's Studies, while emphasizing dialogue and creating a new style
of collective work, still retain the more traditional dialectic methods necessary for dispensing information. This last point seems crucial to me if we
wish to avoid the erroneous associations that often link innovative pedagogy with the absence of hierarchy and that portray didactic teaching as
an inherently repressive activity.

From what we have seen, asking why the university is crumbling and
trying to rebuild its decaying structure is no longer the most fruitful
approach for understanding the institution of education as it exists today.
A more beneficial approach is to examine what precisely is being done
within the confines of the school at the very moment its legitimacy is
being questioned. Such an examination, as I have indicated, reveals several
paradoxes which, rather than marking an impasse in our ability to understand the institution, in fact suggest a new perspective and a new place
from which to view it. While teachers, for example, are not merely impersonal agents transmitting to their students knowledge of a culture, they are
at the same time prevented from speaking in a totally personal voice as
individuals distinct from the institutions. And, whereas teachers by definition function within the confines of the classroom, they are simultaneously
led to speak as if the classroom has receded into the background, their discourse effectively masking the power of the institution. Finally, if by the

very nature of intellectual life, teachers are engaged in a continuous critical process, they must also assume a position of relative mastery for the duration of each lesson.

Teachers, then, can never simultaneously occupy the three places held by the institution, their discipline and their individual situation. The teacher who believes that he or she can truly occupy any one of these positions is living an illusion. It would be vain, of course, to believe that unveiling this illusion will reveal the "truth" of the teacher's place and function. For, ultimately, the only place left for the teacher is a place without place—a place defined by a constant displacement.

An example of this very situation is the woman teacher who decides to speak in the classroom as a woman about women, but who should know that in doing so she is, in relation to the institution, already out of place. Perhaps one additional contribution of Women's Studies will be to look beyond the place of woman in history, literature, society, etc., to the place of woman as questioner of her own place as teacher. The woman in the classroom, thus, finds herself at a crossroads with the possibility of embarking in a new direction—one which would save her from repeating the error of Laius, whose blind belief in his right of way led to his death, and of Oedipus, whose deluded knowledge of his place left him blind.

NOTES

1. Quoted by Alain Schnapp and Pierre Vidal-Naquet, *Journal de la Cummune étudiante: Textes et documents: Novembre 67-juin 68* (Paris: Seuil, 1969), p. 17.

2. Jean-François Lyotard, "L'Endurance et la profession," *Critique*, No. 369 (February 1978), 198.

3. Michel de Certeau, *La Culture au pluriel* (Paris: 10/18, 1974), p. 267.

4. *Tristes Tropiques*, trans. John Russel (New York: Criterion Books, 1961), pp. 45 ff.

5. See Antoine Prost, "De quelques problèmes universitaires en France et aux Etats-Unis," *Esprit* (February 1970), pp. 286-302.

6. *Le Rationalisme appliqué* (Paris: P.U.F., 1962).

7. *Histoire de l'éducation dans l'Antiquité* (Paris: Seuil, 1948), pp. 14 ff. and 145.

8. Another example of the politicization of teaching is the preservation of Latin within the curricular reorganization enacted by the Third Republic in 19th-century France. Alongside such new subjects as experimental sciences and modern history, this apparent anachronism was retained as a way of privileging the texts of ancient Rome and, thus, reinforcing French republican feeling against the menace of the German Empire.

9. See Jean Dubois and Joseph Sumpf, "Un Modèle d'enseignement du français: Analyse linguistique des rapports d'agrégation et du CAPES," *Langue Française*, 5 (1970), 27-44, in which the authors expose the presuppositions directing the exam-

iners' judgment: *"The pedagogical act is a discourse*, and the professor asks his students in turn to proffer a discourse on the text studied, that is to say, to develop a paraphrase on the paradigms of 'man' and 'truth' " (p. 44).

10. *La Culture au pluriel*, p. 146.

11. *De la séduction* (Paris: Galilée, 1979), p. 106.

12. Ibid., p. 93.

13. It seems that, in the United States, most of the studies devoted to the question of education and its reform focus on pedagogy, be it from a sociological, phenomenological or existentialist point of view. The teacher is often described as a "manager of classroom learning" and, as such, occupies a central place in the socio-cultural environment of the school. It is the student, then, who appears as a "stranger" with regard to culture and who must be brought into it through appropriate pedagogical techniques. See, for instance, Clinton Collins, "The Multiple Realities of Schooling," in *Existentialism and Phenomenology in Education*, ed. David Denton (New York: Teachers College Press, Columbia University, 1976), pp. 139-55.

14. "Ja, ou le faux-bond," *Digraphes*, 11 (1977), 110.

15. Speech or discourse: "Concrete manifestation of the language in which must be taken into account not only the linguistic elements, but also the circumstances of their production" (Tzvetan Todorov, *Symbolisme et interprétation* [Paris: Seuil, 1978], p. 9).

16. *Webster's New Twentieth Century Dictionary* (New York: William Collins, Publishers, 1980), p. 1870.

17. *Répétiteurs*, traditionally charged with drilling students between classes, no longer exist in French schools. Ironically, it is only in one of the most prestigious institutions, the Ecole Normale de la Rue d'Ulm, that the title of *répétiteur* has survived—although the function is different—to designate the lower rank in the professorial hierarchy.

18. "Où commence et comment finit un corps enseignant," in *Politiques de la philosophie*, ed. Dominique Grisoni (Paris: Grasset, 1976), p. 62.

19. *Propos* (Paris: N.R.F. Pléiade, 1956), p. 1281.

20. (Paris: Beauchesne, 1958).

21. Quoted by Guitton, p. 11.

22. For a recent reformulation of this problem, see "Avant-projet pour la construction d'un Groupe de Recherches sur l'Enseignement Philosophique (GREPH)," in *Politiques de la philosophie*, pp. 90-91, see also n. 23.

23. "La Détermination philosophique," *Esprit*, No. 50 (1981), 77.

24. *L'Ordre du discours* (Paris: Gallimard, 1971), pp. 7-8. See also "La Pensée du dehors," *Critique*, No. 229 (1966), 523-46. In this article Foucault describes the orientation of speaking ("la pente du 'je parle' ") as a movement of distanciation and dispersion of signs in opposition to the interiority of the *cogito*.

25. *Journal de la Commune étudiante*, esp. pp. 718-24.

26. *Tristes Tropiques*, p. 46.

27. "Toujours ailleurs," in *Université, fécondité d'une crise?*, *Esprit*, Nos. 23-24 (1978), 188.

28. The example of Vincennes, a branch of the University of Paris created after 1968, would be interesting to examine in this respect. See, for example, *Université, fécondité d'une crise?* See also the testimony of J.-F. Lyotard concerning the teaching of philosophy at Vincennes, "L'Endurance et la profession."

29. The ongoing crisis in the teaching of philosophy in France is reflected in the intense debates reported in *Revue de l'Enseignement Philosophique* since the early

fifties. See also Jean-François Revel, *Pourquoi des philosophes* (Paris: Julliard, 1957); François Chatelet, *La Philosophie des professeurs* (Paris: 10/18, 1970); and *Etats-Généraux de la philosophie* (Paris: Flammarion, 1979).

30. See the definition given by Laplanche at Pontalis, *The Language of Psychoanalysis*, trans. Donald Nicholson-Smith (New York: Norton, 1973), pp. 121-23.

31. "Philosophie et sciences humaines," *Revue de l'Enseignement Philosophique*, 13, No. 5 (1963), 4.

32. "Enseignement, séminaire," in *Université, fécondité d'une crise?*, pp. 184-85.

Neal Oxenhandler

Reflections on Literature and Value

> Comment donc poser la valeur d'un texte? . . .
> Notre évaluation ne peut être liée qu'à une pra-
> tique et cette pratique est celle de l'écriture. Il
> y a d'un côté ce qu'il est possible d'écrire et de
> l'autre ce qu'il n'est plus possible d'écrire . . . .
> quels textes accepterais-je d'écrire (de ré-écrire),
> de désirer, d'avancer comme une force dans ce
> monde qui est le mien?
>
> Roland Barthes, *S/Z*

Throughout history reading has implied value. For the ancient Greeks *aretē* (valor) was embodied in the Homeric epics. The *Iliad* and the *Odyssey* were revered not only for their transmission of ethical values, but also because they reflected the will of the gods. No high civilization has survived without sacred texts around which subsequent works unfold, as Dante's *Commedia* echoes and interprets the Bible and the writings of classical antiquity.

The very use of language seems to be value-generating, whether language be used for representation or production (as in the value theory expressed by Roland Barthes). The large proportion of our literature which is based on a theory of imitation gives poetic "pleasure" directly through recognition and more subtly through a kind of proxy stimulation of the reader's senses and imagination. Even if we demur at a theory of imitation, it is difficult to negate the view that human consciousness is mediated by language: "In order to be who we are, we human beings remain committed to and within the being of language, and can never step out of it and look at it from somewhere else." In Heidegger's view, language is value-creating—it is the very "house of Being."[1]

The quotation from Barthes signals an important shift in critical theory, one which casts the critic in a role coequal with that of the poet. This view coincides with the current belief that the principal subject of literature is literature and/or language; whatever the merits of this view, it has made the teaching of literature immeasurably more difficult.

Looking back over thirty years of teaching, I find that the struggle to demonstrate some connection between reading and the meaning of life has been the challenge and criterion for my success or failure as a teacher. Yet the process of communicating value has usually been implicit, marked by almost random success or failure—assuming (not always the case) that I knew what success or failure might be. Together with the relief I feel in realizing that I have not practiced indoctrination, there is some dismay. Alongside the relatively few students with whom there came a spark of genuine intimacy, there were the many who performed the necessary calisthenics and moved on, the only awareness on both sides being that some more essential awareness was lacking. I console myself by thinking that learning is a gift, dependent on the play of affinities. To whom we give and from whom we take often depends on things beyond our control.

I have decided to go back, in a kind of fictionalized memoir, and put the question of when and how value was communicated in my classes.

Twenty-nine years ago, I was a teaching assistant at Yale. I had been given a language course with a literature component and found myself facing twenty Yale undergraduates with the text of Baudelaire's "Le Balcon" in my hand.

I have looked at an essay which I wrote following that class.[2] Its main concern is with the psychological implications of the poem. These are elaborated conceptually around a central metaphor. I was pleased to realize that my article had been created through interaction with two students in my class, Robert and Tonio. They had asked the questions that pushed us day by day towards an interpretation of the poem.

I began the class with the usual remarks about the poet's life. In the case of Baudelaire, poetry had been the counterpart of a life of poverty, alcoholism and mental suffering. Most of the students were satisfied with the perfect justice of this fable.

But Robert and Tonio, who had taken an English course with one of our better new critics, demanded that I turn to the text. Here is the first stanza:

> Mère des souvenirs, maîtresse des maîtresses,
> O toi, tous mes plaisirs! ô toi, tous mes devoirs!
> Tu te rappelleras la beauté des caresses,
> La douceur du foyer et le charme des soirs,
> Mère des souvenirs, maîtresse des maîtresses![3]

Robert asked, "Whom is the poet addressing? If it's his mistress, Jeanne Duval, why does he call her mother?" And Tonio: "What does the use of the future tense in the verb 'rappelleras' have to do with the experience being reported? Why does the poem move from future to past to present and back to future again?"

Although these questions were considered "technical" by the rest of the class, I recognized them as central to understanding the poem. I was committed to the belief that the poem had unity on the levels of emotion and of structure. With the help of Tonio's and Robert's questions, I was able to begin to focus on the "experience" that the poem conveyed.

This approach would be dismissed today as mimetic or representational. Yet even back in 1952 I was aware that the experience is neither described nor enacted in the poem. It is mediated by the poem's language, given in a way by its very absence. Only the absent woman, the absent passion can be suggested by the presence of language.

Robert had read novels and knew that authors often spent pages describing their characters. But in "Le Balcon" the poet's mistress is suggested only by the vaguest of expressions: "Mère des souvenirs, maîtresse des maîtresses." I replied that the precision of poetic language was different from that of the realistic prose he had referred to. By the adjustment of image, rhythm and poetic thought, the poet created a simulacrum of the experience in us. I used the term *harmonie imitative*, not wholly aware of the long tradition of debate over the question of the "motivation" of the poetic sign. As we understand today, the "scientific" position which states that the sign is purely arbitrary is undercut by another view, one first stated in the *Cratylus* of Plato, which sees the poet's task as the creation of a fundamental, if mythical bond between words and things. As Gérard Genette has shown, the mythical status of the ikonic aspect of language appears as nostalgia for a "*lost* linguistic paradise or *linguistic* utopia" in the poetic practice of Mallarmé and the poetics of Valéry.[4]

Tonio mentioned that one thing clearly suggested (if not described) was the apartment and the attached balcony. I added that Baudelaire had changed hotels five times in the year 1855, trying to avoid his creditors. In 1856 he settled in the Hôtel Lauzun on the Ile Saint-Louis, and it was there that he probably wrote the poem, Jeanne Duval being absent as a result of one of their numerous quarrels.

Robert saw this information as interesting, but incidental, since it was not contained in the poem. Tonio insisted, however, that a sense of place was essential to the poem and gave it its structural unity. We puzzled over this, trying to construct scenarios for the poet and his mistress, trying to reproduce their movements at various times in and out of the apartment.

We began to see that the apartment was indeed the focus of the poem. The shifts in verb tenses gave the poem a quality of desperation concealed by its calm surface. The poet seemed to be trying to escape from time. Not only are there shifts in time, but there are also shifts in the poet's mode of address to his mistress: he sees her as Muse, Mother, concubine, sister and, above all, as bringer of memories.

As the sense of the poem's movement within a confined place grew, we began to see that the balcony functions as a symbol. It is first presented as the place where the lovers step, after the physical act of love, to gaze reflectively at night falling over the city. Then little by little it becomes the meditative act itself, it becomes poetry.

By the end of this session, although we did not understand the poem in a coherent way, we had begun to share an experience that came to us through the poem. It seemed to combine in a dramatic form sexual desire, a sense of loss and an almost desperate will to believe in the power of poetry.

A few days later we returned to the poem for the last time. It had made its way in our minds, more in Tonio's than anybody else's.

"We know that the poet is standing on the balcony, remembering the ecstacy of making love with Jeanne. But the tone is very calm, almost depressed. There's an element of threat—he says her breath is 'poison.' In the next line he sees night thickening in front of him like a wall."

The other students were listening. So was I.

"Then for a stanza he tries to reassure himself. He brags about what a great poet he is. But it's not enough. Then . . . ." He hesitated, looked up. "I don't understand the last stanza. He sounds like he's terrified, but I don't know why."

Can students eighteen or nineteen years old project their lives forty years into the future? Can they understand disease, impotency, death? Here is the last stanza of Baudelaire's poem:

> Ces serments, ces parfums, ces baisers infinis,
> Renaîtront-ils d'un gouffre interdit à nos sondes,
> Comme montent au ciel les soleils rajeunis
> Après s'être lavés au fond des mers profondes?
> —O serments! ô parfums! ô baisers infinis!

I hesitated to explain the stanza. Finally, I asked if any of them had wondered if the sun would stop rising every morning.

"But it's 'suns' in the plural," Robert objected.

It's all the suns of our lives. Always renewed by sleep, a kind of purifying innocence. For how many years can each one of us count on its continuing to rise?

In the fullness of their physical and erotic worth, these Yale students caught a glimpse of their own temporality.

Value is given not only by its affirmation, but also by its limits. By following the trajectory of a poem, we were led to the experience of value.

As an infantry soldier in Germany, I had learned a lot about survival. Nothing about value. There was nothing for which I was ready to die.

After the war, at the University of Chicago Robert M. Hutchins assured us that contemplation, the life of the mind, was the only value for a civilized man. I wanted passionately to become a contemplator of works of intellect and of art, but I wouldn't have died for them. The notion of value seemed to recur, but it was something you argued or wrote about. Perhaps, if you were a genius, you lived for some value such as beauty or truth. But who would be crazy enough to die for them? Even Galileo had conceded to force.

In 1952, when I began work on my Ph.D. at Yale, I was fascinated by French existentialism. At first, I couldn't separate the cultural brouhaha from the enterprise itself. Finally I realized that Sartre and the others were involved in a heroic attempt to renew the basic values of Western humanism. They were trying to build a new philosophical basis for freedom, justice, authenticity. It was a rescue mission that failed.

Camus, less enthralled by his own language than Sartre, asked the fundamental question in his book *Le Mythe de Sisyphe*. How is it possible to give meaning to life? What value keeps us from suicide? His answer was the famous appeal to imagination (or was it faith?). Against all evidence, we must believe that life has a purpose. Whatever Camus's purpose might have been, he did not live to find it. On January 4, 1960, his head was crushed against a tree on Route Nationale 7. The only purpose was Michel Gallimard's rush to get to Paris in his new sports car.

When I began teaching, first at Yale and then at U.C.L.A., my approach to literature had been enriched, but had not fundamentally changed. It was most severely tested by three years of collaboration with my friend Robert Nelson. We were in the process of putting together a large anthology of French literature. Nelson, already a theorist, challenged my approach, which remained that of studying tropes of poems in function of an emotional or psychological matrix.

In the fifties and into the sixties, our capital as specialists in 20th-century literature was modernism. I had spent the year 1948-1949 at the Sorbonne, studying under the G.I. Bill. Food was still rationed and memories of the

Occupation fresh. But how overwhelming the cultural life of that period! You could see Jouvet's revival of Giraudoux's *Ondine* or Barrault's of *Le Soulier de satin*. There were exhibits of new works by Picasso and Matisse. You could catch a glimpse of Sartre or De Beauvoir around Saint-Germain-des-Prés. I attended the first postwar showing of Bunuel's *L'Age d'or* at the Cinémathèque and sat on the floor under the screen next to André Breton.

Through modernism and its long twilight we were able to teach literature as the direct mediator of value. Some form of mimetic realism, however qualified, made this possible. Modernist literature was rooted in life. Joyce's Dublin in *Ulysses* is the *eidos* of a real city, based on the maps and directory Joyce carried with him during his long exile. Picasso never painted without some image to give impetus to his imagination. Gide's *Les Faux-Monnayeurs* plays with multiple realities only to affirm their co-existence. Proust, though imbued with Symbolist idealism, insists that value is accessible in concrete experience transformed by art.

Critics at mid-century had seen modernism as a revolutionary movement. Now, some thirty years later, we realize that it was not the beginning of a wholly new concept of the arts. Instead, it was the final flowering of a classical esthetic that goes back to the late Middle Ages and the Renaissance. The key terms of this esthetic are truth and beauty. Modernist mirrorings, breakings, transpositions of forms are always done in the name of truth and beauty, however these terms may be refracted.

Modernism challenges the reader or spectator, but it always respects him, thus following the basic precepts for engaging the reader laid down in 17th-century poetry manuals. Modernism demands co-creation of the work by poet and reader, painter and viewer. For all these reasons and more, modernism is not some kind of beachhead for an invasion that never happened. It is the culmination of a tremendous impulse that played itself out. Modernism, for those of us fortunate to have lived through it, attained in the brief years of the *entre-deux-guerres* a summit point of social, perceptual and spiritual integration. But in 1945, after the end of World War II, for all its richness modernism was exhausted. Existentialism made its rescue attempt and failed. But, as Rimbaud put it, there were other "horrible workers" ready to step in and take their place. We in the 1950s, still going strong with our "masterpieces" and our "great writers," did not realize that in France new modes of thought were being shaped. They were based on restudy of the works of Marx, Freud, Nietzsche and Heidegger. Although the structuralists were continuing the critique of Western culture that their forerunners had made, the possibility of their effecting social change seemed remote. But from the start they transformed our modes of thinking, especially about literature.

In the winter of 1981 I was working with four Dartmouth students in a course on literary criticism. They were French majors. Several, who were seniors, had already decided to go on to graduate school.

We began by studying some recent criticism, ending with several members of the Geneva school. Through the study of Georges Poulet and Jean-Pierre Richard, my students were able to give a precise contour to the term "realism," which poisons so many discussions of literature.

They saw that the text is encountered in consciousness and nowhere else. Whatever we choose to call "real" occurs in the mind and is conditioned by everything the mind brings to the knowing process: its biography, its various horizons, its preconceptions, its beliefs. All these elements contribute to the formation of a system of conventions. Hence, "realism" is no more than the acceptance of a certain set of conventions which happen to coincide with the way a given group of people see the world at a given time.

I went on to show them that structuralism in its early stages had been a version of what Edmond Husserl called "naïve realism." It used the old Cartesian distinction between subject and object. Signifier and signified were seen as mental figments placed over and against the external or "referential" order.

Other structuralists moved towards total separation of signifier and signified. They implied that there was no reality beyond language. This type of neo-nominalism gives up the hard struggle to validate knowledge or to incorporate in some adequate way the intrusive, but necessary external order. Nominalistic structuralism produced some truly delirious works of fiction and criticism. I showed some of this work to my students to remind them that criticism must aim for some kind of truth and that truth must be not merely self-referential, but contextual.

In the historical overview that I was proposing to my students, I suggested that structuralism was in many ways the true revolution that modernism had not been. Through its spin-offs into different disciplines, structuralism attacked Western society and thought on both the macro-level of institutions and the micro-level of language. It was an approach that was deeply hostile to the values that were assumed to sustain our civilization.

Literary structuralism attacked mimesis or representation, which it saw as far more than a mere literary convention. Mimesis was based on a system of educational nurture whereby signs were permanently attached to signifieds which were coded into systems of established value. A child's ego-formation consisted of his or her internalization of a system of power relations. Literature was the extension of these power relations back and forward into history.

There was a vast amount of material accumulated under the structuralism/post-structuralism rubric. We could only scratch the surface, using as our sourcebook *Textual Strategies* by Josué V. Harari. My aim was to show that any form of thought is self-limiting. There is no single system that can account for the totality of a poem. I wanted to demonstrate also that literature was value-bearing in a more complete way than criticism. The distinction between them was not, as a distinguished critic had written, "delusive." Literature carried the values while criticism discerned them, validated them or disputed them.

Barthes's distinction between "work and text" was subtle and convincing. It was the beginning of a lexical curettage that radically changed the teaching of literature. The notion of "work" had allowed us to single out masterpieces as paradigms of excellence, hence privileged vehicles for the transmission of value. By what criteria did one now decide which books were worth teaching? Barthes's own formula, the "writability" of the text, produces a radical skewing of the traditional value position. The text is valued for its usefulness to the critic. In Barthes's view, the text takes its value from the degree to which I can use it "as a force within this world which is my own." Under such a dispensation the notion of the text as a repository of cultural values is bound to fail.

After the disappearance of the work came the disappearance of the author, argued in Foucault's essay in the Harari anthology. My own work in psychoanalytic theory had convinced me that the historical author is not recoverable. Yet the notion of an authorial "presence" cannot be wholly abandoned, as certain deconstructionists demand. Rather, it remains one of the text's horizons, a limiting boundary towards which criticism must be directed, but beyond which it cannot go. I remain convinced that there is a "consciousness" not so much behind as *within* the words of the text. This consciousness or voice or presence is not merely a metaphor and not merely "the initiator of a chain of signification." To Foucault's question, "What difference does it make who is speaking?" I would answer that the difference is precisely in the speaking; the poem's language carries the indelible voice-print of its absent creator.

I tried to overcome my students' initial aversion to the abstractness of structuralist language. At the same time, I turned their attention to some of the vulnerabilities of structuralism. One of these was the kind of truth-value one could get from it. Structuralism presented itself as a kind of radical doubt. It turned this doubt upon language itself, thus suspending or bracketing the very instrument of inquiry. The unexamined Cartesianism of much structuralist writing formed only a shaky alliance with its skeptical posture. Hence, the arguments that were put forward could lead at best to tentative conclusions. In general, structuralist thought lacked the rigor necessary to question its own foundations, in the way that had been done by British analytic philosophy.

There was a subversive strain in structuralism, but most of its practitioners were paper tigers. The gurus of structuralism traveled around the world analyzing texts, not preaching revolutions. They believed that social change would take place in the civilized countries through the work of critical intelligence. Meanwhile, they undermined our linguistic conditioning by teaching us word games and deconditioning our automatic mental behavior. The linguistic revolution is with us. The cultural and social consequences are still to be tallied.

We had studied theory. Now it was time to put the theory to work. I chose stanza three from the fifth Canto of Lautréamont's *Les Chants de Maldoror*.[5] I liked the violence of the text and its flagrant obscurity. In this passage, Maldoror, hero and narrator of the work, describes his struggle to refuse sleep. He is like the mountain climber or the channel swimmer, someone who assumes a gratuitous task. He risks his life for no apparent reason.

The students reported on the text over a period of several weeks. The first to present his view was a student who had used Foucault's essay on the author to examine the identity of Ducasse/Lautréamont. He was able to show that, despite the mythical biographies invented by critics and archivists, the author of this text is unrecoverable. Almost nothing is known about Isidore Ducasse, the young Frenchman from Montevideo.

But the text remains unattributable for purely textual reasons. Among these are the constant shifts in tone and register. The student gave as an example the heavy latinity of the first line, a parody of Moliéresque medicine. This gives way to several deceptively simple statements: "Qu'il lève la main . . . ," "Qu'il redresse la tête . . . ." The didactic tone reminds us that painful experiences of the Tarbes *lycée* are still close in time. There is also an echo of the New Testament command "Let him who is without sin among you cast the first stone." This ploy, which involves casting back the sin on the accuser, is a frequent device of that great sinner and rhetorician, Maldoror.

The text is a series of rhetorical boxes, parodies containing other parodies, leading always to a regress that annihilates the "meanings" of the text while seeming to generate them. The dandyism of "sur le satin de mon front" conveys a grimace of self-deprecation which continues until interrupted by the ruthless slaughter of frogs by voracious herons and flamingos. The alternation between the abstract (spirit) and the concrete (voracious birds, tropical wetlands) sets one of the rhythms of the text.

The studied self-punishment of the stanza defines a pose of bravado tinctured with self-pity. Buried under his pseudonyms, Lautréamont/Maldoror becomes a juncture of mid-19th-century rhetorics. Reinvented by the Surrealists fifty years later, he became yet another avatar of the *poète maudit*, prophet and priest. Yet this conventional literary typification does not make Ducasse/Lautréamont recoverable. The problem of the poet's identity led us to a consideration of history itself.

We once believed that history was easy to teach. History was not merely anchored to wars, natural catastrophes, the rise and fall of kings—it *was* these events. Only slowly, as we grew aware of our own historicity, did we realize that the historical sense was a complex form of awareness that one could attain only by fits and starts, something never wholly graspable once and for all. We taught literature in order to convey the mind and mores of an epoch, yet we realized that stories have a way of abolishing history by the fact of their repetition. They anchor us to some transhistorical dimension, itself an ultimate value.

If the signs of the text both reveal and conceal history, they do the same for the presence of the author. In every text the author is both absent and present—absent in his biographical or empirical reality, present as a foretokened horizon, a voice at once both full and empty. We would return frequently during the entire course to this perplexing question of the author's status.

Another student read the text from the viewpoint of myth. Since she was of Hindu extraction, she knew myth by experience. Her experience did not coincide, however, with the theories she found in Jung, Eliade and Lévi-Strauss. What she found was that the text did not embody any theory. Instead, it aspired directly to the status of myth. This was apparent in the repetitions of formal patterns and in the inventory of divine/demonic beings. Once again, the question of history arose. Myth seemed to be yet another way of abolishing history.

A student named Jacques decided to look at the stanza intertextually. We agreed that the intertext would probably be a passage from Romanticism which would contain the same semantic matrix as the text from Lautréamont.

While there were several kernel phrases in the text on which we agreed, Jacques stood his ground against the rest of the class and myself. He saw the principal semantic matrix as having to do with nature, being in fact a reversal of the normal Romantic celebration of plants, animals and the like. He insisted that the revulsion inspired by the frogs, herons and flamingos which abound in the poem indicates conversion of a normal Romantic topos. The rest of us, on the other hand, found the matrix in the hero's refusal to sleep.

While the students researched their reports I reread *Les Chants* with an emotion equally composed of tedium and pleasure. The tedium came from the obsessional quality of the book, the endless repetition of sado-masochistic fantasies making use of devices such as exaggeration, homeric simile, *mise en abyme*; protrope or exhortation within the lengthy period sentences emphasizes the archaic flavor of these schoolboy parodies. Yet my pleasure in *Les Chants* was equally real, arising from the discovery of a complete fictional world. It is the same discovery that one makes, on a larger scale, in Tasso or in *Don Quixote*. Everything is grounded in imagination, all traces of representation expunged in favor of a wholly productive use of language. References to Lautréamont's life (as in my remark on p. 40 about memories of the *lycée*) serve rather to reveal the critic's insecurities than to "explain" the text. Just as in the *Gerusalemme liberata* or the *Quixote*, there is a perfectly articulated rhetorical system combined with high fantasy and unusual precision in the control of language.

The question of value may seem remote from this project. Thinking back, I find that value was involved simply in our willingness to invest effort in a critical method that was not only difficult, but in some respects also hostile to our personal values. Even more important, though, was the question of what we took poetry to be. Would we be convinced that, as structuralism had it, poems were simply signifying structures? The theory of intertextuality showed how sign systems interpenetrate and regenerate each other. A system of disvalue (later codified as "deconstruction") is· brought to bear on prior uses of poetry, beginning with the invalidation of "mimesis" and the skepticism attached to "interpretation." The notion of "mimesis" is narrowed to "significance," and the rebirth of the critical spirit is consecrated by the prevalence of the deconstructive method, which aims at reading the text as some form of fundamental contradiction. Whatever the validity of these approaches (and they can provide extraordinary insight), the overall effect is to kill the poem's ability to produce an emotional response. Professional critics are not interested in the emotional response, which is both transient and largely beyond analysis. I tried to make a cautious statement about the choice of a critical method. I suggested that one could not argue for any particular kind of heuristic procedure as being necessary preparation for the act of reading. Criticism, considered not as a profession, but simply as a preparation for reading, could serve in many ways to make the poem available to the reader. And yet there was evidence that poems could be effective even for readers who had only a vague knowledge of the language in which the poem was written. As evidence for this assertion, I read the class several pages by Jacques Lusseyran, the blind poet and Resistance fighter who recounted how poetry had served as a survival value for the prisoners of Buchenwald.[6]

We argued Jacques's theory of the text which he supported by quotations from Romantic nature poetry. The class disagreed. Finally, we decided that any interpretation of the poem must unite two semantic kernels: (1) the hero's boast that he never sleeps and (2) the punishments he must endure for this apparent transgression.

The connection between the two kernels then became obvious. It was based on the cliché "God never sleeps." Maldoror considers God his supreme enemy. Here he assumes one of the divine attributes. First resisted, then willingly assumed, it is his chosen destiny: "C'est moi qui l'ai voulu; que nul ne soit accusé." Maldoror props his eyelids apart with splinters, somewhat like what is done to the sinister hero of *A Clockwork Orange*.

The first intertext suggested by the searing stare is the eye image in Hugo's "La Conscience." Lautréamont's text is a reversal of the Hugolian intertext. It is God's eye that tracks Cain, the infamous murderer who is a worthy progenitor for Maldoror: "Il vit un œil tout grand ouvert dans les ténèbres, / Et qui le regardait fixement."[7] In our text it is Maldoror who stares back at God, repaying the "curiosité farouche du Céleste Bandit." By his self-imposed discipline, he resists "le Grand Objet Extérieur." He is unlike other mortals, who by night fall victim to this horrible brain surgeon: ". . . oh! voir son intellect entre les sacrilèges / mains d'un étranger. Un implacable scalpel en scrute / les broussailles, épaisses."

The torments that Maldoror undergoes during his insomnia are violent and horrible, caused not only by lack of sleep, but also by guilt at having usurped the divine role. Too proud to admit it, he suffers what Hugo called "conscience." Like Milton's Satan or Goethe's Faust, Maldoror has chosen freedom over obedience. Like them, he is willing to pay the price.

Hugo had a god-complex equal, if not superior to that of Lautréamont, but he never allowed it to disturb his serenity. But then, Hugo's God is not the personal God of Lautréamont. Like the Brahman of Hinduism, he is in all things and everywhere: "Monde noir qui te tais et qui dors! Dieu se lève. / Ombre! il est le regard; sommeil! il est le rêve; / Silence, il est la voix!"[8]

I asked the students to wait until we had done a little more textual analysis before we asked any more interpretative questions: Why does Maldoror hate God? What does God represent here? In continuing with the text, we found that each sentence developed, through the use of exaggeration,[9] the long and delectable amplification of each rhetorical unit to a point of excess where the form outran the meaning. Each sentence changed in mid-career, as in the following long sentence which begins with the impersonal "il m'arrive," then shifts to the imperative "sachez," then returns at the end to the impersonal with "c'est ma volonté":

Cependant, il m'arrive de rêver, mais sans perdre un seul instant le vivace sentiment de ma personnalité et la libre faculté de me mouvoir: sachez que le cauchemar qui se cache dans les angles phosphoriques de l'ombre, la fièvre qui palpe mon visage avec son moignon, chaque animal impur qui dresse sa griffe sanglante, eh bien, c'est ma volonté qui, pour donner un aliment stable à son activité perpétuelle, les fait tourner en rond.

In the sentence quoted above, he makes an apparent concession. But it is no more than a feint designed to distract the reader, whom he is trying to convince of his divine insomnia. He then gives a sampling of his dreams, images that emerge in a kind of mechanical parade till cut off by the urgency to return to his argument.

The speaker has shown us these images, which constitute a weakness, only to prove his strength of will. Several logics support this strategy. Psychoanalysis is familiar with a process, the repetition compulsion, by which the subject takes over suffering inflicted from without and assumes responsibility for it. The motive for this is to avoid passive suffering, which is intolerable. Hence Lautréamont's assertion that he alone is responsible for his nightmares.

In his study of modern mythologies, Roland Barthes has spoken of a process by which one admits a small failure, which is then made to function as a "vaccination." Maldoror's hallucinations are the weakened strains of virus that innoculate him against sleep.

In general and throughout the entire work, the use of images is controled by rhetorical urgency.

Having done our close analysis, we tried to look at the text in a broader context. It was possible to see a multitude of connections, backwards and forwards in time. So the Sadean obsession with the mechanics of torture is energized by the rhetorical machinery of Romanticism. The obsession with God as "thief of energies" coincides with the violent deicide of Lautréamont's contemporaries, Nietzsche and Rimbaud. The fall into abjection anticipates Kafka, Genet, Burroughs.

It was a relief, after the constraints of even our modest intertextual study, to allow free play again to the belief in representationalism, to acknowledge that texts are full of flotsam and jetsam, accretions from everyday life. Voices in the street, the color of a wall, the odor of a park or a latrine, the roar of the sea. Lautréamont is no realist, and any evocations of Montevideo, of Tarbes or of Paris are not only disguised, but also irretrievable. Yet the impulse to mimetic reading is not merely a reprehensible tic; it is the acknowledgement of our link with the poet as denizens of the same world, as pilgrims through the same history.

As we isolated fragments of discourse, we made connections with other voices, other circumstances. We allowed ourselves yet another of the critic's naïve dreams, the belief in unity. I suggested that Baudelaire's notion of "correspondances" among things and our ideas of those things were yet another return to the unity that is argued against in the *Cratylus*. The impulse to connect and the impulse to break play through all literature. Early structuralism, with its dream of systematization, gave way to a second generation of critics, who looked for the breaks and fissures in texts, the multiplication of voices and points of view. Lautréamont's satanic pathos conceals both desire and dread of breaking the order of things.

We concluded with a digression on the theme of power, seen as a subtext in *Les Chants*. Foucault and Lacan were right in their insistence that the text tells us something about power relations. Lautréamont created his Maldoror as a Prometheus who protests against life as a system of constraints. Who is "le Céleste Bandit," if not the great power broker, God himself? All our life he molds our psyche not merely when we are awake, but far more powerfully when we sleep. In the passivity of sleep, the pulsions and the defenses of the unconscious are rearranged like so many molecules.

Maldoror is a mirror image of his great predecessor, Don Quixote. His dedication to a career of crime is every bit as absolute as Quixote's dedication to chivalry. In both cases the consequences of their deeds are unpredictable, with Quixote's occasional blunder into wrong-doing symmetrical with Maldoror's occasional expression of compassion or generosity.

There is no final answer to Barthes's question, "How, then, pose the value of a text?" The text *is* the value; otherwise, it would never have survived. The reverence that we accord to the works in our keeping acknowledges value without making it explicit. We once were priests; later, legislators; later still, humanists; today many are content to be umpires of linguistic games. The job of the teacher-critic is not to teach value, but to let value reveal itself. How this happens will vary endlessly. We must continue to allow this to happen; if the splinters slip and our eyes shut even for a blink, we may find that civilization has gone by.

NOTES

1. Martin Heidegger, *On the Way to Language* (New York: Harper and Row, 1971), pp. 134, 135.

2. Neal Oxenhandler, "The Balcony of Charles Baudelaire," *Yale French Studies*, No. 9 (Spring 1952), 56-62.

3. Charles Baudelaire, *Oeuvres complètes*, Bibliothèque de la Pléiade (Paris: Gallimard, 1961), p. 34.

    4. In the words of Josué V. Harari, Genette provides "a typology of Cratylism" broad enough to include not only Mallarmé and Valéry, but also Claudel, Sartre, Proust and Jakobson. Josué V. Harari, *Textual Strategies* (Ithaca: Cornell Univ. Press, 1979), p. 66.

    5. Lautréamont, *Les Chants de Maldoror*, in *Oeuvres complètes*, Bibliothèque de la Pléiade (Paris: Gallimard, 1970), pp. 195-98.

    6. Jacques Lusseyran, *Le monde commence aujourd'hui* (Paris: La Table Ronde, 1959), pp. 115-33.

    7. Victor Hugo, "La Conscience," from *La Légende des siècles*, in *Oeuvres*, vol. I, Bibliothèque de la Pléiade (Paris: Gallimard, 1950), p. 25.

    8. Victor Hugo, *Dieu, l'océan d'en haut* (Paris: Nizet, 1960), p. 146.

    9. Michael Riffaterre's essay on Lautréamont (also in the Harari anthology) provided an analytic model for the study of linguistic clichés and their variants.

Glyn P. Norton

Images of Transfigured Space:
The Inflections of Energy in the Renaissance Classroom

Language, Wilhelm von Humboldt once asserted, is a gesture of *energeia*, "a continual intellectual effort to make the articulated sound capable of expressing thought,"[1] its reality borne not in the emptiness of graphological or typographical alignments and surfaces, but in the moment of speech becoming thought. By the 19th century, both term and concept were, of course, nothing new, already belonging to an ancient tradition that assigned to words powers of sacrament and substitution. What, in fact, Humboldt was alluding to as an act of thought and articulation had its origins in rhetorical theory, where *energeia* and its paronym, *enargeia*, had long described the capacity of language to effect qualitative and quantitative changes in reality, or the perception thereof. In other words, any process of articulation is predicated on the mind's urge to connect, to seek out metaphorical affinities and ratios. In *Rhetoric* (1412[a]), for instance, Aristotle discovers in Homeric language "active" metaphors (or *energeias*) that represent everything "as moving and living; and activity is movement." For Demetrius, in his treatise *On Style, energeias* are similarly invoked as foci of action, units charged with portative force and displacement fundamental to the term *translatio* in Latin rhetoric.[2] A battle, Demetrius imagines, "shivers" and is brought to life through the animism of Homeric style. As readers, we experience a figurative migration from space once inhabited by the text, tabular and typographical, to space that seems at once transformed, able to encompass us in a fullness transcending linguistic structures.

In Renaissance settings, perhaps the most vivid reminder of Demetrius' "shivering" battle occurs in Rabelais's well-known episode of the Frozen

Words (*Quart Livre*, 15-16). Again, it is a question here of an epic battle reformulated through the tactile, animizing commodities of language, and again Rabelais, like Demetrius before him, refers to Aristotle's text on Homeric *energeias*, where words are perceived as "voltigeantes, volantes, movantes et par conséquent animées."[3] Later, in the Temple of the Divine Bottle (*Cinquiesme Livre*, 38-40), the more visually oriented notion of *enargeia* dramatizes a similar moment of spatial epiphany, the Pantagruelists drawn beyond the cubic limits of a room into the lived-in presence of still another epic battle.[4] The point is that language and thought have the capacity to transform our very sense of space, to engage in what I.A. Richards called a *delegated efficacy* "exerting the powers of what is not there."[5] And, on the most primal level, it is the power of rhetoric to be translative, to replenish and delegate the absent moment, that makes it a living repertory of energy. In a sense, then, rhetoric labors in the rewriting and re-creation of a textual past, whether through imitation or translation, and it is the attempt by Renaissance teachers and theorists to articulate these energic states that brings the student, like Rabelais's Pantagruelists, into his own theater of textual and intramural relationships.

In his *Thesaurus Graecae Linguae*, Henri Estienne, the great 16th-century Hellenist, calls attention to the activating, almost displacing force concealed by the term *energeia*, along with its Latin synonym, *actio*. This basic meaning, especially as it relates to the oral production of speech, appears validated in several early settings and definitions. At the entry for *energeia* in his *Dictionarium* (1502), Calepinus draws on a passage in Saint Jerome where "the activity (*actus*) of the living voice" is said to harbor a "latent *energeia*."[6] A practical dimension to this notion had already surfaced among the reforms of the University of Paris in 1452, with the Regent Teachers admonished to recite their lessons *ore proprio* to their pupils; likewise, on that occasion, Saint Jerome's text is adduced as the authority.[7] By the early 16th century, the Patristic text seems sufficiently commonplace to appear unattributed in a revealing passage from Jacopo di Porcia's *De generosa liberorum educatione*: "For just as the living voice has a certain latent *energeia*, penetrating more effectively the heart of the listener than those things which are read; so also fame inheres more tenaciously in living men and inflames [children] more urgently to virtue than in dead men."[8] What is new here is the way the Patristic reference in the first half of the passage, already a metaphor for speech, finds itself articulating a second figurative relationship directly proportional to the first. The same passing of vital spirit into words projected orally to a listener likewise expresses the parallel force of a living moral example. In dead men fame lies congealed, much as do words on the surface of the text. *Energeia*

is thereby caught up in the deeper revitalizing spirit of Renaissance pedagogy, the classroom transformed into a place in which thought and language
are both activated as agents of motion and displacement.

This notion of an animized classroom space where children are infected
by a transcendent presence quickly becomes the defining feature of *energeia*. Even images of the text itself are not immune from this development.
An early anonymous translation of Ovid claims that the "énergie" of Homer
passes to the child through a form of nocturnal osmosis, with book replacing pillow.[9] Similar qualities, according to Coelius Curio's *Schola* (1555),
are clearly among the interests of poetry. In a remarkable description of
this process, Curio makes specific reference to Aristotle and stresses the
innate pleasure of children in poetic harmony and imitation. Appropriately,
the entire passage is centered around a definition of *energeia*:

> There are in words qualities that are either proper or figurative, lofty, sublime and
> brilliant. They have the material of vast powers, the admirable force of feeling which
> is called *energeia*. They breathe with a certain great and lofty spirit, as if they are
> themselves blown out, so that they even seem to rise above the comprehension of
> their own substance and natural qualities.[10]

No longer is it a question here of the sonic ascendancy of spoken word
over written text, but of writing that undoes its own texture, the reflexes
of pen becoming those of breath. This eradication of scriptural surface in
favor of an aerial, pulmonary space into which words are "blown," like so
many iridescent bubbles, recalls precisely Aristotelian settings of *energeia*.
Curio, however, provides a special added insight into this process, suggesting that words are able "to rise above the comprehension of their own substance and natural qualities." In language, he seems to be saying, there are
often disproportionate gaps between the word as a lexical artifact, dense,
consolidated into the mass of all its possible glosses, and the word in its
capacity to transcend that density, to be etherealized. Energic language is,
by definition, buoyant language, able to jettison the encumbrance of mass
that seems otherwise bent on restricting it to non-poetic expression. The
impelling force behind this buoyancy is, of course, the mind, that organ
which first conceptualizes "the admirable force of feeling" called *energeia*.
Later on, Joannes Sturmius, the Strasbourg schoolmaster, builds on this
concept in *De imitatione* (1574).

Like Curio's, Sturmius' subject is imitation. In his scholia on Chapter
III, he first asks "what kind of mind we should require in the imitator"[11]
He then concludes that such a mind develops largely through a special tem-
perament (*natura bona*) composed, in turn, of three successive steps: the
first is that of ability (*facultas*), latently present "in the cradle," but per-
ceptible early on in children; the second, which "reveals itself in school,"

is that of *energeia*; the third is that of memory. It is the second, however, that emerges as the crucial element in the child imitator's formation. *Energeia*, along with its Latin analogues, *actio* and *efficacia*, is defined as a quality of effort and zeal, the desire for learning and, ultimately, a sign that *euphuia*, or *natura bona*, "is living, not mute."[12] In the cradle and in infancy, Sturmius repeats, *energeia* and its various forms remain previously silent, but "begin to unfold and reveal themselves in school."[13] Within the classroom, a new vitality takes over, making possible the mind's easy apprehension of all that is uttered by the Master.[14]

Taken in their entirety, the insights of Di Porcia, Curio and Sturmius all localize the classroom as the creative epicenter of *energeia*. It is the place in which reserves of muteness, whether the unvoiced capacities of speech, the blank moral slate of the child or his untested vigors of mind, are each compelled to speak and to speak, no doubt, as one. Words are made to levitate, bodies inflamed by the brilliance of exemplary living flesh, and minds invigorated with the force of thought and inquiry; in short, an Aristotelian progress of life being brought to fulfillment. *Energeia*, so conceived, is an intensification of every living fiber of the child, his projects of action, speech and thought. As such, the term appears central to the concept of imitation, not as a sterile textual exercise, but as a process or revival, the text becoming the negative on which an image has been refracted through the imitator's own transfused being.

The implications for the term *energeia*, used in this broadly versatile way, now become more apparent. In one sense, it may be seen as a metaphor for the way in which the classroom and its occupants are thought to be destabilized. The walls are thrown back, the contained, opaque space of life *intra muros* made somehow translucent by an aggression of imitated forms. Just as the confines of Rabelais's temple seem to dissolve into a pictural horizon, so imitation implies an ability to bring into the classroom, into the text itself, the distant reaches of historically and physically remote expression. From this perspective, there thus emerges a plan of cross-reference, enabling Renaissance thinkers to infer connections between something that happens within the larger intramural space of the classroom, within the performer and his own text, and, on occasion, within the resonance of the Master's voice. It is in the very complexity of these cross-references that one begins to glimpse the potential overlap between the energic paronyms, the one (*enargeia*) dramatizing a level of pictural fulfillment, the other (*energeia*) a totally revitalized space.[15]

Despite Erasmus' lucid account of *enargeia* in the *De copia*, there is little evidence that the work's wide influence on pedagogical techniques helped deter the ensuing lexical confusion.[16] In a treatise popular early on in France, the English humanist Thomas Linacre defines *energeia* as a grammatical device in which the present tense is thought to create, in prose and poetry, an effect of immediacy, "as if we seek to display and place the subject (*res*) in front of our eyes."[17] Traditional associations of the other paronym, *enargeia*, with features of narrative presentation suggest that Linacre has transposed the terms in the above passage, for it is not so much poetic vitality as visual impact that appears to be at stake. In the case of *emphasis*, a common synonym for *enargeia*, a later commentary on Erasmus' *De constructione* is no less problematic. *Emphasis*, the commentator insists, occurs when less is said and more understood, as when Dontaus describes the entry of "power" and "meaning" into the pronoun.[18] "What is *emphasis*?" asks Maturinus Samuel later on in the *Elementaria principia grammatices*: "it is a figure offering the higher intellect whatever the words reveal in themselves."[19] Both definitions, however, are describing an intensification not of narrative detail, but of the revelatory potential of the word itself, its correlation of "power" and "meaning." In the former work, understanding is said to expand in proportion to a net compression of language, a condition more related to *energeia* than to Erasmus' view of linguistic *copia*. What strikes us in each of these settings, in contrast to the preceding descriptions of *energeia*, is their relatively narrow scope of application. Their purview is largely that of grammar and syntax, of phases within certain wider pedagogical concerns. Thus, their individual blurring of terminology notwithstanding, they draw on those same reserves of activity and presence fulfilled in the spatial, intramural depths of the classroom. On the tabular plane of desk and text, *enargeia* and its analogues extend the reach of these depths. They suggest that those most seminal of classroom disciplines, grammar and syntax, are no less enriched by their own force of thought and statement, their potential for *sententia*.

None of the above passages, however, quite succeeds in doing justice to the terms within the wider problem of textual articulation. It is thus appropriate that the very schoolmaster who depicted *energeia* as an animizing impulse of the student's mind should later class variants of this notion among the features of rhetoric. In his commentary on Hermogenes, *De universa ratione elocutionis rhetoricae* (1576), Joannes Sturmius devotes an entire chapter to the subject of *energeia*, but not without compounding the lexical difficulties already encountered. He begins by comparing *evidentia* and *illustratio*, "what the Greeks call *energeia*," to the act of *amplificatio*, a medieval term transformed in the Renaissance to the more evocative *copia*.[20] But, he cautions, "although *illustratio* may amplify the body of the entire speech, to amplify and to illustrate are nonetheless two different things."[21] *Amplificatio*, he stresses, refers to a technique for enlarging the *res*, increasing its "magnitude"; alternatively, *illustratio* or *evidentia* renders it luminous and resplendent.[22] The one deals in quantity, the other in quality ("Amplificatio est quantitatis, evidentia qualitatis," p. 163). To a degree, the entire chapter will stand or fall on this distinction because Sturmius' aim is to preempt and dispense with the fallacy that *evidentia* comes about through a simple arithmetic inflation of the text. Yet neither are the two terms antithetical, for the clarity of choice they seem to present is, in fact, blurred. "*Res*," Sturmius asserts, "is illustrated by modes of amplification," and, while amplification is itself not a figure of speech, it is an end of such figures.[23]

Evidentia, on the other hand, is described not only as an end of figures, but more precisely as *energeia*, "the extreme end of all figures," by which *res* become evident.[24] It is the all-encompassing result of figurative language, broader and more inclusive than *amplificatio*. Up to this point, however, what Sturmius has labeled as *energeia* has undeniably all the attributes of visually oriented *enargeia*. While he does nothing to erase this overall impression, he is, nonetheless, conscious of a vague lexical nuance that turns out to pose more of a dilemma than it does a resolution. "Certain people," he continues, "think it necessary to call artistic style *energeia*," but, alluding to a Ciceronian distinction between *energeia* and *enargeia*, he finds it more convenient to account for the latter as a body of techniques systematized according to their use of narrative material.[25] En*argic* narrative thus depends on a descriptive orchestration of *res* (divisible into deeds and abstractions, *facta* and *formae*), character, place and time. Within the declared topic of the chapter, it plays a contributory role, establishing a complex of articulating methods by which an articulated result, *energeia/ evidentia* is achieved. From this range of expression, the text emerges as a finished picture, analogous, in turn, to the terminal perfection of Nature.[26] *Enargeia*, in a sense, fashions one of many impressions, but the quality of those impressions lies in the converging action of all the rhetorical figures, in their distilled *energeia*. Here we are closer once again to the animizing features of the latter term. Its effect is to trigger a response mechanism deep within us, heightening our awareness and, for Sturmius, bringing on the spiritual reflexes of *voluptas* and *animorum permotio*, pleasure and agitation of minds.[27]

No doubt one of Sturmius's aims has been to stress the inherent compatibility of the Greek paronyms while remaining true to the etymological tradition behind the terms. In the discussion, both retain vestiges of earlier forms, *energeia* referring to the animizing consequence of language, *enargeia* to functions of narrative treatment. And more significantly, perhaps, they portray rhetorical vividness as a unitary event predicated on the coalition and mutual dependency of all its components; *energeia* is summoned from an arsenal of *enargic* materials. If we now recall once more, however, the wider intramural context in which this rhetorical activity occurs, the compatibility is even more dramatic, with the culminating *energeia* of the rhetorical text and that of Sturmius' blossoming imitator both evoked as forces that transcend the media which have given them life. Just as the stimuli of the text converge on an emotive center beyond the surface of the page, so the classroom's opaque enclosure is somehow transfused by a living energy of thought greater than any plane or surface. Where this lexical compatibility remains flawed, not to say confusing, is in the latitude of analogy that brings the Latin terms *actio/efficacia* and *illustratio/evidentia* roughly into alignment with each other. Indeed, they are each cited by Sturmius as synonyms for *energeia*.

All this suggests that *energeia* and its forms enjoy a versatility of cross-reference permeating most levels of curricular awareness. That the terms are often semantically intertwined does not, perhaps, so much reflect badly on the users themselves as expose the deeper patterns of reciprocity that enable the terms to merge, yet, at the same time, to keep their differences intact. Within the classroom, they come to imply a broad convertibility between environments that are identifiably and functionally separate from each other. To the student, attentively positioned in the midst of the enclosure, sone of these paired environments could be more dramatically explicit than that illustrated by two linguistically alien texts. Composed of identical materials and located in the same field of vision, the source work and its translation form perhaps the most radical expression of the "energies" described above. That arc of mystery enabling words to agitate and pleasure the mind, thought to be displaced, and patterns of conduct to be transferred is not only repeated, but, in a sense, also desacralized by the two coexisting texts. They become the *exempla*, gathering together and imprinting these various transmissions within the graphic format of the book. Translation can simply not resist the theoretical infiltration enacted by the Greek paronyms.

Accordingly, evidence of the terms in pedagogical settings of translation is supported in two important works. In the *De laudibus graecarum literarum* (1551), the German teacher Conrad Heresbach defines the goal of translation, for students, as the power to retain "through clearness and distinctiveness (*proprietas*) the same emphasis, pleasantness of allusion, *energeia* of figure (*schema*) and of like thought (*sententia*)."[28] This instructively concise passage clusters together several concepts whose individual resonance is largely a function of their relationship to each other. *Emphasis* becomes more meaningful when we are aware of its collateral ties with *enargeia*, *perspicuitas* when we know that *enargeia* is seen as a process of translucence, *proprietas* when we consider its adjacency to *enargeia/energeia* in other Renaissance settings,[29] *schema* and *sententia* when we comprehend the overlapping interests of visual and revelatory aspects of language. In other words, here *enargeia* seems to be a gravitational center from which various dependencies emanate. As a concept, it seeks to bridge the imagined separateness of the two texts, accounting, on the one hand, for arrangements of language and articulation common to the source (its *enargeia/emphasis*) and, on the other, for the replenishment of those arrangements, their sameness, through *perspicuitas* and *proprietas*, qualities invested through the translator's own discourse. On closer study, there emerges from the opposing ends of this passage a further set of symmetrical terms, the one (*proprietas/schema*) depicting factors of linguistic particularity, the other (*perspicuitas/sententia*) the clarifying force of thought. In keeping with the basic pictographic sense of *enargeia*, the first refers, then, to the substances that paint the picture, the second to its transcendent statement. Heresbach's remarks on *enargeia* have the merit of preserving the term's viability as an ingredient of both source and target texts. What he seems bound not to avoid is the reasserted tension between a possibility framed within an impossibility, of translation as an object militating against its own fulfillment.

The second of the pedagogical examples explores these issues in a far less cursory way. In the subtitle of his *Obstetrix animorum* (1600), Edmond Richer, a late-16th-century pedagogical reformer and Syndic of the University of Paris, defines his work as "the clear doctrine of instruction, study, conversation, imitation, judgment and composition," with a generous segment devoted to classroom uses of translation. Typically, *energeia* first makes its appearance in a discussion of grammar, the discipline compared by Richer to a corporal structure and groundwork of all the other arts. It is the function of grammar, Richer asserts, "to attend to the meaning (*significatio*) of every word, its power (*vis*), distinctiveness (*proprietas*), *energeia* and small figures (*sigilla*)."[30] Unlike Heresbach, who uses the more picturally significant term *enargeia*, Richer opts for the other paronym, but ascribes to it no precise links with Aristotelian usage. What is especially striking, however, is the fact that, despite these orthographic differences, the two terms are located amidst similar clusters of companion words, thereby calling attention to a consistency of purpose between translation and grammar in the school program. In both settings, *enargeia/energeia* draws to itself certain classes of words that assist in its own self-definition. Indeed, without this pattern of self-reference, established through a vocabulary that reflects back on the lexical core, the paronyms would remain impenetrable. As with Heresbach, each of the appending terms relates to a sequence of disclosure in language, the distinctiveness (*proprietas*) that sets words (or texts) apart from each other, their figurative effects (*sigilla*), their reserves of meaning (*significatio*) and intensity (*vis*). Richer's *energeia*, like Heresbach's *enargeia*, functions as an aggregate of translative impulses not directly attributable to either of the Greek forms, but with characteristics of both.

Grammar refers, then, to the preordained identity of a language and *energeia* to the structure of that identity. To describe and assimilate the structure, one must look beyond its morphological carapace to the transforming qualities within, those features that determine the force and clarity of statement, how sense may be articulated. The investigation launched by the student into the grammatical system is, consequently, a labor of translation mimicking, albeit intralingually, the same strategies that permit the translator to breach the linguistic obstacles of source text. In fact, when Richer takes up, soon after, the subject of translation, he embarks on what appears to be a deliberate rephrasing of his grammatical definition of *energeia*, once again assembling around it the familiar cluster of terms. "All learned men," he begins, "propose in books and treatises on translation that authors be translated not so much *ad verbum* as *ad sensum* and *ad mentem*, not rendered word for word, but expressed especially according to the thought."[31] As a result, the translation of the thought (*sententiae explicatio*) "depends on emphasis, *energeia*, distinctiveness (*proprietas*) and the exact meaning of the words, that is to say, on the sense of the grammar."[32] In this respect, the *energeia* referred to is located in the grammar of the target text, those resources of expression summoned by the translator from himself. Certain languages, Richer claims, are furnished with a more accurate grammar and greater emphasis, a case in point being that of German, which "expresses more exactly and meaningfully the mind of authors and explains better the sense."[33] The capacity of a given translator to translate *ad sensum* and *ad mentem* is seen as a response to these latent "energies" of the target grammar. *Energeia* is, thus, a force of revelation within that grammar, translation the operative reach of such force into another grammatical superstructure inhabited, in turn, by its own *energeia*. Here, however, Richer cannot avoid the dilemma imposed by this dual placement of *energeia*. He acknowledges there to be few translators who have grasped successfully the thought and mind of authors and, consequently, few who have retained their textual *emphasis*.[34] When once we accept the fact that *energeia*, along with its analogue, *emphasis*, refers to the grammatical identity that distinguishes languages from each other and establishes the autonomous conditions under which they make sense, then we must also accept the reality that an energic aggression in behalf of one will be met by an energic resistance by another.

Richer's solution to these self-canceling motions lies in the comparison of translation to an architectural edifice ("velut in aedificiis"). The components of any building, he continues, are selected either from necessity or pleasure of ornamentation, what we might term its structure and texture. By extension, translation, too, is obliged to consider both necessity and the illuminating features of ornamentation, the former in the guise of grammar and sense, the latter as the "ornaments and lights of speech," the figures of rhetoric.[35] Richer is suggesting that one cannot postulate the presence of a grammatically authentic sense without postulating, at the same time, its containment and revelation in language. The structure remains immanent in its own expressive texture. This is true of the translative text no less than it is of the source. Because languages embed sense in an articulating medium, translation must be seen to reduplicate the implantation that first gave life to the source text—it must create a new *energeia*. The focus of Richer's interest is, thus, not only on the autonomy of the two *energeias*, but also on the fulfillment of source structure in the figurative, textural forms of the translation. As we have already observed in Curio's *Schola*, the text of these energic effects lies in the capacity of texture to seem not to be a texture at all, but to vaporize, as it were, the scriptural surface. Similarly, for Richer certain languages are capable of emissions that reflect the "more impelling motions of mind" ("in vehementioribus animi motibus," p. 150^r) and appear to "unwind speech from the very edge of the lips rather than from the chest or entrails."[36] It is as though we, as readers, were present at the labial and mental *locus* of the utterance, a place where speech makes contact with air, no longer muffled or engulfed in an articulating cavity. Coelius Curio had written in non-translative terms of the frontal buoyancy of words, of their tendency "to rise above the comprehension of their own substance." In adapting this Aristotelian concept to translation, Richer contributes to a theoretical refinement of *energeia* hitherto only implicit in pedagogical settings. Through this refinement, *energeia* comes to represent a process in which the dynamic, thought-impelling movements of mind become palpable in the act of verbal creation. Hence, the lopsided attention given here to the role of figurative language in translation. And what figures have the power to accomplish is to commemorate, like Aristotle's "active" metaphors, the urgency of an agonistically replete moment when we grasp the thought at its instant of uttered fullness.

Translative *energeia* might, therefore, be described as a transfiguration of space in which the scriptural surface of the target text is rendered transparent, its texture imagined to reverse the reader's sense of temporal removal from the source. Sturmius' definition of *energeia* as "the extreme end of all figures" is reaffirmed by Richer for the status of translation and made even more explicit in his later pedagogical manual, the *Grammatica obstetricia* (1607). Under the first rule of figurative usage, he defines *figura* as "a type of speech which either transforms (*immutare*) with restraint the familiar manner of speaking or renews (*innovare*) it with credibility and thus unites with style the great charm and emphasis of novelty."[37] This definition then devolves into a transformational exercise, with its main elements filtered down into a systematic fission of parts. The dependencies of *figura* meld immediately with those of *energeia* and are dispersed into a new definition: "*Emphasis*, or *energeia*, is a certain power (*vis*) and charm of speech which proceeds from the credible renewal (*innovatio*) of words or the moderate transformation (*immutatio*) of speech and which produces the variations of Auxesis and Hypocorismos."[38] Since "the credible renewal of words" and "the moderate transformation of speech" have already been seen to underwrite the entire process of figurative expression, *energeia*, by inference, refers to the broad, calculated effect of *figura*. It is a commodity transmitted from all the possible inflections of renewal and transformation. *Figura* merely describes an articulated system, a category within the greater phenomenon of speech; *energeia*, however, describes the affective action (*vis*) of that system. As the major subspecies of *energeia*, auxesis and hypocorismos carry the fission of *figura* ever deeper. Auxesis, or amplification, Richer resumes, "is a kind of power and stretching of language which proceeds from the credible renewal of words or the moderate transformation of speech."[39] Hypocorismos (diminution), on the other hand, "is the breaking off and diminishing of language which derives from the credible renewal of words or the moderate transformation of speech."[40] While each of these terms retains, in common, a pattern initiated by *figura* (renewal and transformation), as mirrors they carry the reverse images of each other, auxesis activated by a tensile stretching (*intentio*) of language, hypocorismos by its constrictive severance (*remissio*). *Energeia*, the encompassing agent of the two, thereby emerges as a pulsation between more words and fewer words.

Richer's contribution to this theoretical issue derives principally from the way he views *energeia* as a methodized response to a problem of writing. More than a vaguely defined effect of grammatical or figurative expression, it is a process with its own system and organized relationships. No less at home in the contexts of grammar than in those of translation and figure, *energeia* permeates a full sequence of classifications, from the identifying force it gives to particular words within the grammar down to the categories and subcategories of figure that reveal how the young writer can accomplish certain behavioral modifications in words. The tensile and contractive motions of discourse, its reserves of transformation and renewal, are the axes of these modifications, each one composed of smaller elements that can, in turn, be named and defined. As a consequence, *energeia* is projected down through the entire system, diffused even into the lesser, more subordinate forms. Referring to just such a form, Richer defines the syllepsis of a construction, for instance, as "that which expresses the greater *energeia* of style—the sense—and, thus, transposes its nature and rhythm, often its entire form, and includes *Appositio* and *Epexegesis*."[41] Of the varied pedagogical settings of *energeia* that we have examined, none is as explicit as this one in establishing the term's interconnection of sense with stylistic arrangement. More than this, however, the definition shares with the broader, upper categories the perception that where there is no concerted action to transform the text in some way, there can be no *energeia*. Both *appositio* and *epexegesis*, in fact, conspire to supplement the text through parenthetical and explanatory expansion, at the same time altering the stylistic rhythm while revitalizing the textual message, bringing to it previously unimagined detail. So, although Richer in his *Grammatica* does not make an overt connection between translation and *energeia*, as he had done earlier in the *Obstetricia animorum*, there does appear a deliberate consistency between the term's figurative application in the later work and its service to grammar, translation and figure in the earlier one. It finds itself absorbed by a porous assortment of terminologies, all of which assist in clarifying its functions and in establishing its commitment to a methodology of writing and translation.

What becomes clear from the analyses of both Richer and Sturmius, and reaffirmed throughout this survey of Renaissance pedagogical literature, is the fact that *enargeia/energeia* and their analogues are not definable outside a figurative environment. In this, they assume, with translation, an entire range of shared values. As figurative concepts, both practice the ultimate illusion, a perception that things can be as they once were, yet in the here and now fabricate a new identity discontinuous with the past. The classroom becomes the architectural structure in which this illusion is reenacted, the various modes and allocations of *energeia* making their respective appeals to the student, dismantling the mural and textual barriers that might otherwise quarantine him within the structure. This tendency to externalize *energeia*, however, to impute it to conditions that encircle and act upon the student, obscures a more vital truth: the notion that *energeia* cannot exist independently from the creative force that fashions it, the self that brings it to life. In the classroom practice of translation, the student emerges as the *locus* of that self and *energeia* as an illusionistic ploy that defines the relationships between two interlingual texts, the one doubling for the other.

Several factors conspire to underwrite this illusion. First, *energeia* contains a paradox of removal and delivery, a sense that any qualities brought to an object must necessarily be removed from something else, the second object existing potentially within the configurations of the first, and all the while safeguarding their own autonomy. A related illusion has to do with the problem of motion: objects that are energically forceful have the power to animize space in such a way that things appear to contract and expand, much like the figures of auxesis and hypocorismos. In temporal terms, *energeia* also has the capacity to dissolve historiographic distance and establish bonds of renewal (*innovatio*) between rekindled events, rekindled words and rekindled texts. Taken in their entirety, all these illusions seem dependent on a much broader energic principle. There exists in *energeia* and its variants the impression that their effects form around a network of axial tensions, alternative surges between transformation and renewal (*immutatio* and *innovatio*), expansion and contraction (*intentio* and *remissio*), difference and sameness, more language and less language, and ultimately the view that any text negotiates its own treaty between quantity and quality, a substantialist feeling for words determining their Orphic revelation. At the imaginative extreme, *energeia* strives, inside language, for an extralinguistic experience; it works towards an ultimate dispensation from describing something in order to reconstitute the emotion of simply being there and not having to talk about it from the reality of a mediating texture. Illusion it well may be, but one that is calculated to engulf the Renaissance student within the living tissue of thought.

NOTES

1. Wilhelm von Humboldt, *Linguistic Variability and Intellectual Development*, trans. George C. Buck and Frithjof A. Raven (Miami: Univ. of Miami Press, 1971), p. 27.

2. *A Greek Critic: Demetrius on Style*, ed. and trans. G.M.A. Grube (Toronto: Univ. of Toronto Press, 1961), pp. 80-81.

3. François Rabelais, *Oeuvres complètes*, ed. Jacques Boulenger and Lucien Scheler (Paris: Gallimard, 1955), p. 691.

4. On this later text, see G.P. Norton, "Rabelais and the Epic of Palpability: *Enargeia* and History (*Cinquiesme Livre*: 38-40)," *Symposium*, 33 (1979), 171-85. For a more general discussion of *enargeia*, see Terence Cave, "*Enargeia*: Erasmus and the Rhetoric of Presence in the Sixteenth Century," *L'Esprit Créateur*, 16 (1976), 5-19, and *The Cornucopian Text: Problems of Writing in the French Renaissance* (Oxford: Oxford Univ. Press, 1979), pp. 27-34.

5. I.A. Richards, *The Philosophy of Rhetoric* (Oxford: Oxford Univ. Press, 1936), p. 32.

6. *Ambrosii Calepini Bergomatis Eremitani Dictionarium* (Reggio, 1501), n.p. The source text is from Saint Jerome's *Ad Paulinum presbyterum*: "habet nescio quid latentis [*energeias*] viva vox et in aures discipuli de auctoris transfusa fortius insonat" (*Lettres*, ed. J. Labourt, vol. 3 [Paris: Les Belles Lettres, 1953], p. 10). Translation of all Neo-Latin texts, unless noted otherwise, is my own and has been done in the

interests of accuracy rather than stylistic merit. In Renaissance texts, I have deleted at all times the standard orthographic contractions.

7. "... ita quod lectiones suas elaborato studio suis Discipulis ore proprio dicunt & pronuntient: quia, ut Hieronymus ait, habet nescio quid latentis energiae vivae vocis actus, & in aures discipuli de authoris ore transfusa fortius sonat." César Egasse Du Boulay, *Historia Universitatis parisiensis*, vol. 5 (Paris: Petrus de Bresche, 1673), p. 572. A similar precept, under the synonym *efficace*, is repeated early on in an edition of Agostino Dato: "Ceulx sont bien abusez qui cuydent autant aprendre en luysant les livres: comme en oyant ceulx qui les exposent: car la voix vive ainsi que dit Quintilien a grant efficace." *Praecepta elegantiae latinae, versu ab Roberto Dumo expressa, adjunctis non illepidi viri Guillermi Gueroaldi thematibus vernaculis* (Caen: Laurens Hostingue, 1525), n.p. (B.N. Rés. X.2080). A sign that this precept later comes under a cloud appears in a late-16th-century pedagogical reform, with a knowledge of things declared superior to the *energeia* of language: "Aristotelis contextus Philosophorum, non Grammaticorum, modo exponatur, ut magis pateat rei scientia, quam vocum *energia*." *Réformation de l'Université de Paris* (Paris: I. Mettayer & P. L'Huillier, 1601), p. 32; see statute no. 42.

8. In L. Vitruvio Roscio, *De docendi studiendique modo, ac de claris puerorum moribus* (Basel: Robertus Winter, 1541), p. 114 (Arsenal 8⁰ B77). Porcia's work appears to have been first published at Treviso in 1492.

9. *Le Grand Olympe* (Paris: P. Sergent, 1537), sig. ai^v. This work is in the Grenville collection of the British Library, shelfmark G.9674. G. Lanson cites a 1532 edition at Lyons in his *Manuel bibliographique*.

10. Coelius Secondus Curio, *Schola, sive de perfecto grammatico, libri tres* (Basel: Ioan. Oporinus, 1555), p. 52.

11. *De imitatione libri tres* (Strasbourg: Bernhardus Jobinus, 1574), sig. A7^r.

12. Ibid.

13. Ibid.

14. Ibid.

15. W. Rhys Roberts has proposed the English synonyms vividness, realism, lifelike, telling, graphic, for *enargeia*, and activity, actuality, for *energeia*. *Demetrius on Style* (Cambridge: Cambridge Univ. Press, 1902), p. 279.

16. Terence Cave calls attention to the replacement of *energeia* for *enargeia* in Weltkirchius' commentary on *De copia. The Cornucopian Text*, p. 28.

17. *De emendata structura latini sermonis libri sex* (Paris: C. Wechelus, 1533), p. 401. First published in London, 1524; other Paris editions printed by Robert Estienne appear in 1527 and 1532.

18. D. Erasmus, *De constructione, libellus, Scholiis Henrici Primaei illustratus* (Lyons: Io. et Franciscus Frellionios, 1546), f⁰ A3^r.

19. Maturinus Samuel, *Elementaria Principia grammatices è gallica interpretatione in latinam traducta* ... (Paris: Gab. Buon, 1559), p. 58^v (Mazarine 20172).

20. See Cave, *The Cornucopian Text*, pp. 8-9.

21. *De universa ratione elocutionis rhetoricae, libri IIII* (Strasbourg: Bern. Jobinus, 1576), p. 159 (Arsenal 8⁰ B2459).

22. Ibid.

23. Ibid., pp. 159-60.

24. Ibid., p. 160.

25. Ibid., p. 161. Elsewhere, Sturmius refers to the four parts of *enargeia*: "Postremô ostendimus quatripartitam esse materiam [*enargeias*]" (p. 163).

26. Ibid., p. 161.

27. Ibid., p. 177.

28. (Strasbourg: Wendelinus Rihelius, 1551), f⁰ 23^r (Mazarine 22680 [2e pièce]).

29. See, for example, Henri Estienne, *Conformité du langage français avec le grec*, ed. L. Feugère (1853; rpt. Geneva: Slatkine, 1970), p. 35.

30. *Obstetrix animorum, hoc est brevis et expedita ratio dicendi, conversandi, imitandi, iudicandi, componendi* (Paris: Ambrosius Drouart, 1600), pp. 136^v-137^r (Mazarine 22337).

31. Ibid., pp. 149^v-150^r.

32. Ibid., p. 150^r.

33. Ibid.

34. Ibid., p. 149^r.

35. Ibid., pp. 149^{r-v}.

36. Ibid., pp. 150^{r-v}.

37. (Paris: Petrus Ludovicus Feburier, 1607), p. 126^r (Arsenal 8⁰ B743).

38. Ibid.

39. Ibid., pp. 126^{r-v}.

40. Ibid.

41. Ibid., p. 137^r.

Elias L. Rivers

The Spoken and the Written Word

I

Human beings, that is, talking animals, existed for hundreds of millenia before inventing ways of writing down their words and sentences. Without the full development of this invention, it is hard to imagine the teaching of literature as we have known it from Classical antiquity until the present. In fact, one may question the existence of literature, in our sense of the word, in an illiterate or preliterate world. The word itself, "literature," deriving from *littera* (or *litera*), refers to alphabetic writing and the analysis (grammar and rhetoric) associated with written texts. To speak self-contradictorily of "oral literature" is to project into non-literate culture a concept directly dependent upon literacy. Strictly speaking, then, before writing there were songs and stories and ritualistic entertainments, but there was no literature. The writing down of songs and stories inevitably made people conscious of songs and stories in a different way; this new consciousness, or awareness of textuality, constituted in itself the invention of literature.[1]

It is, nevertheless, helpful to speculate briefly about how literature may be said to have existed in some sense "avant la lettre." A fully developed model for the mode of existence of such pre-literary institutions is described in Albert Lord's *The Singer of Tales.*[2] Although many aspects of Lord's dogmatism have rightly been criticized, no one can deny the value of his direct observation of the process of chanting long epic tales in an act of simultaneous composition and performance. The functionally illiterate singer relied heavily upon his memory and repeated practice in combining metric formulas, or brief set phrases, with traditional motifs and plots to produce the uninterrupted flow of stylized narrative. The short, fixed formulas can be seen as anticipating microtextuality; but the fluid oral composition-performance as a whole is a very different sort of verbal substance from the fixed literary text, which may be revised by the author and repeated by the reader, with a new sort of control over identity and variation. It is only this fixed text, not the fluid oral performance, which can be studied, and taught in the classroom, as literature.

The oral singer of tales memorized and/or composed and performed his rhythmic sequence of declaimed words in the same place and at the same time as the audience which listened and responded. In principle, community and communication coincided perfectly; performance as repeated public events provided constant training for singer and listeners alike. But in the case of a written text, there is no such simultaneous presence and comprehension, no such guarantee of community: composition took place at some time in the past, and reading as a performance will take place at some time in the future, and meanwhile there is only a sequence of letters written on the page. Teaching became necessary to provide a way of bridging the gap, of forming a new and different community by the academic institutionalization of reading. The teacher, I suggest, is there to help the student reconvert into a possible "oral" performance that inert text, those dead letters, by breathing into them a new spirit of life. If this sounds mystical, it is because the whole process of reading is much more complex, more difficult to understand, than we usually take it to be.

Fortunately for the teacher, the world or oral-aural language and the world of writer-text-reader are not altogether mutually exclusive; the latter is usually grafted upon the former and displaces it only in part. We know that there is a great range of differences among literate societies in the way that they manage diglossia, that is, the co-existence of oral and written systems of language.[3] Every normal child learns his mother tongue at home before going to school; then he learns a textual mode of language within a different social context. In all literate societies there is a difference between the written standard learned at school and the various dialects spoken at home; in some societies these two modes of language overlap only slightly. In the United States today one seldom reads black English; obviously, diglossia everywhere has social and political implications. The literate American often retains and even strengthens his roots in one or more spoken dialects as he develops his diverging skills in reading a wide range of texts, from Chaucer to William Carlos Williams. (The American teacher of literature written in a foreign language is faced by one further complication: he himself and his students have frequently learned that language as a second language. This may well mean that, in the case of foreign language, the written standard has been learned first; the foreign language is in no case a mother tongue, but rather, like Latin, constitutes a new level of school-taught diglossia.)

II

Let us assume, then, that literature, by definition, is a series of letter-constituted texts. Without a competent reader, however, literature cannot be said to exist in any meaningful sense. The teacher must be a competent reader and must be able to show students how to read: he reads and talks to them about the process and strategies of reading, that is, about how to "perform" a text. Reading a text in class replaces the rhapsode's performance, not as an authoritative declamatory interpretation, but as a tentative model for the ultimately solitary, yet socially conditioned, process of making sense out of a text, or naturalizing it. The reader must take a much more active and self-conscious role than the listener within an oral community; the reader is engaged in a process of decoding for which he must have some social preparation, which makes him ready to draw tentatively upon all the relevant codes at his disposal. As a first example of how this process may work, I have chosen a sonnet written in Spanish about 1530-1535 by Garcilaso de la Vega (1501?-1536):

> Escrito está en mi alma vuestro gesto
> y cuanto yo escribir de vos deseo:
> vos sola lo escribistes; yo lo leo
> tan solo que aun de vos me guardo en esto.
>
> En esto estoy y estaré siempre puesto,
> que aunque no cabe en mí cuanto en vos veo,
> de tanto bien lo que no entiendo creo,
> tomado ya la fe por presupuesto.
>
> Yo no nací sino para quereros;
> mi alma os ha cortado a su medida;
> por hábito del alma misma os quiero.
>
> Cuanto tengo confieso yo deberos:
> por vos nací, por vos tengo la vida,
> por vos he de morir, y por vos muero.[4]

At a strictly lexical level this sonnet offers few problems to the 20th-century reader of basic Spanish: perhaps only "gesto," meaning "facial expression" or "face," and "vos," an archaic polite second-person form of address. But it is hard to see how any 20th-century American reader could begin to make coherent sense of this sonnet as a whole without some historical or social knowledge of the written poetic code of courtly love and its Christian allegories. Grammatical gender reveals only the sexual contrast of "yo" (masculine) and "vos" (feminine); the reader can hardly avoid identifying the first person as a devout poet-lover, but is the second person a lady, let us say, or Our Lady? This erotic/religious ambiguity is built into the sonnet's primary code.

In the first quatrain the verb "to write" occurs three times and the verb "to read" once. We are accustomed to the poet-lover who presents himself as a singer, speaker or writer, but here, surprisingly, he first presents himself as the reader of what the lady has already written. Polyptoton brings changes of voice and subject on the verb of writing, from passive "escrito" to active first person ("yo escribir de vos deseo") and second person ("vos sola lo escribistes"), after which the first person takes over as subject of the complementary or reciprocal verb of reading ("yo lo leo"). The reader of the sonnet, led through this maze of verbs, suddenly finds his own activity reflected in that of the poet-lover, who reads the total image of the lady inscribed within his own soul. The frustrated passion of love is rooted in the solitary separation of writer from reader and of reader from writer: it seems that the reader cannot trust anyone, not even the writer ("aun de vos me guardo").

In the second quatrain, the poet-lover's constant devotion to this practice of reading is declared to be at least in part dependent upon the act of faith: the image of the lady exceeds the dimensions of his soul, but he can still believe what he cannot comprehend. Here a religious metaphor, with the theological overtones of a Thomistic sequence for Corpus Christi ("quod non vides, animosa firmat fides": "What you do not see is confirmed by a lively faith"), begins to displace the metaphor of writing and reading, as faith compensates for alienation and makes understanding possible. The implications of all this for the process of reading are suggestive: the poetic text itself provides clues for the teacher-reader-student, who is cut off by time and space from the historical roots and codes of this sonnet, but is given insight by certain universals of human language and experience, which he accepts on faith.

In the tercets there is no further reference to the inscriptional metaphor. The poet-lover's life, he now declares, is devoted to love. His soul is no longer like a piece of paper upon which the lady is inscribed, but is like a body which has cut her to its own measure in order to clothe itself. She had exceeded him; first by faith and now by reduction they are made commensurate. He wants her to be the "habit" of his soul, in both senses of the word: a religious garment, precisely tailored, and a customary action, which, according to Aristotle and popular wisdom, becomes a "second nature." This equation is no mere pun: artificial exercise clothes and shapes the self. In the second tercet the poet-lover declares himself entirely dependent upon that other person for his existence: for birth, for life and for death. The phrase "por vos" is repeated with emphatic anaphora four times, with four different verbs: "nací" in the past perfective, "tengo la vida" in the present imperfective, "he de morir" as a future perfective and "muero" as another present imperfective, which seems to be equated paradoxically with "tengo la vida." This tercet, if taken literally, that is, physiologically, could properly be addressed only to the Deity, with the traditional Christian characterization of life on earth as a process of suffering and dying, of mystic passion and longing for God. But this same language could be addressed to a deified lady, with erotic masochism, passion in the modern sense. And perhaps the lady is a metaphor for the source of written poetry: she writes muse-like upon the poet's soul, and his poem is a mere reading of her script, to which he devotes his life.

Can the teacher tell the class authoritatively what this sonnet is really about? I suggest that, as perhaps in the case of all literary texts, and certainly in the case of this sonnet, the teacher can give no such final answer because there is none. A written text is cut off from a determining social context, a living community, in a way that no oral performance is; a written text provides the basis for many different reading performances, and our teacher will try out several of these in his attempt to convert his class into a new hermeneutic community.

III

Georges Poulet has described the alienation of the subject which takes place within the reader's mind: "As soon as I replace my direct perception of reality by the words of a book, I deliver myself, bound hand and foot, to the omnipotence of fiction. I say farewell to what is, in order to feign belief in what is not. I surround myself with fictitious beings; I become the prey of language."[5] The letters of the literary text are dead until they have been experienced in this way by a reader. The writer as a source is inaccessible except insofar as the reader takes on faith the intelligibility, linguistic and literary, of the text. The only immediate presence is that of the reader, that hybrid subject, trying to make sense out of the text. Like the child who discovers its own subjectivity when it appropriates the first-person singular pronoun, the reader of our sonnet assumes the identity of the poet-lover as he speaks, converting the text into an actual or virtual oral performance.[6]

According to Eric Havelock, for a long time after the invention of the alphabet, the preliterate oral performance of Homeric poems continued to be the basis of Greek education; traditional rhapsodic experiences, rather than grammatical or rhetorical analyses of texts, still provided collective indoctrination in tribal mythology and military enthusiasm. Such an anti-intellectual *paideia*, in Havelock's opinion, explains Plato's opposition to poetry, that is, his opposition to the singer of tales as schoolmaster.[7] The ideal Socratic teacher, on the other hand, would use dialogue to analyse the meanings of words by putting them in different contexts and thus create a new philosophical community rooted in rational agreement on first principles. Poetry would have to be discarded by the philosopher-king; Homeric texts would be relegated, if not to the dustbin of history, to the sophists, grammarians and rhetoricians.

The modern teacher of literature, with a modesty less ironic than that of Socrates, shows his student-reader how to invent a literary subjectivity appropriate for the performance of each text and then, after performing the text, how to analyze this subjective process objectively, as correlated to significant features of the text. This is what Dámaso Alonso called for over thirty years ago, when he published *Poesía española*.[8] According to him, one cannot simply analyze a text as a linguistic object, but must first experience it in the way described by Poulet; it is this subjective experience which enables the reader to identify those critical points that give structure to the process of reading. One must lose oneself as a reader before being able to find oneself as a literary critic, that is, as an analyst, not of isolated texts, but of readings correlated to texts and to other readings. One cannot analyze a poem by gazing at it from a distance as though it were a well-wrought urn; one must first enter and listen to the resonances of its interiority.

IV

The dialectical process of critical reading and writing is everywhere implied in Cervantes' *Don Quixote*. The opening words of the narrative ("In a village of La Mancha . . .") seem to invite the reader to plunge in uncritically, but, as the protagonist is presented, the reader of the first chapter quickly discovers that that ridiculous old man is the archetypal uncritical reader:

Es, pues, de saber que este sobredicho hidalgo, los ratos que estaba ocioso—que eran los más del año,—se daba a leer libros de caballerías con tanto afición y gusto, que olvidó casi de todo punto el ejercicio de la caza, y aun la administración de su hacienda; y llegó a tanto su curiosidad y desatino en esto, que vendió muchas hanegas de tierra de sembradura para comprar libros de caballerías en que leer, y así llevó a su casa todos cuantos pudo heber dellos . . . .[9]

Like the Greek schoolboy reciting Homer and imagining himself to be a hero on the plains of Troy, Don Quixote subjectively identifies himself so completely with Amadís de Gaula and other knights errant that he no longer has a self of his own. When, in Chapter 5, a neighborhood peasant tells Don Quixote that he is not Baldwin or any other literary character, our hero declares, "I know who I am, and I know I can be not only the persons I've said I am, but all twelve Peers of France . . . ." His first phrase, "Yo sé quién soy," was the traditional Jehovah-like assertion of absolute and honorable social identity and integrity; the words that follow, however, are not those of the Spanish *hidalgo* affirming his ancestry and status, his immutable selfhood, but are those of the avid, uncritical reader who identifies fully with each hero that he reads about.

Don Quixote describes more fully the subjective experience of naïve reading in Chapter 50 of Part I, when he defends romances of chivalry against the Canon's criticisms; for him the proof of the pudding is the pleasure of the text, or, more precisely, the pleasure of the reader's response:

¿Hay mayor contento que ver, como si dijésemos, aquí ahora se muestra delante de nosostros un gran lago de pez hirviendo a borbollones, y que andan nadando y cruzando por él muchas serpientes, culebras y lagartos, y otros muchos géneros de animales feroces y espantables, y que del medio del lago sale una voz tristísima que dice: "Tú, caballero, quienquiera que seas, que el temeroso lago estás mirando, si quieres alcanzar el bien que debajo destas negras aguas se encubre, muestra el valor de tu fuerte pecho y arrójate en mitad de su negro y encendido licor; porque si así no lo haces, no serás digno de ver las altas maravillas que en sí encierran y contienen los siete castillos de las siete fadas que debajo desta negregura yacen"? (I, 499-500)

The reader-knight, of course, takes the fateful plunge into the black lake of the text and is immediately rewarded by finding himself in a subterranean *locus amoenus* of art and nature, of lovely damsels who bathe him and dress him in the finest clothes.

The ability to participate vicariously in another person's experience is based upon the "I" who can perceive a thou, or even a third person, as a potential first person. This ability, rooted in the linguistic competence of speakers who have learned how to use grammatical shifters, is further developed in the intense oral exchanges of neighborhood gossip and other forms of social conversation; it may then lead to the total alienation of the Quixotic reader, the disintegration of self. The reader of *Don Quixote* slowly comes to see himself rejuvenated among lovely damsels. No matter how much the reader may laugh at that poor old madman, he finds himself slipping inevitably into the same naïve role: if the giants are mere fantasies, the windmills must be real. Immersed in the text, the reader inevitably loses his footing and finds himself drowning in another subterranean world.

But Cervantes' novel also provides fictitious models for the reintegration of self, that is, for the construction of the critical, or self-conscious, writerly reader. Throughout the novel the implied narrator winks at this reader over the heads, or behind the backs, of his characters and surrogate narrators. Playfulness on the part of the narrator creates an implied reader capable of coping with such playfulness.[10] The implied narrator-writer presents himself more directly to the reader in his prologue to Part I of *Don Quixote*; in this self-portrait of the author as an old man,[11] the writer addresses the reader ("desocupado lector") in such a way as to insinuate the complicity of their roles. The writer's attitude towards *Don Quixote*, his book (or Don Quixote, his character), is less that of a proud parent than that of an ambiguous stepfather; hence, the reader is free to think and say whatever he will of the book, the story or the character. The substance of this prologue, however, is not a defense or critique of the book, but rather a deconstruction of the prologue itself as an academic genre of written discourse. The writer's "real" problem is posed as the composition and conventional scholarly ornamentation of a prologue, with its sonnets and epigrams, "this preface which you are now in the process of reading"; the writer presents himself as at a loss, with paper in front of him, pen behind his ear, elbow on desk and chin resting on hand, when an anonymous friend enters and asks him what his problem is. Their pseudo-oral dialogue and, in particular, the friend's cynical advice constitute the rest of the prologue's text, the conclusion of which begins with these words: "Con silencio grande estuve escuchando lo que mi amigo me decía, y de tal manera se imprimieron en mí sus razones, que, sin ponerlas en disputa, las aprobé por buenas y de ellas mismas quise hacer este prólogo . . ." (I, 25).

The text of *Don Quixote* is, thus, a Protean interplay of discourse, narrative and dialogue, each undermining and replacing the other. The reader must have his eye, or inner ear, attuned to many voices. As he is implied within the text, the reader is always in the presence of the narrator, with whom he overhears the unending dialogue between Don Quixote and Sancho Panza, between the tall, thin gentleman who speaks in the style of the romances which he has read and the short, fat peasant who speaks more fluently, in his illiterate way, but quickly absorbs Don Quixote's literary style as it has been retailed to him orally. This dialogue is a diagram of the coexistence of written and oral cultures; Don Quixote is the schoolmaster who corrects the peasant's grammar, and Sancho is the bright learner who eventually governs his village more ably than any duke. Within its ludic text, *Don Quixote* presents the reader with a wide range of shifting roles to play. The teacher of literature has only to accompany the student as he plunges into the text, and snaps out of it, with a subjectivity that is increasingly aware of its own fragility.

V

Let us return once more to our imaginary prehistoric mode of existence within a completely oral language. The simultaneous presence of "speaker and listener, event and discourse, intention and context" made possible an unequivocal comprehension, a mystic tribal community for which we are all nostalgic. Writing represents our alienation from this community: "absence of the reader in the act of writing, absence of the writer in the act of reading, absence of reader and writer in the text itself."[12] It would seem to be no accident that literature written in the modern European languages began with the strange poetic cult of courtly love, in which the absence of the lady provoked the production of literary texts; sexual frustration, alienation, parodies of divine love are the powerful motifs behind these texts, from Guillaume d'Aquitaine to Ausias March and Garcilaso. Petrarch, in his Sonnet V, writes of speaking aloud "il nome che nel cor mi scrisse Amore," but Laura's name remains concealed anagrammatically in his text.

The teacher talks about a written text; he reinvents the oral community of Edenic understanding. But the silent presence of the text is a constant reminder of the *felix culpa* of writing's invention, the fortunate fall which made literature, and the teaching of it, possible and necessary. Reading and writing have become our soul's habit, our second nature; the writer projects an ideal reader into the text, and the reader evokes from the text a persona for the writer. But writers and readers die; scripture remains inexhaustible in its meanings, accumulating oral and written glosses, midrashim which uncover new meanings for each generation and each historical context. The teacher is the ideal reader, performing orally, suggesting models; the student, after class, is on his own, caught in the radical solitude of that real reader who faces the text by himself. The teacher-student's passionate, yet undeceived search for a lost community is what generates meanings; according to Garcilaso's Sonnet V, the search depends upon an act of faith, the reader's conviction that meaning is there and is somehow comprehensible or at least believable. But the process of reading continues to be a mysterious one, alienating and alienated. Saint Augustine, accustomed to the oral community of the pagan schools, records his amazement at seeing Saint Ambrose read silently to himself, in Christian alienation: "But as he read, his eyes traveled over the pages and his heart dug out the meaning, and yet his voice and tongue were motionless."[13] Jorge Luis Borges imagines an eventual utopian culmination of the process: "Ya se practica la lectura en silencio, síntoma venturoso. Ya hay lector callando de versos. De esa capacidad sigilosa a una escritura puramente ideográfica—directa comunicación de experiencias, no de sonidos—hay una distancia incansable, pero siempre menos dilatada que el porvenir."[14] And between the distant centuries of these two writers, between Augustine and Borges, we have *Don Quixote*'s playful text about the madness of reading and Garcilaso's evocation of writer and reader as separate and solitary and liberated centers of power: "vos sola lo escribistes; yo lo leo / tan solo que aun de vos me guardo en esto."

NOTES

1. For an elaboration upon this idea, see my "Prolegomena Grammatologica ...," in *What Is Literature?*, ed. Paul Hernadl (Bloomington: Indiana Univ. Press, 1978), pp. 79-88.

2. (Cambridge, Mass.: Harvard Univ. Press, 1960).

3. The concept of diglossia was first defined by the sociolinguist Charles A. Ferguson in his now classic article entitled "Diglossia," *Word*, 15 (1959), 325-40.

4. Text based on my edition, Carcilaso de la Vega, *Obras completas con comentario* (Columbus: Ohio State Univ. Press, 1974), pp. 77-79.

5. Georges Poulet, "Criticism and the Experience of Interiority," in *Reader-Response Criticism*, ed. Jane P. Tompkins (Baltimore: Johns Hopkins Univ. Press, 1980), pp. 41-49. This collection of critical essays defines the tradition to which the present essay in part belongs.

6. See Emile Benveniste, "Subjectivity in Language," ch. 21 of his *Problems in General Linguistics* (Miami: Univ. of Miami Press, 1971).

7. See *Prologue to Greek Literacy* (Cincinnati: Univ. of Cincinnati Press, 1971); *Preface to Plato* (Cambridge, Mass.: Harvard Univ. Press, 1963); and "The Preliteracy of the Greeks," *New Literary History*, 8 (1977), 369-91.

8. Dámaso Alonso, *Poesía española: Ensayo de métodos y límites estilísticos* (Madrid: Gredos, 1950).

9. Miguel de Cervantes, *Don Quijote de la Mancha*, ed. Martín de Riquer, 2 vols. (New York: Las Américas, 1965), I, 36-37.

10. Walter J. Ong, S.J., "The Writer's Audience Is Always a Fiction," *PMLA*, 90 (1975), 9-21.

11. Elias Rivers, "Cervantes' Art of the Prologue," in *Estudios literarios de hispanistas norteamericanos dedicados a Helmut Hatzfeld en su 80 aniversario* (Barcelona: Ediciones Hispam, 1974), pp. 167-71.

12. See Inés Azar, "Meaning, Intention and Written Text ...," *MLN*, 96 (1981), 440-44.

13. *Confessions*, VI, iii, 3.

14. Jorge Luis Borges, *Discusión* (Buenos Aires: Emecé, 1957), p. 49.

Hugh M. Davidson

Voltaire Explains Newton:
An Episode in the History of Rhetoric

I

In the half-century stretching from about 1685 to 1735, two new views of the world and of the natural systems into which it fits competed for acceptance. Both were contrary to traditional geocentric habits of mind. Both had been worked out by great technical thinkers—Descartes and Newton—who wrote treatises, not popular accounts. Those who thought of themselves as lovers of truth and as bearers of some responsibility to spread it had to solve the rhetorical problem of how to bring about in a wide audience assent to new views. Two people in particular took up the challenge and gave classic responses to it: Fontenelle, in his *Entretiens sur la pluralité des mondes* (1686) (and in the series of *Eloges* that he wrote during his long tenure as *secrétaire perpétuel* of the Académie des Sciences—these were not, of course, limited to Descartes and Cartesianism); and Voltaire, in his *Eléments de la philosophie de Newton* (1st ed., 1738). I have decided to concentrate here on Voltaire, but Fontenelle saw the nature of the problem first, and he noted its connection with an ancient parallel. Here is the opening sentence of the preface to the *Entretiens*: "Je suis à peu près dans le même cas où se trouve Cicéron, lorsqu'il entreprit de mettre en sa langue des matières de philosophie, qui jusque-là n'avaient été traitées qu'en grec."[1] Fontenelle first and then Voltaire were mediators between the "philosophie" of their time—more specifically, the new physics written in its technical language—and an audience unaccustomed to such language. Like Cicero, they wished to join knowledge to effective expression, wisdom to eloquence.

The three works I have just mentioned go over the same or similar ground, but with different emphases. In the *Entretiens* Fontenelle constantly shapes his material so as to make it easy for his *audience*, which is summed up in the figure of the Marquise, who is beautiful and intelligent, but no great reader; in the *Eloges* he keeps our attention constantly on the *inventors* of new theories; and Voltaire, finally, in his *Eléments*, makes an impressive attempt to convey the conclusions, method and spirit of Newton's *theories*. We can see, therefore, in these remarkable texts a series of experiments in *vulgarisation* centering by turns (1) on the audience, (2) on the philosopher/scientist or (3) on the inquiry itself—though, of course, none of these factors is ever completely absent. In fact, my remarks on Voltaire treat his way of conceiving audience as well as theory and, in passing, his image of Newton as a man. Actually, if one takes the three terms in the order 2, 3, 1, they form a triad that resembles speaker-speech-audience or writer-work-reader. They put the new science at once and axiomatically into a rhetorical context.

II

The first edition of the *Eléments de la philosophie de Newton* had as its subtitle the phrase "mis à la portée de tout le monde," which suggested to some a bad joke to the effect that the elements in question had been "mis à la porte de tout le monde." The publishers had invented the subtitle, but it was fair enough. Voltaire himself had spoken in a letter two years earlier (1736) of Newton's philosophy and of the need to make it accessible to the public: "mis à la portée du public."

Clearly, he thought of his *Eléments* as a replacement for Fontenelle's *Entretiens*, which—with its plenum, its *matière fluide*, its fixed stars, its vortices—was unswervingly Cartesian. In his *avant-propos* Voltaire hastens to separate himself from his predecessor, though without naming him:

Ce n'est point ici une marquise ni une philosophie imaginaire. L'étude solide que vous avez faite de plusieurs vérités, et le fruit d'un travail respectable, sont ce que j'offre au public pour votre gloire, pour celle de votre sexe, et pour l'utilité de quiconque voudra cultiver sa raison et jouir sans peine de vos recherches.[2]

The contrast with the *Entretiens* is total. Instead of imagined conversations with an imaginary marquise about a philosophy that he takes to be a product of the imagination, Voltaire evokes a real marquise, Mme du Châtelet, who has herself carried out—with Voltaire as a collaborator—investigations on a genuine subject matter that yielded or confirmed truths useful to anyone wishing to cultivate his mind.

The Marquise represents, in fact, only one of the categories of readers Voltaire thinks he is addressing. He says in one place that he writes for himself and for a few others: "Mon principal but, dans la recherche que je vais faire, est de me donner à moi-même, et peut-être à quelques lecteurs, des idées nettes de ces lois primitives de la nature que Newton a trouvées" (p. 438, Introduction to the 2e Partie, in 1741). But elsewhere he asserts that philosophy and science are widely pertinent:

La philosophie est de tout état et de tout sexe: elle est compatible avec la culture des belles-lettres, et même avec ce que l'imagination a de plus brillant, pourvu qu'on n'ait point permis à cette imagination de s'accoutumer à orner des faussetés, ni de trop voltiger sur la surface des objets. (p. 401)

He sees no necessary tension between the "two cultures" (here again he is perhaps disagreeing with Fontenelle, who had promoted physics, mathematics and medicine at the expense of poetry and eloquence during the Quarrel of the Ancients and Moderns). *Belles-lettres* can coexist with *philosophie*. But so can civil life and one kind of thinking, at least, that goes with it: "Elle s'accorde encore très bien avec l'esprit d'affaires pourvu que, dans les emplois de la vie civile, on se soit accoutumé à ramener les choses à des principes, et qu'on n'ait point trop appesanti son esprit dans les détails" (ibid.). And, of course, women can do philosophy; Mme du Châtelet had shown the way: "Elle est certainement du ressort des femmes lorsqu'elles ont su mêler aux amusements de leur sexe cette application constante qui est peut-être le don de l'esprit le plus rare. Qui jamais a mieux prouvé que vous, Madame, cette vérité?" (ibid.). The most formal statement concerning the size of his audience comes in the Introduction, after the compliments have been made and the body of the work is approached:

On tâchera de mettre ces Eléments à la portée de ceux qui ne connaissent de Newton et de la philosophie que le nom seul. La science de la nature est un bien qui appartient à tous les hommes. Tous voudraient avoir connaissance de leur bien, peu ont le temps ou la patience de le calculer; Newton a compté pour eux. (p. 438)

Whatever the number of readers may be, in fact, Voltaire thinks that what he is about to treat belongs by right to all; and it is precisely there that the need for rhetoric arises. Voltaire would not have used that word to characterize his *Eléments*; indeed, he was probably referring to rhetoric when he used the disdainful phrases cited above apropos of the imagination and its tendencies: "orner des faussetés," "trop voltiger sur la surface des choses." I suspect that in the back of his mind are the old prejudices about rhetoric as an art of ornament and verbiage. But the fact remains that he has written a rhetorical work, in the sense that it depends on a mediating discipline of composition and communication. Newton inventoried our common property, but the calculations are obscure; he shed a great deal of light, but it is too far from our eyes. Voltaire must interpret him to us. He will go down into the *abîme* that hides the light and bring it up to where all may see and understand:

La philosophie de Newton a semblé jusqu'à présent à beaucoup de personnes aussi inintelligible que celle des anciens; mais l'obscurité des Grecs venait de ce qu'en effet ils n'avaient point de lumière, et les ténèbres de Newton viennent de ce que sa lumière était trop loin de nos yeux. Il a trouvé des vérités; mais il les a cherchées et placées dans un abîme: il faut y descendre et les apporter au grand jour. (p. 439)

Through these passages Voltaire shows us who his addressees are: himself, a few readers, those interested in literature (broadly defined), all ranks and callings in society, women—in other words, everybody; and this ever-widening focus is an indispensable clue to the importance and essential nature of his undertaking.

III

Voltaire is now ready to approach his reader. He regularly avoids offering on the printed page an exposition to be read in cold blood. Again and again he turns his reader into an interlocutor; he engages him in something like a dialogue that may often become three-sided, involving philosophers and scientists as well. Almost any chapter will do as a case in point. Chapter X ("De la réfrangibilité") begins: "Si vous demandez aux philosophes ce qui produit les couleurs . . ." (p. 483)—and right away you have the device of direct address, something, incidentally, that Pascal used repeatedly to good effect in the *Provinciales,* and we know that Voltaire admired that work as an example of argument in prose. The sentence continues: ". . . Descartes vous répondra que 'les globules de ses éléments sont déterminés à tournoyer sur eux-mêmes, outre leur tendance au mouvement en ligne droite, et que ce sont les différents tournoiements qui font les différents couleurs' " (ibid.). The next word that Voltaire writes is "Mais . . . ." With relish he begins a refutation of Descartes. There is no need to carry out experiments in order to prove him wrong; easily accessible demonstrations will do: "Mais ses éléments, ses globules, son tournoiement, ont-ils même besoin de la pierre de touche de l'expérience pour que le faux s'en fasse sentir? Une foule de démonstrations anéantit ces chimères. Voici les plus simples et les plus sensibles" (ibid.). There follows a page in the demonstrative, or, as I think we may say, the dialectical, mode. Here are some phrases, chosen at points of articulation in the argument; they will suffice to give an impression of Voltaire's manner of reasoning with his imagined interlocutor:

Rangez des boules les unes contre les autres: supposez-les poussées en tout sens . . . . il est impossible que . . . . De plus, comment verriez-vous . . . . Un jésuite flamand fit cette objection à Descartes; celui-ci en sentit toute la force, mais que croiriez-vous qu'il répondit? . . . Vous me direz sans doute que . . . . Vous me direz que . . . mais ce scrupule sera bientôt levé, si vous considérez que . . . . Mais direz-vous . . . . Cela est vrai . . . . Mais . . . . Il faut avouer que dans le plein de Descartes, cette intersection de rayons est impossible; mais tout est également impossible dans le plein, et il n'y a aucun mouvement, quel qu'il soit, qui ne suppose et ne prouve le vide. (pp. 483-84)

So much for Descartes here. But Voltaire has not finished with the philosophers. "Malebranche vint à son tour et vous dit . . ." (p. 484). This little opening, no doubt inspired by the line from "Les Animaux malades de la peste" ("L'Ane vint à son tour et dit . . ."), leads us off on a different track. Malebranche denies the Cartesian explanation of colors and brings forward his own solution: "petits tourbillons tournoyants de matière subtile, capables de compression" (ibid.). These replace the "globules de lumière" of Descartes, and their vibrations under pressure constitute the various colors. Voltaire quotes Malebranche's statement that it is impossible to determine the exact relationships or proportions of these vibrations, and then he plays his ace of trumps:

Vous remarquerez qu'il parlait ainsi dans l'Académie des sciences en 1699, et que l'on avait déjà découvert ces proportions en 1675, non pas des proportions de vibration de petits tourbillons, qui n'existent point, mais proportions de la réfrangibilité des rayons, qui contiennent les couleurs, comme nous le dirons bientôt. Ce qu'il croyait impossible était déjà démontré aux yeux, reconnu vrai par le sens, ce qui aurait bien déplu au P. Malebranche. (ibid.)

Malebranche is dismissed with less reasoning and ceremony than was Descartes. Still, Voltaire is making an important point, in fact *the* point, from the Newtonian approach: Malebranche gives us an impressive example of hypothesis-framing that takes place apart from observed phenomena, and even with systematic distrust of the senses.

In the third page of his presentation Voltaire refers to "d'autres philosophes" without naming them. According to their view, color results from the amount of reflected rays coming from an object; thus, white reflects the most, black the least. An easily performed experiment will disprove this. The *vous* so constantly appealed to in this chapter can do it:

Cette hypothèse (déjà suspecte, puisqu'elle est hypothèse) ne paraît qu'une erreur grossière, dès l'instant que l'on daigne considérer un tableau à un jour faible, et ensuite à un grand jour. Vous voyez toujours les mêmes couleurs. Du blanc, qui n'est éclairé que d'une bougie, est toujours blanc; et le vert, éclairé de mille bougies, sera toujours vert. (p. 485)

This passage concludes what might be called the opening *refutatio* (it has taken up two-plus pages of the total of six). The time has come for the *confirmatio*. Voltaire continues in the mode of quasi-dialogue:

> Adressez-vous enfin à Newton. Il vous dira: Ne m'en croyez pas; n'en croyez que vos yeux et les mathématiques; mettez-vous dans une chambre tout à fait obscure, où le jour n'entre que par un trou extrêmement petit: le rayon de la lumière viendra sur un papier vous donner la couleur de la blancheur. (ibid.)

Voltaire/Newton then tells us exactly what to do with prisms and lenses in this darkened room in order to find out some essential things about light: the division of the single ray of white light into seven distinct colors or rays, the different degrees of refrangibility that are characteristic of the rays, the possibility of recombining the separate strands of color so as to make white again, the unalterable character of the seven colors taken one at a time.

What is happening here? We have already seen one transformation in the addressee of these *Eléments*—from reader to interlocutor—in a conversation involving Voltaire, Descartes, Malebranche and others. Now *words* are giving way to *actions*: the interlocutor learns how to become an amateur investigator. References to proper names and authorities drop out. Nature is the authority—or rather witness, since she is being interrogated in special circumstances and with special equipment, with the idea that she will give answers to be assembled and judged by the observer. It seems to me that we have reached a decisive point in understanding how Voltaire proceeds in these *Eléments de la philosophie de Newton*. Rhetoric does its job and in so doing establishes its proper bounds. At a certain moment it falls silent, because an argument to which one assents by the force of words is yielding to a conclusion at which one arrives by oneself in the presence of things. At first Voltaire's efforts to win and hold his reader's attention called for drawing science into the rhetorical situation and its familiar tropes; but here rhetoric is disappearing into the operation of inquiry. The nature and cause of the paradox will be clear, I hope, in sections V and VI of this discussion.

IV

Voltaire's "petit traité d'optique," as he calls it—from which I have chosen one chapter for comment—ends with a conjecture connecting the behavior of light with the principle of gravitational attraction. In the second part of the *Eléments* he studies that principle, that force, as it applies everywhere to all things. As before, he is concerned to adjust his presentation to the experience and capacity of his reader; and once more there is a *pars destruens* in the argument, even more imposing than before, through which we must go before settling down to the *pars construens*. Again the idealistic constructions of Descartes must be laid low before the discoveries of Newton—shown to be rooted in work done by Galileo, Kepler and Copernicus—are reviewed and summarized. Voltaire concentrates his fire against the *plein* and the *tourbillons*. Against the latter he offers eleven numbered refutations, or "demonstrations." Most of them consist of a single paragraph, and five are set up as single sentences.

Here is the first one, which refers to Descartes's assumption that the earth and the moon are caught up in a vortex causing them to move rapidly from west to east and that this vortex is located in another, even more vast, and so on:

1º Si cela était, le tourbillon qui est supposé se mouvoir autour de la terre d'occident en orient devrait chasser les corps sur la terre d'occident en orient; or, les corps en tombant décrivent tous une ligne qui, étant prolongée, passerait à peu près par le centre de la terre: donc ce tourbillon n'existe pas. (p. 512)

The formula and the principle of demonstration are perfectly clear: if X, then Y; but observation shows Z instead of Y; hence, we may deny X. By discrediting the consequent we destroy the antecedent.

With slight variations Voltaire follows this pattern through the series. The conclusion—"donc ces tourbillons n'existent pas"—becomes a kind of refrain. This figure of proof makes minimal demands on the reader. He need not have any direct knowledge of Descartes's problematic and method; he need not know what lies behind the critical observations of natural phenomena; and he certainly is not called on to repeat the experiments leading to them. He is asked to do only two things, both matters of immediate judgment: (1) to see the connection between what is said in the if-clause and what is said in the consequent, and (2) to see the contradiction between the alleged observation and what is affirmed in the consequent.

The next chapter starts a series written in the constructive mode, though the side remarks against the Cartesians never let up. Voltaire radically changes his style of presentation. He gives an account that is essentially *narrative*, taking us in a half-dozen pages from falling bodies to universal gravitation. At each stage he finds some way to make the story vivid, convincing, instructive.

He constructs the situation and thoughts of Newton:

Un jour, en l'année 1666, Newton, retiré à la campagne, et voyant tomber des fruits d'un arbre, à ce que m'a conté sa nièce (Mme Conduit), se laissa aller à une méditation profonde sur la cause qui entraîne ainsi tous les corps dans une ligne qui, si elle était prolongée, passerait à peu près par le centre de la terre. (p. 520)

Newton recognizes in a short inner monologue that it cannot be what Descartes thought it to be: "Quelle est, se demandait-il, cette force qui ne peut venir de tous ces tourbillons imaginaires démontrés si faux?" (ibid.). After Newton has his basic intuition and as he begins to think of lines of possible proof, Voltaire points out a lesson in method:

> Mais ce n'est pas ici une hypothèse qu'on ajuste comme on peut à un système; ce n'est point un calcul où l'on doive se contenter de l'à-peu-près. Il faut commencer par connaître au juste la distance de la lune à la terre, et, pour la connaître, il est nécessaire d'avoir la mesure de notre globe. C'est ainsi que raisonna Newton . . . . (ibid.)

Our lesson is completed as we note the proper attitude and morality that any student of nature should have. When his theory failed to conform to what he thought to be accurate observations, Newton reacted in an exemplary way:

> Il ne crut pas qu'il lui fût permis de rien suppléer, et d'accommoder la nature à ses idées; il voulait accommoder ses idées à la nature: il abandonna donc cette belle découverte, que l'analogie avec les autres astres rendait si vraisemblable, et à laquelle il manquait si peu pour être démontrée; bonne foi bien rare, et qui seule doit donner un grand poids à ses opinions. (p. 521)

Although, as I say, this chapter has a strongly narrative aspect, the next ten chapters emphasize demonstrations and necessarily become more technical. New proofs of gravitation are found in the orbit of the moon and in the irregularities of that orbit, in the elliptical character of the orbits described by the other planets as they move about the sun, in the studies of distances and revolutions of planets with reference to the sun, in the movement of tides on earth, in a general "théorie de la lune et du reste des planètes," and so on.

Sometimes Voltaire shunts into notes the longer and more difficult developments. One long passage in Chapter VII was originally printed in italics. Voltaire explains: "Tout ceci est mis en lettres italiques pour avertir les lecteurs peu exercés qu'on peut passer les calculs et aller tout d'un coup au chapitre VIII" (p. 537). By thus writing on different levels of technicality (and marking them clearly), he makes it possible to satisfy more than one kind of reader. He also includes 73 illustrative figures, which are great helps, in spite of the fact that they fall below the kind of presentation to which we have become accustomed in modern textbooks.

V

Voltaire's reader, as he goes through the chapters on optics, can have from time to time a sense of participating in scientific investigation and in rediscovering for himself what Newton had learned about light. I suspect that, as he gets into the chapters on gravitation and the system of the world, he is likely to revert to his original status as Voltaire's pupil. The subject matter of the *Principia mathematica philosophiae naturalis* does not lend itself readily to vulgarization. If we compare the *Principia* with the *Eléments*, it is apparent that the substance of Books I and II, where Newton expounds the theory of motions and of motions "in resisting mediums," has been largely omitted, and what remains has been modified considerably.

Newton's plan was first to set up his theory and then to provide a large-scale application of it in Book III, which he entitled "The System of the World (in Mathematical Treatment)." In fact, the treatment in Books I and II is even more strictly mathematical than in Book III, moving steadily from definitions and axioms to propositions and proofs, with additional matter set down in corollaries and scholia. At the time of composing Book III, Newton made a very significant choice, which he explains in a prefatory note:

> It remains that, from the same principles, I now demonstrate the frame of the System of the World. Upon this subject I had indeed composed the third book in a popular method, that it might be read by many; but afterwards, considering that such as had not sufficiently entered into the principles could not easily discern the strength of the consequences, nor lay aside the prejudices to which they had been many years accustomed, therefore, to prevent the disputes which might be raised upon such accounts, I chose to reduce the substance of this book into the form of Propositions (in the mathematical way), which should be read by those only who had first made themselves masters of the principles established in the preceding books.[3]

He adds that one need not study every proposition in the previous books; it would be enough to read carefully the definitions, the laws of motion and the first three sections of Book I, consulting the remaining portions as references and needs require.

Voltaire seems to have taken this suggestion to heart: he concentrates on Book III and makes selections from Books I and II. But with regard to exposition, he cast his chapters in a non-geometrical format, thus choosing precisely the alternative that Newton says he discarded.

It would not be fair to criticize Voltaire for not doing exactly what Newton does. As a matter of fact, the *Eléments* was a successful and influential work. However, it *is* fair to say that, when Voltaire set out to popularize Newtonianism, he became involved in a complex problem of interdisciplinary relations. Rhetoric and mathematical physics are quite distinct modes of discourse.

What happened in this episode in the history of rhetoric is that (1) the subject matter, (2) the principles and (3) the method of science had to be

transformed so as to enter into the economy of rhetoric, which has its own
(1) subject matter, (2) principles and (3) method. (1) Bodies in motion,
(2) attractions and ratios, and (3) observations, measurements and deduc-
tions had to be transformed so that they could function in the framework
of rhetoric, where the essential factors are (1) a public and its opinions, (2)
a writer and (3) a way of combining appropriately a content and a manner
of expression. Some changes must take place. Newtonianism, which was
elaborated in *inquiry*, becomes a content to be expressed in accessible
prose instead of the esoteric language of geometry; and, thus transformed,
it emerges in a new perspective and is elaborated in *communication*. Moreover, the problem is not really one of technical vs. non-technical ways of
saying the same things. The *Principia* and the *Eléments* embody two distinct kinds of technicality. They are incommensurable, and yet rhetoric, as
a comprehensive attitude and discipline, has the power to overcome in its
way the obstacles and to free truth that otherwise would be held captive
in specialized treatises. Of course, the subject of discourse loses something
as it passes from the first mode to the second, but it also gains something—a
new life in a wider circle of minds than before. The *Eléments* are a genuine
work of enlightenment and of the Enlightenment.

Much more could be said about the indefatigable rhetoric of Voltaire;
Newtonianism was only one article in his gospel for his age. And Voltaire
was only one of the *philosophes*, each of whom had a grip on some technical wisdom that needed to be made accessible to all.

VI

This episode illustrates a tension or paradox that recurs in the history
of rhetoric. In Voltaire's treatment of optics, rhetoric prepares the way for
science and by moments becomes indistinguishable from it; in his treatment of gravitation, however, rhetoric does not abdicate—it stands finally
as a sovereign discipline in counterdistinction to science. It states *in its
way* truths that science states *in its way*. The relationship between the two
accounts is guaranteed by the productive force of ambiguity and by the
analogies that it engenders. In other words, we can see in the *Eléments de
la philosophie de Newton* how the status, scope and function of rhetoric
may evolve in two directions: it may be derivative, limited and propae-
deutic, or it may be independent, comprehensive and judicial.

With a few changes in wording we could make the same points about
Fontenelle and his effort to popularize the Cartesian world view, and also

about Cicero and his attempt to interpret Greek philosophy to Roman readers. In all three instances, there is no doubt what the choice has been: Cicero, Fontenelle and Voltaire opt for an art of composition and communication belonging more often than not to the independent, comprehensive and judicial kind. For representatives of the other option one might mention Plato, Saint Augustine and Pascal. I cannot here develop this line of thought; my point is that the discipline of rhetoric—which takes its point of departure in commonplaces—behaves itself like a commonplace, i.e., a locus of possibilities; and, as it plays its role in intellectual and artistic history, now this and now that possibility is realized, in versions that are more or less pure.

The period of the Enlightenment would seem to be a particularly fertile field for studies of the changing faces and uses of rhetoric. The very notion of Enlightenment implies a distinction between knowledge and opinion and a desire to replace the latter by the former. In such an atmosphere rhetoric is bound to flourish. Although Voltaire, Montesquieu, Diderot and Rousseau—to mention only some French examples—make disparaging remarks about rhetoric as an art of ornaments, flights of the imagination and appeals to feeling, the fact is that rhetoric understood in a more authentic sense is something they produced and consumed on a very large scale.

NOTES

1. *Entretiens sur la pluralité des mondes*, ed. Robert Shackleton (Oxford, 1955), p. 53.

2. *Oeuvres complètes de Voltaire* (Paris: Garnier, 1879), XXII, 400n. All further citations refer to this edition.

3. *Mathematical Principles of Natural Philosophy*, Great Books of the Western World, 34 (Chicago: Encyclopedia Britannica, 1952), p. 269.

John D. Lyons

Belief and Representation in a Renaissance Novella

A novella seems easy to read. After wending through the fantastic realms of *Orlando furioso* or *Gerusalemme liberata*, many a student has been happy to rest, to enjoy a good story about ordinary life. Yet often our relaxed familiarity with the novella makes us forget that its apparent "realism" is an artful and not a spontaneous quality. We may forget that we are not reading picturesque scenes taken from everyday 16th-century life, but narrative based on a social consensus of beliefs about the world, a consensus that should be conceived as a process and not as a stable and timeless object.

The widely influential *Novelle* of Matteo Bandello (1485-1561) offer particularly good opportunities to explore the social role of belief and the relationship between belief and the novella as genre. Indeed, Bandello's work has traditionally been subjected to a kind of criticism that makes an approach through this problematic particularly useful.[1]

I

Let us look closely at one story, the *Mirabil beffa fatta da una gentil-donna a dui baroni del regno d'Ongaria.*[2]

The principal elements of Bandello's story can be summarized quickly. A Bohemian knight (Ulrico), vassal of King Mattia of Hungary, marries a young Bohemian lady (Barbara), whose family fortune, like her husband's, has been squandered. Moved by ambition, he wants to improve his estate through royal service, but fears to leave his beautiful wife, lest she succumb to the advances of other neighboring barons. She promises to remain faithful and even to allow him to lock her in the tower in order to assure himself of her virtue. He promises to leave her in full liberty and in charge of their castle if he does go away, but he still hesitates. Hearing of a renowned Polish doctor, he asks for some means to be certain of his wife's fidelity. The Pole tells him that there is no means to constrain her to fidelity, but gives him an image of a woman which will always appear brightly colored if his wife is faithful. If she is tempted, the image will become pale during the moments of temptation and then return to its normal color. If she is actively unfaithful, the image will become black and will stink. With this image in a little box, the knight goes to court and wins great favor. Certain Hungarian gentlemen are puzzled that Ulrico would leave a beautiful wife, and to his claim of trusting her virtue they reply that women are naturally and easily seduced. Two of the Hungarians wager all their goods that one of them can seduce Barbara. Each of the Hungarians separately attempts and fails to win the lady. She tricks both by imprisoning them and making them work at a spinning wheel. The lady writes her husband, and the king and queen, after sending counselors to confirm the situation of the barons, reward the Bohemian couple.

Clearly a central subject of the novella is how qualities become known through what people say. The problem of discourse, or of *fama* (reputation, rumor), is introduced by Ulrico's wife very early in the tale when she describes what men say about women ("voi uomini diciate le donne esser di povero core," p. 245). Public esteem affects Ulrico directly and through his wife, who would not be called the same thing if she became unfaithful ("come la donna ha perduto l'onore ha perduto quanto di bene possa avere in questa vita e non merita piú esser nomata donna," he reminds his wife, speaking of unfaithful women, p. 247). In the court Ulrico soon wins a reputation ("acquistando nome," p. 249), and the word also spreads that he has a beautiful wife. By far the most important display of the power of what people say is the court dispute about the nature of women. Here there is a veritable battle of maxims, common opinions as solidified into traditional sayings. On the one hand, there is the belief in difference between individuals ("dui fratelli e due sorelle, ad un medesimo parto nati, saranno il più de le volte di contrario temperamento e di costumi diversissimi," p. 252, and "Ciascuno sa i casi suoi, e il pazzo sa meglio ciò che ha, che non sanno i suoi vicini ancor che siano savii," p. 251), and, on the other hand, a belief in uniformity within categories. In this latter perspective comments on women abound: "le donne esser naturalmente pieghevoli . . . ," etc. (p. 253).

The narrative is not neutral in this quarrel between the tenants of sameness and the partisans of individual difference. It comes down strongly on the side of difference, for it asserts not only that the court dispute is *about* the variety of individuals, but also that it is *caused* by that variety: "... perché gli uomini tutti non sono d'un temperamento e molti si persuadeno saper piú del compagno, e ne le chimere loro sono di maniere ostinati che de la ragione punto no si appagano, quasi che i ragionamenti vennero in gridi ed in romori" (p. 251). Even after the queen's intervention on the side of multiplicity, the two Hungarians persist in proclaiming the universal *sameness* of female nature because men are all *different* from one another, as the narrator says: "perché, come si vede, ... un uomo più di un altro è ardito, anzi, per meglio dire, ostinato e temerario ..." (p. 252).

These contradictory opinions would lead to a dead end if it were not for the empirical option—the proof, *prova*—that is organized by the court. After all, Ulrico goes to the court to seek recognition for his valor by demonstrating it. But demonstration, through which action influences the world of words, or *fama*, is divided into two parts. One is the argumentative aspect, the formation of hypotheses and the judgment of experience, and the other is the active experience itself. In the *Mirabil beffa* these two parts are separated spatially.

The story, even in the simplest form, could not exist without the separation of the husband and the wife. But in Bandello's tale it is not only the spouses who are separated. The distinction between the Hungarian court and the Bohemian castle incorporates the division between the center of judgment and the place of experience. The distance between the spouses permits a transfer of responsibility from husband to wife; she assumes the defense of honor normally assumed by him and, thus, takes on part of his role. Her failure in that role would ruin not only her, but also—and this consideration is stated first in the narrative—her husband ("temo ... che io non ricevessi alcun disonore," says Ulrico of his wife's potential infidelity in his absence, p. 245). This honor, which is not the virtue of chastity, but the specific power of reputation, is mentioned in the context of the spouses' common desire for the benefits offered by the royal court, benefits which are counterbalanced by a feudal rivalry expressed in sexual terms: "Che subito ch'io fossi partito, dubito che i baroni e gentiluomini ne la contrada non si mettano con ogni loro sforzo per acquistare il vostro amore" (p. 245). By leaving her "padrona di tutto e signora," Ulrico places responsibility for his position as a local baron in the hands of his wife while he advances the reputation of the family at court. Thus, a hierarchy is established in space. The *active* pursuit of honor takes place at the royal court. The passive defense of honor is regional or provincial.

This hierarchical difference is coupled with a temporal one, for the Bohemian castle is the vestige of former nobiliary glory, a formal political system. Ulrico refuses to force his subjects to pay more than "quel censo che ai suoi avoli erano consueti pagare, che era molto poca moneta" (p. 243). His wife insists on the decadence of their state: "che il vostro et mio padri hanno logorati molti beni" (p. 244). The wife describes the bedroom to which she confines the first Hungarian as an ancient prison ("una prigione fortissima, che fatta fu anticamente," p. 255). King Mattia's court, on the other hand, is the place of contemporary glory, the unique avenue towards honor. Bandello's lengthy development of Ulrico's motivation underscores the lack of alternatives to the court. The court is the modern, adaptive locus of achievement in a centralized monarchy, a monarchy which supersedes, and consequently requires also the subjection of, regional interests, in this case, the subordination of Bohemia to Hungary.

This historical situation casts the king and queen in a very specific role, one which is less the direction of the state than the judgment of value (of *virtù*). The initiative comes from within the dynamic structure of the court over which the royal figures preside and where they serve as arbiters. Both husband and wife insist on this function. Ulrico describes the king as "liberalissimo principe ed amando gli uomini che il vagliono" (p. 245), and the wife refers to him as "giudicose estimatore . . . de l'altrui vertú" (p. 246). So important is this function that the court becomes almost a "court" in the different sense of "tribunal," for here active discussions take place and the royal couple makes decisions concerning rewards for individuals on the basis of their demonstrated accomplishments.

In this court the queen has a role developed especially by Bandello.[3] She is not only the defender of women—though one of the Hungarian gentlemen attributes her opinion to her sex: "fate bene a mantener la ragione de le donne, poi che sète donna" (p. 252)—but the promoter of consensus in general. Hearing that the conflicting claims of Ulrico and the Hungarians had led to "gridi ed . . . romori,"

Ella, che donna era a cui le gare e questioni in corte meravigliosamente dispiacevano, fatti a sé chiamar coloro che ragionato avevano, volle puntalmente che i parlamenti avuti le fossero narrati. E avendo il tutto inteso, disse che in effetto ciascuno poteva a suo piacer credere in tel materia ciò che voleva; ma che era bene presontuosa e temeraria pazzia giudicar tutte le donne d'una maniera, come anco errore grandissimo esser si conoscceva a dire che tutti gli uomini fossero di medesimi costumi . . . . (pp. 251-52)

In other words, the queen is not simply the champion of women, but the principal proponent of the great variety of individual characteristics among members of both sexes. At the same time she opposes conflict which arises from such multiplicity. She has the paradoxical role of advocating a unitary opinion of diversity, advocating discursive consensus about the variations of extra-discursive, concrete reality. The Hungarian gentlemen, on the other hand, approve discursive disagreement about the underlying unity of non-discursive reality—e.g., the sameness of all women. This symmetry of stances towards the relationship of language to reality reveals a political as well as a philosophical tension. The existence of a court supposes a hierarchical ordering of persons in a non-egalitarian, yet strangely interchangeable way. The project of forming a "perfect courtier" in Castiglione and the prescriptions for courtly conduct in the other courtesy books of the period are evidence of a standardization of courtiers. Such a standardization permits the rise and fall of individuals in the court without altering the court framework itself. The emphasis on courtesy makes achievement in court, in the eyes of the ruler, more important than purely inherited property (i.e., real estate). Though courtiers may differ in their accomplishment of courtly acts, such accomplishment is never an end in itself, but a means of attracting admiration and the respect of the prince. Initiative is encouraged and conflict is permitted so long as it is merely verbal conflict which submits itself to the ruler as arbiter. The centripetal energy of such a system contrasts with the centrifugal rivalry of provincial aristocracy mentioned by Ulrico before his departure for the court. In this provincial or feudal system, multiplicity of "centers of power," so to speak, coexists with a unity of goal (possessing the coveted woman). The Hungarian gentlemen consider it normal that the queen defends a position favorable to women, because they believe that a multiplicity of discourse is inevitable despite the monotonous sameness of the world, for this concept parallels their view of the world as perpetual rivalry never coalescing around an effective, hierarchical and non-violent center of power.

The contrast between these two structures of power (and their corollary structures of belief) is evoked spatially in the novella. The movement towards the court (Ulrico, the wife's messenger, the returning chancellor and counselors) denotes the appeal to the king's power as controller of discourse, as the one who decides what is established as a statement of truth. The movement away from the court (the Hungarian gentlemen, the inquiring chancellor and counselors) is from language towards what the characters call *prova*, proof by action. But such proof is firmly subordinated to argumentation as it occurs under the king's direction. On the return of the mission of inquiry, a full judicial proceeding gives the property of the defeated barons to Ulrico. On one level, therefore, the story moves in a circle, from courtly discussion back to courtly discussion. But perhaps the spiral would be a better image, for the return to discussion occurs with a higher degree of authority.

II

There is another authority in this story, an authority that is never opposed to the royal power and remains unknown to the king and queen, the magic picture. This authority and the belief it permits differ spatially from the procedure of assertion/proof, which originates in the courtly discussion and then returns to the court for final confirmation of the findings of experience. The magic picture is brought to the court and provides information in one direction only and to a single person. With his magic portrait in its *scatolino*, Ulrico possesses an individual knowledge that places him outside the social system. Significantly, he is not a major party to the general discussion about the nature of women because his ideas are not based on deduction from general principles or indeed, despite the queen's assertion to the contrary ("ella portava fermissima openione che il cavalier boemo avesse ragione di credere de la sua moglie . . . avendola per lungo tempo praticata," p. 252), on inductive experiential knowledge. The portrait, which I have called magic, is described as being based on the research of a learned medical doctor, who has a reputation as a sorcerer. It is not clear whether we should call it technology or magic, categories not strictly separated at the time (cf. Della Porta's *Magia naturalis*, 1558). Whatever it is called, the picture gives Ulrico the means to succeed at court. He can concentrate on his achievement without afterthought for his wife, remain passive in the discussion about the nature of women, and observe the pact he has made with the two Hungarian gentlemen: he promises that he will send no messages *to* his wife, but he continues to receive information from her through his magic picture. This passivity, similar in many ways to the effortless grace of achievement recommended by Castiglione for those who can conceal their extraordinary preparation, undercuts the political structure and the beliefs implicit in the court/province opposition. Ulrico can go anywhere with his portrait. It liberates him from the day-to-day defense of his castle and from the cares of petty baronial rivalry. Secure in his faith, Ulrico can remain at court while the Hungarians travel on their mission of conquest. They show in this way a continued preoccupation with provincial conquest, while Ulrico is an accomplished modern courtier attentive to his position in the center of power. He is Bohemian, yet he is a better vassal of the Hungarian king than the Hungarian gentlemen.

So the portrait works. It lets Ulrico do what he wants to do. But does the portrait do what the doctor says it will? Is it a placebo, this portrait? Has the Polish doctor treated Ulrico's fears of being "sent to Cornwall" by giving him an object that only reflects the faith of the one who uses it?

Would the portrait really turn black and stink? Ulrico never knows, but he has an almost religious faith in this picture and in his lady: "per fermo teneva la sua donna esser onestissima e leale e fedele, e credeva come al Vangelo al paragone de l'imagine" (p. 253). This belief is essential to his actions, but Ulrico's faith would not work without the portrait. He could not leave his province on the strength of his own estimation of his wife's virtue. He needs some external representation of what he wants to believe. Curiously, the portrait and Ulrico's already great faith in his wife must co-exist and are stated together in the text. When the other courtiers see the Bohemian's serenity at court, they are unaware that this manifestation of trust is based in part on an instrument conceived in the greatest of mistrust and acquired on account of the proverbial fear of "Cornwall." The doctor who makes it considers women to be "naturalmente fragili ed inclinatissime a la libidine" (p. 248). Perhaps it is not a mere accident that the image of the faithful wife should be fabricated by a skeptical doctor, for this image is necessary only as an antidote to another contrary representation. No belief is spontaneous and unmediated in this novella. The husband's distrust does not come from any experience of disloyalty in his wife, but from a general discourse about women. The portrait is a representation destined to combat Ulrico's belief in what people say about women, or at least about one woman. By playing one representation against another, Ulrico can approximate a kind of spontaneous trust, a return to his own belief in the honesty of his lady. In this respect the spontaneity simulated by the perfect courtier parallels this highly mediated return to a "natural" contact with reality.

III

Although the magic portrait is an important and rather startling part of the story of the *Mirabil beffa*, it is clear that the making of the portrait is much less important than the use to which the portrait is put. In seeing how Bandello centers his tale on the courtly discussion, it is helpful, therefore, to note the changes in event and emphasis from two earlier stories—one in the *Gesta Romanorum* and the other in the romance of *Perceforest*—in which similar magic objects represent the fidelity of one or both spouses. In the *Gesta* story of the faithful carpenter, the husband goes off to work at court with a white shirt given to him by the mother of his bride. It has the unusual property of remaining always immaculate unless one of the two spouses is unfaithful. The court in this story plays very little role in the discovery of virtue; knowledge and the creation of consensus about what is true have much less importance than the instance on moral conduct, moral conduct which can be seen as the manifestation of grace and as an allegory for our relationship to God and the Church: "Uxor est sancta mater ecclesia," concludes the "moralization" at the end of the tale: "The wife is the holy mother Church, the carpenter is the good Christian, who accepted that maiden as wife. The shirt is our faith, because, as the apostle said, without faith it is impossible to please God." It is true that this tale and Bandello's have in common a concern for what is believed about the wife's conduct, but in the *Gesta* only the spouses' belief in one another, not the general agreement at court, matters. Finally, in the *Gesta* the text presents itself as a detached and impersonal legend without internal marks of its origin. "The very wise Gallus was king," it begins, leaving out any indication of who tells the story. In the romance of *Perceforest*, the section called the "Lai de la rose" is much closer to Bandello's tale in its events (the punishment of the would-be seducers, the desire of husband and wife to improve their state by obtaining regocnition from the king, the rivalry between courtiers, etc.), but it remains within a moral tradition, presenting the issue primarily as the triumph of chastity (a virtue) over jealousy (a vice). When the wife gives her departing husband a rose that does not fade, she offers him a chance to demonstrate his faith in her, and this faith constitutes a moral strength. The court is not foregrounded. Instead, the individual noble characters *as* individuals have first place, right from the beginning.

In Bandello's story, as we have seen, there is strong emphasis on belief about generalities and how one can speak about that belief. The actions of characters no ionger appear primarily as moral (and much less as religious), but as matters of civic concern in a courtly society. There is a certain irony in the fact that, while the central individual accomplishment of the story is the wife's fidelity, this triumph is cast into the periphery of the actions by the narrator's insistence on the court as the place of judgment and discourse. Conjugal fidelity, primary in the other two texts, is secondary in Bandello, for the real grain of sand in this pearl is not sexual jealousy, but the disturbance caused by a difference of opinion at court. The restoration of courtly harmony is, therefore, paramount, and in some senses it is not important whether Ulrico's wife is faithful, provided that there is no disorder in the royal presence.

This modification in emphasis in Bandello's text responds to a certain conception of the novella, which is not considered as a finished product, but as the result—or the embodiment—of a process: *novellare*, to tell a tale. This is an act, repeatedly accentuated by Bandello in a way that in part conforms to the novella tradition and in part indicates preoccupations peculiar to the 16th century. To the extent that the novella, since Boccaccio, traditionally includes the frame situation of those telling the tales, Bandello is loosely adapting his work to that tradition, both in his dedications and in his opening paragraphs. But Bandello here goes further towards the integration of frame and tale, making the process of telling tales part of the courtly demonstration of quality, of the courtly conversational exchange and of the system that can accept diversity within the "content" of its discussions, provided that certain formal relationships remain intact.

In the dedicatory letter to the *Mirabil beffa* Bandello had created a *locus amoenus* in a spa—in other words, centered, like so many fictive utopias, about a fountain. This place is inhabited by an idealized company of courtiers whose pastime comes directly out of a book. A copy of Boccaccio's *Decameron* circulates among this company, and from this book comes the example of the pleasure of telling novellas. Far from hiding the bookish sources of the novella, Bandello uses this volume, supreme among novella collections, to start a process in which the contours of book and world flicker and blur. The dedication is a letter (therefore, written) about a conversation (not previously written) in which a book provides the model of discourse. This discursive exchange contains a novella which is written by Bandello.

The narrator of the novella begins by blurring the distinction between the realm of what I have called the body of the novella and the court in which he speaks:

Io non so, signora Cecilia molto amabile ed onoranda, se cosí di leggero mi debbia, avendomene voi pregato, porre a novellare, non essendo io molto pratico di cotal mestiero, nel quale veggio alcuni in questa nobile ed onorata compagnia, che vie meglio di me e con maggior sodisfazione di tutti, essendo in quello essercitati, si diporterebbero.

Manfredi himself is simply retelling a story that he has heard from another courtier, his uncle. This uncle belongs to the Sforza court, but has also witnessed the Hungarian court. Mediator between the two courts, he also straddles the two realms of the telling of the tale (the "factual" context) and the tale itself (the exotic, uncertain, even "fictive" Hungarian world). Through this figure Bandello integrates the ancient story of the faithful spouses into the historical proximity of the Sforza court while maintaining a certain distance. Through the uncle, Manfredi tells the story as purely objective, passing from his own discourse to "history" (in Benveniste's terms).

By drawing attention to the environment in which the novella claims its place (and in which it claims to take place), Bandello opens for us fascinating questions about the relationship of text and society in the courtly literature of the 16th century. This relationship appears in the *Mirabil beffa* as a mirroring. The story that arises out of courtly discussion is about courtly discussion; the kind of noble character who tells the tale has his counter-part in the noble hero who proves his worth at court; etc. By proposing such a mirror, the novella becomes a genre that makes us forget that it is a literary genre at all, for its public is also its *dramatis personae*. This transparency, however, is undermined by Bandello's reminders that everything in this story is a *mise en scène*, a studied performance of spontaneity.

The paradoxical conclusion to which the *Mirabil beffa* leads us is that the realism of the novella, its conformity to our beliefs about the world around us, is the result of a particular process by which we agree about the world, a process in which we "produce" that world by telling one another about it. The important historical evolution in narrative that is foreshadowed by Bandello's work is the rise of the novel, a genre that continues for centuries to be preoccupied with questions about how a genre can conform to a consensus about the world (verisimilitude) while thriving on the representation of departures from that consensus, characters who break down the notions of what *all* members of a certain category are like.[4] Yet we sometimes forget that both novella and novel are only instruments, however magic, that reflect what we want to believe.

NOTES

1. A good summary of the controversy about fiction and history in Bandello can be found in T. Gwynfor Griffith, *Bandello's Fiction* (Oxford: Blackwell, 1955), pp. 1-22. Di Francia's articles appeared in 1921-1923 in the *Giornale Storico della Letteratura Italiana*, 78, 80 and 81. Brognoligo's reply was published in 1928 in the *Atti dell'Accademia Pontaniana*, 58.

2. I have used Francesco Flora's edition, *Tutte le Opere di Matteo Bandello*, I Classici Mondadori (Milan: Arnoldo Mondadori, 1934).

3. The figure of the queen is much less important in the "Lai de la rose" in *Perceforest* and altogether absent in the story of the carpenter in the *Gesta Romanorum*. For the "Lai de la rose" I have used the text published by Gaston Paris in his article, "Le Conte de la rose dans le roman de Perceforest," *Romania*, 23 (1894), 78-140. The tale "De castitate," beginning "Gallus regnavit prudens valde . . . ," can be found in *Gesta Romanorum*, ed. Hermann Oesterley (Berlin: Weidmannsche Buchhandlung, 1872), Capitulum 69, pp. 381-83.

4. The novel's delight in eccentrics can be seen in two of the works often hailed as the "first" novels, *Don Quixote* and *La Princesse de Clèves*.

Stephen G. Nichols, Jr.

The Promise of Performance:
Discourse and Desire in Early Troubadour Lyric[1]

What makes the early troubadours so special? Why do we feel that an aura of beginnings, a mystique of origins, marks the poetic tradition with particular force? It has become a commonplace of the teaching of Old Provensal poetry, for example, to say that the eleven extant songs of the first troubadour, Guilhem IX, Count of Toulouse and Duke of Aquitaine (1071-1127), adumbrate the basic elements of nearly all subsequent developments in the troubadour canon.

The works of the first troubadours undeniably occupy a more prominent position in the teaching and scholarship of Old Provensal poetry. Few students of the troubadours can quote a line from or even the title of a song by Guiraut d'Espanha (1240-1270) or Blacasset (ca. 1240-1280), to name but two troubadours of the last generation. Yet we unhesitatingly name Guilhem IX, Cercamon, Marcabru and Jaufré Rudel when asked to list the early troubadours and cite Bernart de Ventadorn as the transitional figure between the first generation and its successors. Furthermore, we can quote from memory first lines, favorite lines, themes and images from all of these poets. Could we do the same for the poets of the generation of 1200-1220?

The fascination surrounding the first generation of troubadours derives in part from the relative obscurity of their beginnings, but even more from the apparent freedom, the flexibility and openness that lay before these poets. Even though we know that a poetic movement does not generate spontaneously *ex nihilo*, we still feel a fascination with the infinite potential that confronted the founders, a potential we can identify retrospectively. Faced with the absence of a language, with no set genres, lacking the techniques that would be commonplace for their successors, in short, faced with a void, they appear—in a Promethean gesture—to invent a complex poetic movement. This movement generated the image of the so-called courtly universe and established the standard of lyric poetry that remained a model for the Middle Ages.

As the Russian semiotician Michael Meylakh recently reminded us:

> The language of the troubadours served as the universal language of courtly poetry of the twelfth and thirteenth centuries in many Romance countries. Parallel with dialectical unification, this language spontaneously achieved in the process of poetic practice a high degree of regulation and refinement which replaced the fixed grammatical norm . . . .[2]

Maylakh's remarks reinforce the notion of an inchoate early period marked by a "high degree of regulation and refinement." Consciously or not, he by a "high degree of regularion and refinement." Consciously or not, he, too, incorporates the aura of origins in his formulation of the troubadours' extraordinary achievement.

Would this myth of beginnings assume such important dimensions if the subsequent tradition were not perceived as so highly codified? Is the mystique of origins simply a romantic and modern view of a phenomenon that appeared far less extraordinary to the later troubadours themselves and the late medieval scholars who compiled such compendia of poetic rules as the *Leys d'amor* ("The Rules of Poetry") or those "biographies" of the troubadours called the *vidas* ("lives") and *razos* ("explanations," "defenses")? In short, what is there in this myth?

Judging by formal indices, the early troubadours, particularly Guilhem IX and Marcabru,[3] do utilize a number of unique metrical schemas and stanza configurations which fall outside the norms favored by their successors. Similarly, certain subjects, tones, images—such as the explicit sexual references—exceed the canon of taste to which later troubadours subscribed. Even the taxonomy of lyric forms exhibits instability in the first generation, where the term *canso*—the generic designation for the best-known Provensal lyric form—does not occur. Instead, the vague term *vers* serves to designate a wide variety of lyric forms.

The *vida* of Marcabru, composed sometime in the 13th century, cites this generic designation as an important, albeit quaint, distinguishing mark of the early period: "et en aqel temps non appellava hom cansson, mas tot qant hom cantava eron vers" ("and at that time people did not use the term *canso*, but rather everything that people sang was called *vers*)."[4] Something similar appears in the *vida* of Marcabru's contemporary Cercamon (ca. 1137-1152), which adds that this was the "old-fashioned way": "cercamons si fo uns joglars de Gascoingna, e trobet vers e pastoretas a la usanza antiga" ("A jongleur from Gascony, Cercamon made *pastorellas* and *vers* in the old way").[5]

We could adduce further evidence to demonstrate the ambivalence evinced by the tradition towards the early troubadours. But is it necessary? Clearly, this generation occupies a paradoxical place in the canon of Old Provensal poetry. Acknowledged as founders of a tradition, the early poets then appear to have been permitted only marginal participation in the canon. As another of Marcabru's *vidas* demonstrates, this ambivalence rested upon strong normative presuppositions: "Trobaire fo dels premiers c'om se recort. De caitivetz vers e de caitivetz serventes fez, e dis mal de las femnas e d'amor" ("He was one of the first troubadours that we remember. He made wretched songs and wretched *sirventés* and spoke ill of women and of love").[6]

The *vidas*, *razos* and other early documents do not deny the primordial role of these poets, but they emphasize a deviant cast to these poems. In stressing the problematic, rather than the normative, the *vidas* suggest to us that the precursors were rather uncomfortably housed in the edifice they helped to construct.

This ambivalence illustrates how a naïve reading may contain a profound if undeveloped insight. For, if we stop to analyze comments like the ones quoted above, we recognize that they actually do attribute to the work of these poets what we would term a dialectics of imitation and differentiation. On the one hand, they point to the existence of a recognizable poetic tradition consisting of a special language, generic distinctions, a poetic code and a socio-political orientation. These characteristics enabled a reader to move from one poet to another, from one poem to another with a clear sense of commonality.

On the other hand, the *vidas* call attention, in accordance with their name, to aspects of the lives of the poets—often derived from a literal-minded reading of the poems—which somehow mark them as eccentric according to the norms of a later age. And, as we have seen, the poets do turn out to have strong or deviant personalities by subsequent standards.[7]

In other words, the *vidas* recognize the existence of a dominant speaker in the poems who controls the poetic discourse, but, more specifically, an enunciating subject which deflects the imitative process onto a path of differentiation.[8] This tension, however crudely adumbrated in the *vidas*, may be shown to constitute an integral part of the poetic process from the work of the earliest troubadours down through the entire corpus of Old Provensal poetry.

Perhaps the greatest contribution of the poets of the first generation, as the *vidas* crudely perceived, really did lie in the nature of the speaker inscribed in their work. A close look at their poems reveals a dialectical matrix within which an enunciating subject could define itself with great flexibility. Indeed, the protean character of the speaking subject in the early troubadours constitutes a key to understanding the extraordinary virtuosity and variety of the Provensal lyric from its inception.

The speaking subject ran the gamut from expressing the crudest desires or exploits to philosophical thoughts of an exalted, spiritual nature. This subject could assert and define itself in a number of ways, but three modes in particular seem to cover the majority of situations. First, the subject could articulate authoritatively such universals as philosophy, politics, religion or ethics. We might call this phase the *didactic speaker*.

A second mode of subjectivity conveys the viewpoint of the individual *qua* problematic being. This speaker opposes itself to the idealized cogito of the didactic mode, the model being-in-the-text. It does so by adumbrating an uncensored being, a self deflected from the social or religious norms espoused by the didactic speaker. A language of desire unresponsive to moral maxims, however apposite, defines this differentiated being. We may term it the *hedonistic speaker*.

Yet a third possibility may be seen. The dialectical matrix of the lyric could readily juxtapose conflicting aspects of the subject, the didactic and the hedonistic, in a discourse which represented the complexities of a psyche that poetic language unveiled, attempted to limit and ultimately showed to be unattainable. In my view, this persona constitutes the real enunciating subject of the poetic project, and so I call it the *lyric subject*.

Such insights suggest that a coherent and complex theory of imitation underlay the early lyric forms of the troubadours. One could look almost anywhere in the *œuvre* of the first generation to find examples of these three speaking subjects and their interaction. For purposes of economy, however, let us concentrate on one song by Marcabru to show how highly developed a theory of imitation may be found at this early stage and, consequently, how justified our regard is for the founders of the tradition.

Marcabru's song "Al departir del brau tempier" (BdT 293, 3) illustrates dramatically how the three speaking subjects function dialectically within a given poem to promote a series of progressively more complex readings. Almost never do we perceive the existence of all three voices on a first reading, although we do perceive elements of them, generally as unresolved contradictions or questions raised by the text. From the very first reading, however, we do recognize the presence of a strong, controlling voice.

The poem consists of six stanzas. In stanzas 1 and 2, we find two progressive and distinct images of nature: the first, a general evocation of the natural state, the second, an orchard. These images do not succeed one another directly, but are separated by the intervention of a speaker whose statement that he is "minded to make a poem" delineates the two images of nature in several ways.

The conventional nature opening works to establish a contrast between the objective/universal discourse—an impersonal "weather report" on the change of season—and the subjective and personal reaction of the speaker. This opposition receives reinforcement from the space that lies between them; only after seven full lines of natural description does the speaker intervene in the first person, in the eighth and final line of the stanza.

Yet the irruption of first-person discourse decisively explodes the illusory identity acquired by the pastoral mode of the first seven lines. And, if we may anticipate, it also convincingly forewarns the reader against taking the second nature image, that of the orchard, at face value when it appears, immediately afterwards, in line 9 at the beginning of stanza 2.

The explicit appearance of the speaker in line 8 wrenches our perspective. It breaks the illusion of an objective narrative—an account told by itself—and reveals the presence of a maker. In deflecting attention from the world of pre-existent objects to the work itself—a shift from objective to subjective representation—the speaking voice obliges the reader to recognize the different levels of mimesis at work in the first stanza. Initially, the first seven lines offer themselves as a straightforward imitation of nature, on the one hand—and were so read as recently as the beginning of this century[9]—and, on the other hand, as a conventional sign equating nature and lyric poetry. Both views postulate a transparent language; they make an unproblematic assumption that natural description reflects nature and the beginning of a poem.

The irruption of a speaker who announces his intention "to make a poem" radically alters the situation by calling into question the lyrical project as understood in lines 1-7. This assertion, coming at *the end* of the first stanza, after the poem has already begun its trajectory, has a different status than if it came earlier. For we now see that the statement asserts the presence of two kinds of mimetic activity. Since it represents the subjective mode that calls attention to the work as artifact, we may see it as a declaration of intent to transform the poetic project from the simple imitation of nature or the conventional opening that the exordium at first seemed to promise.

The abrupt shift in mimetic mode allows the speaker to transform the closure of the stanza—the last line—into a new beginning. The end calls into question our initial reading by explicitly acknowledging the conventionality of the first seven lines. The overt declaration of intent to make a *vers* forces us to see these initial lines as imitating *not* nature, but *vers*, and a quite self-consciously conventional poetry at that. Line 8, then, comes as an explicit rejection of conventional imitation of the kind illustrated above. This line deflects the poem onto a path of differentiation by introducing an explicit persona, a speaker who literally takes control from the implied poet, the conventionalist of lines 1-7. From a transparent and unproblematic text, the stanza has been transformed into a palimpsest. But we now face the question as to the nature of the rewriting that will be imposed on the old text so forcefully expunged.

The topic of the rewritten stanza lies in the reconsideration the speaker's forceful personality imposes by its sudden intervention. By obliging the reader to revise the initial reading of the stanza, the speaker establishes the concept of a text that represents thought or reflection, a text that asserts itself as a product of a continual motion of the mind. This mind motion, mimetically inscribed in the text, as we have just seen, multiplies the possibility of meaning, and yet anchors the mental activity in an historical and philosophical context. The textual cogito which we see here emerging may stretch, but not exceed the limits of contemporary thought. But those limits, as recent studies by M.-M. Davy, M.-D. Chenu, Bernard Cerquiglini and others have shown, were much more expansive than students of the early troubadours have been accustomed to recognize.[10]

We shall see, however, that the status of the text derives from its ability to transcend the meanings it appears to postulate as limits; in this sense, our reading of the first stanza proved paradigmatic. By way of illustration, we have only to recall how line 8 placed the intellectualized cogito between the reader and any facile assumptions about the transparency of nature conventions within the song.

Any doubts on this score must be dispelled by comparing the conventional nature imagery in the early part of stanza 1 and the allegorical orchard of stanza 2, introduced in line 9, immediately following the intervention of the intellectual cogito. The allegorical orchard establishes the dialectic for the rest of the song. By way of testing the reader's newly sharpened intellectual reflexes, line 9 links two words, *cossiros* ("mindful," "anxious") and *vergier* ("orchard"), in a proximate repetition of the coupling of *vers* and *cossirier* in line 8 ("Suy d'un vers far en cossirier," "I am minded to make a poem"). The two lines thereby establish a clear equation between mental activity and poetic discourse, thought and the images it produces. The chiastic sequence *vers:cossirier::cossiros:vergier* assures that even the least promising reader would see the *vers* in the *vergier* and vice versa. As a gross marker or blatant overdetermination, it signals yet another transformation of the discourse from the simple metaphorical equivalence of nature and *vers* in stanza 1 to the allegorical mode of stanza 2. These various markers begin to suggest the reason for the shift from the implied poet of lines 1-7 to the explicit speaker in line 8. For in the chiasmus of lines 8-9 the poet emerges as a didactic speaker with a definite program of instruction.

The allegorical mode that begins in line 9 plays upon the opposition between the natural world evoked early on and a posited and purposeful world announced in lines 8-9. The opposition lies between drift and mastery, in political terms, or will versus desire in psychological and philosophical terms. It posits a dialectical matrix for the song which moves it inexorably away from the celebratory mode of the beginning to one of analysis, criticism and instruction.

Let there be no mistake. The role predicated for the didactic speaker is nothing short of grandiose. It constitutes a challenge to represent in seven stanzas not simply the proposition that the orchard is a microcosm of the universe, but also that the struggle between order and entropy—the carefully tended orchard versus the wild state of nature—reflects the conflict between will and desire in the human psyche.

Allegory will be the vehicle for the didactic project. And yet the allegorical mode initiated by the didactic speaker in stanza 2, like the conventional nature opening, offers little of interest once the reader grasps the mechanism:

> Cossiros suy d'un gran vergier
> Ont a de bellis plansos mans lucs;
> Gent sont l'empeut e·l frugs bacucs,
> Selh qu'esser degran sordegier,
> Fuelhs e flors paron de pomier,
> Son al fruchar sautz' e saucs,
>
> · · · · · · · · · ·
>
> (9-14)

(I am concerned about a great orchard where there are beautiful saplings all about: the grafts are fine and the fruit fleshy; those (trees) that ought to be worse appear to flower and leaf like an apple tree; but at harvest time they are rather like willows and elders . . . .)

No sooner have we begun to register the allegorical elements, and even become a bit jaded by their facility, then something goes askew: the anticipated meanings necessary to complete the paradigm fail to materialize. Just when the reader expects a satisfactory, if conventional ending for the first image, a substitution occurs. The refrain element, "sauzes e saucx" ("willows and elders"), interposes itself between the anticipated result and the reality. *Sauzes e saucx* could never be the harvest of *pommier* no matter how many *fuelhs e flors* it might have. But in this case the symbolic vehicles, the trees, alter their identity between the allegorical spring and harvest.

They have the blossoms and leaves of apple trees in the spring, but by fall look more like willows and elders.

The problem here lies not with the allegorical potential of *sauzes e saucx* —which is rich enough as we shall see—but with the context of the stanza. In its present configuration, the stanza activates a simple nature allegory insufficiently dense to allow for an elevation of connotation to religious allegory that would permit *sauzes e saucx* to assume their full symbolic potential. The form of the stanza requires the refrain words to retain their natural connotation of sterile, non-fruit-bearing trees that have been substituted for the promise of rich yields from the *pommiers*: fruit versus the absence of fruit; promise or disappointment.

The form of the stanza, with its fixed refrain element—the only occurrence of such a feature within this metrical schema in all of troubadour poetry[11]—has, of course, predetermined the failure of allegorical fruition. Although the mode of the second stanza differentiates it from the first, it cannot accommodate the refrain element repeated from the first. The refrain originated in the pre-allegorized state of the poem. *Sauzes e saucx* belong to the entropic, *sauvage* order of the natural world rather than to the courtly world of allegory, where the gardener is supposed to root out such unpromising "trash trees" as willows and elders. Their survival here prevents the rhetoric from making good on its promise to allegorize, at least in the direction the stanza apparently began to take. By way of confirmation, stanza 3 consecrates this deflection by taking it as the basis of its didactic narrative. It extends the imagery of the failed orchard by remarking that the "trees" within make expansive promises which they ultimately fail to perform.

We have now witnessed in stanzas 2 and 3 a repeat of the techniques used in the first one. The speaker initiated a highly conventional allegory—the equivalent of the conventional nature opening—which short-circuits because an antithetical figurative language has been grafted on, to use the image of the stanza. Or, rather, the allegory fails because the palimpsest has not been sufficiently forceful. The allegorical rewriting is so faint as to allow traces of the first mode, the refrain, to show through and contaminate the image. Now, if we back away and look at stanzas 2 and 3 in perspective, we see that they do not simply present an image of failed performance, they actually represent it; they perform it themselves, as it were. The two parts of stanza 2, followed by stanza 3, provide a *mise en abyme*, a graphic image, of the failure of promise which the speaker sees as a major problem in the world. At the same time, by engaging the reader's mental activity at so many levels, the stanzas provide a text that is a product of incessant mind motion: that of the cogito of the didactic speaker which has by now also become ours. It is this cogito, functioning in and above the text, that will point the way to the ultimate resolution.

In stanza 6 we witness another failure to realize allegorical promise when the gardener and the gatekeeper of the orchard flee with their eyes closed. In a rather curious passage, the text says that they have exchanged their elegant clothes, the marks of courtly status, for the dress of vagabonds or peasants (II. 43-44). This image represents the flight of the allegorical gardener and gatekeeper into literality; it is a refusal of meaning, a failure to fulfill their promised allegorical function. And, as we know, the function of the gatekeeper in courtly allegory is one of the more highly codified figures, as Guillaume de Lorris' lover found when, at a later moment in the tradition, he approached another orchard.

The flight into literality of Marcabru's gardener and doorman suggests a turning away from the nascent world of courtly allegory. In fact, it replicates the failure of another set of archetypal gardeners—they also failed as gatekeepers—Adam and Eve, to realize the promise of meaning in their orchard. Suddenly, the apple tree of stanza 2 begins to take on new significance. Stanza 6 supplies the contextual setting that allows for the introduction of religious allegory; it activates an intertextual dialectic not previously apparent. As a result, we reflect that Adam and Eve, consumed with a literal-minded curiosity, exchanged a richer language potential for the letter of the word. For them, too, an exchange of garments marked the fall from promise of being, as it does for Marcabru's gardeners, whose sartorial degradation from courtly to servile dress signifies their exclusion from the language of the courtly lyric and their translation to the fallen world of the villain.

This flight, like the other moments of crisis in the poem, leads us to reconsider the nature of the discourse, and to recognize a further transformation of the allegory, now raised to yet another level of meaning. For, just as we prepare to conclude that the poet and we have been designated to tend the garden—that he, in fact, pruned and trimmed the discourse all along, thus bringing the text to fruition—just as we prepare to settle on this meaning, the refrain recurs to render such claims problematic: "tal hira'm fan sautz' e saucx!" (l. 46) ("What anger willows and elders fill me with!").

The anger may indeed be directed against the real-life equivalents of the willows and elders who refuse to realize their promise, but, even more, it concerns the inability of the poem, up to this point, to accommodate the allegorical potential of these recurrent images. Throughout the poem we have witnessed a struggle between will and pleasure, didacticism and hedonism, and we have naturally assumed, since the didactic speaker identified so strongly with the path of duty, that this voice would ultimately produce a triumph of the will. In fact, we reach stanza 6 only to discover the didactic speaker exploding in anger at the *sautz' e saucx* which have consistently undercut the conventional language and expectation. And, at each recurrence of the refrain, a new level of meaning emerges from the confrontation between the conventional and the intellectual.

We realize that the text consists of several different poetic voices, several personae. Heretofore, we have been aware of two, but this awareness itself suggests the possibility of a third. Throughout the poem we have witnessed a conflict between the hedonistic speaker—the conventional poet satisfied with imitating modish verse that sounds good, but does not test the intelligence or require one to think too deeply about the meaning of appearances —and a didactic speaker who represents a more thoughtful approach, and one more closely allied with what we come eventually to recognize as the poet's first-person voice. We see the necessity for the ultimate intervention of that voice because of what the didactic speaker finally cannot accomplish. The rules and moral principles of this figurative gardener, the didactic speaker, cannot banish the *sautz' e saucx* from the garden. It is, rather, the gardener, as we saw, who, at least figuratively, throws up his hands and flees. The equation cannot come out right, by the end of stanza 6; the garden still contains the irrational, self-indulgent elements who promise, but cannot produce.

The poem reaches a stalemate, rather than a conclusion, at the end of this stanza. The symmetry of the poem—twice three or thrice two stanzas, each stanza itself a square of sorts (eight lines of eight syllables each)—corresponds to the symmetry of the two voices, the didactic and the hedonistic. In many ways it represents a typical debate between the mind and the soul, the head and the heart, a favorite medieval genre. Another binary element, the refrain words *sautzes e saucx*, symbolizes this stalemate. They have yet to be set in a context that can fully activate their allegorical meaning. Stanza 6 begins the task, but cannot realize it, since it remains largely a product of the didactic speaker, a frustrated and defeated speaker by now.

The seventh stanza disrupts the symmetry, in a purely arithmatic sense, but completes it in another way. Here a third level of speaking voice intervenes to evoke God and the concept of *pretz entier*, an almost untranslatable expression, signifying a spiritual wholeness of great value. The idea here will not be simply to respect the letter of the rules and conventions, as the didactic speaker repeatedly insisted, but rather to achieve a total union, a spiritual harmony that transcends external *convenances*. In a text devoted to fragmented values, this concept of spiritual harmony, *pretz entiers*, resonates meaningfully.

The contextual symmetry of this stanza permits the *saucx* finally to cast off literality and to function as a fully allegorized element. "God saves," says the first line, "those who have *pretz entier*." Who else could these be but the *imitationes Christi* who practice some form of christological dialectic? These people "speak" a meta-historical language with and through the wood of the Cross, that allegorical tree *par excellence* on which performance redeems promise. In the dialectics of philosophical anthropology, *pretz entier* can never come *before* the deed, but only with and through performance. Therein lay the lesson of the *arbor vitae* for the Middle Ages.

The second line of the stanza now stands boldly juxtaposed with the first in a resolution of the dualistic debate of the preceeding stanzas. Taken together, the first two lines of stanza 7—a cruciform number in the 11th and 12th centuries, as we know—underline the christological dialectic by revealing that the arborial imagery focuses on the emblematic nature of the Cross. The agenda of the third voice, thus, differs radically from the other two. This speaker takes as intertext the cruciform mythology that was so dominant a theme in the Romanesque period. From this perspective the elder tree serves as a crucial arbiter of performance. Since it lacked a firm heartwood, and was seen as a tree that rotted from within, it could be perceived as a vehicle which derived its symbolic status from the value of the person associated with it. It could be positive or negative. According to medieval legend, the Cross was made of elder wood, but, at the same time, legend held that Judas hanged himself on an elder.[12]

This double signification made the elder a kind of litmus test of intentionality. For Christ, and the *imitatio Christi*, it served as a vehicle demonstrating how the coincidence of promise and performance could transform an object, or being, demonstrating the harmony, or reconciliation, of opposing forces within that distinguished those who had achieved *pretz entier*. For the Judas figure, the person who betrayed his promise, the elder stood as a cursed symbol: a sign of the disjunction between act and intention, and an image of the heartless wood that rotted from within. In both cases, though, the test comes at the end: only in the closure—or in the envoy, as here—can one tell the one from the other and make the judgment. Death provides the real allegorical context that determines the meaning, the true nature, really, of the life that preceded it. The manner of death, or the mode of closure, thus obliged a rereading and new interpretation of what had appeared to be a closed text.

In the case of Marcabru's poem, a new horizon of meaning thus opens up as the third voice, the lyric speaker, lifts the reader's vision beyond the particular image of historical accident towards a universal goal of spiritual perfection. That goal is, of course, *pretz entier* that God, not the poet, will bestow on those who care to perform the christological dialectic necessary to reach the state of grace in which it can be conferred. Now we find that we must reread the poem yet again from the perspective of this third speaker. As we do so, we discover that it does not simply mirror a divided and fragmented world. Rather, it appears as a mimesis of spiritual exercise, a hermeneutics of the world that Marcabru says Christians must perform in order to demonstrate the harmony in *pretz entier*.

Modern symbol theory offers yet another sense for the ambivalent symmetry of the tree. The double meaning of the elder—both cross and gallows—corresponds to what Carl Jung recognized as a projection of the duality of the human psyche. For Jung, "the double meaning of the tree symbolizes the process of individuation during which the contradictions within us unite."[13]

Now, one very profound purpose of Romanesque art lay in demonstrating the harmony, and the possibility for harmony in humans. For it was in such demonstrations that the poets, artists and philosophers of the period strove to show that humans, in their works, could reflect the cadences and patterns of the Prime Mover, who was, as they thought, both the supreme gardener and the musician "who created the universe like an immense cithara."[14] The lyric speaker attempts no less than to make his *vers entier* an instrument for hearing the secret harmonies of that other music.

This transcendent goal of the lyric speaker helps to explain in large part the question posed at the beginning of this study. We can now understand how the poetic persona of the early troubadour imprinted a powerful intellectual—and spiritual—goal on the discourse. The cogito revealed in our analysis must have contributed enormously to the sense of authority projected by the troubadour lyric at this early stage. It guaranteed that the poetry would have to be taken seriously, even viewed as a worthy complement to the Latin lyric.

Now, this multiform poetic persona did not just happen. We should expect to discover at least an implicit theory of representation underlying the concept of *voces*, a theory which could link the poetics of the troubadour to the literary, historical and philosophical concerns of the period. Ultimately, the anticipated mimetic theory—as much as or even more than its practical application in poems like Marcabru's—will show how the early troubadours succeeded in establishing so strong a poetic canon.

Nature, presented in an astonishing variety of forms, provides one of the most pervasive themes in early troubadour poetry. "Al departir del brau tempier" shows just how varied and expressive the symbolic vocabulary of Nature could be in the hands of so skilled a poet as Marcabru. Like him, Guilhem IX, Cercamon and Jaufré Rudel often juxtapose nature, society and human existence.

Reflecting on the equation of nature, humanity and the social order, M.-D. Chenu, the French theologian and historian, pointed out that nature constituted one of the two broad categories of symbolism in the 12th century, the other being history. Nature and history—space and time—between themselves encompassed the physical world, allowing it—when properly interpreted—to be seen as a mirror reflecting the creative imprint of the Prime Mover.[15] Chenu reminds us that Saint Augustine had laid the groundwork for this division between the symbolism of nature and that of history, between the natural universe and the human one, by arguing that what was found in nature was the *vestigia* of God, the divine imprint, whereas in humans and human history might be seen the *imago* of God.[16]

Such concepts appeared compelling in the neoplatonic ambiance of the 12th century, where the purpose of representation in the plastic, graphic and verbal arts was to demonstrate the transcendent knowledge to be found in the physical world. The definition of the symbol, according to Hugh of Saint Victor, presumed just such a progression: "The symbol is a juxtaposition, that is a coaptation of visible forms brought forth to demonstrate some invisible matter."[17]

If we review the structure of "Al departir del brau tempier" with this background in mind, we recognize that it divides symmetrically in half, with three stanzas devoted to nature symbolism and three to the human, historical world. The first three stanzas use the nature imagery as a metaphor for human society, as we saw, while the continued echoes of the nature metaphors in the second part make the equation of nature and society even more explicit.

The nature/history dichotomy in each part may be further refined to reveal a fundamental opposition between present and past. The new summer season not only highlights more starkly the decadence of the "natural" world or its cultivated surrogate, the garden, but also evokes a primordial garden of unimpeachable perfection. Similarly, the human/historical dimension, implicit in the first three stanzas, but progressively more explicit in the final ones, culminating in stanza 6, contrasts a primordial human society of real distinction to contemporary degeneracy. The major signifying systems in the poem situate themselves in the gap, pointed out in each stanza, between promise and performance: "Qu'ieu sai quals mortz foron primier! / E·l mais dels vius son vers saucx" (ll. 37-38) ("The old ones made death mean! And those that live? They're the real elders").

Nature symbolism provides the satiric elements that make this poem a *sirventés*, that is, a caustic commentary on the present state of the world. The metaphors of nature furnish the imagery of *disharmony* between the new season of growth, cultivation and productivity—a pattern of performance established by the primordial garden—and the decadent horticultural practices recorded by the poem. On the historical level, the same disharmony exists between the predecessor aristocrats and their craven, vain and slovenly ephebes. We now see why the poet announces, in the first stanza, his intention to write *against* the season, that is, to argue that history and nature, in their present form, belie their models: "Contra·l termini qu'es yssucs / Suy d'un vers far en cossirier" (ll. 7-8) ("Against this new dry season I am minded to make a *vers*").

The mimetic project of the poem thus proposes a double specularity. It "reflects" the natural and historical world not passively, but dialectically, comparing contemporary vision of a primordial order evoked negatively in the poem by its absence. The point of Marcabru's satire lies precisely in the *inability* of the poet to find the *vestigia Dei* in Nature or the *imago Dei* in man.

The text of the poem thus assumes a crucial importance. If the *world* fails to yield the *vestigia et imagines Dei* so important to the microcosmic theories of the period on which the concept of world harmony rested, then the *poem* must provide a new, para-scriptural model of a world in which these transcendent signs might again be found. *Pretz entier* would, thus, be found in the *vers* which becomes *entier*, in its turn, by virtue of its status as the new matrix for the divine vestiges now obliterated, or obscured, in the phenomenal world. All this obviously affects the role of the poet, giving him the status of an *alter deus* engaged in a second level of creative activity. In this view, the world appears not as a given, immutable reality, but as a construct, like the text itself, formed to be perceived, interpreted and re-formed.

Marcabru thus shows us a theory of representation grounded in a dual movement of objective and subjective mimesis. Besides the depiction of phenomenal reality that we associated with objective representation, we also discover, in the poetic *voces*, the portrayal of a subjective and intellective consciousness. This subjective dimension underlines the problematics of the representational process: it stresses *representing*, rather than *representation*. [18] Representing incorporates into the figurative act the difficulties inherent in portrayal: how the sheer fact of reproducing the world as sign can expose and call into question precisely those conventions meant to systematize and objectify representation. In Marcabru's poem, the agonistic dimension that struck us as so exciting derives from the strongly marked presence of the subjective and intellective elements.

They circumscribe the domain of validity of the exemplary models posited by the objective representation. And they do so by emphasizing the distance that separates the model from the subjects to whom it is meant to apply. Once again we see a differentiation between the two mimetic modes. If representation makes us conscious of the proximity of historical models, representing accentuates the enormous space standing between such exemplary paradigms and the present. We might say, then, that *representation* stresses the force and continuity of cultural and religious models, while *representing* stresses their vulnerability.

When one stops to think about it, these observations may shed light on our original question. The early troubadours did manage to establish a poetic canon whose force and continuity derived precisely, as Michael Meylakh put it in the quotation cited earlier, from its success as "a highly organized modelling system," with the added power of registering contextual reality as it changed over time. This dialogic capacity, which Meylakh calls "the peculiar 'constituting' function inherent in it," made the troubadour canon "one of the most important subsystems of the courtly universe."[19]

In other words, the strength of the canon established by the early troubadours lay in its doubly specular nature: to represent a tradition which could be seen as unvarying from the 12th to the 14th centuries—what Zumthor calls the *grand chant courtois*[20]—while at the same time encouraging the expression of altered worldviews—intellectual, spiritual, political—from generation to generation. From this point of view, the founders of the tradition would necessarily be viewed ambiguously: recognition for their achievement, but acknowledgement of their difference as well. The subjective and intellective elements we associate with that part of the mimetic process we call "representing" would naturally register the difference between and distance separating founders and successors. So what we saw in the few *vidas* quoted earlier was at once a demonstration of the force and continuity of the early troubadours, and also a poignant testimony to their vulnerability.

NOTES

1. I read an earlier version of this paper in October 1981 at the Third Annual Congress of the Centre Guillaume IX devoted to "The Early Troubadours."

2. Michael Meylakh, "The Structure of the Courtly Universe of the Troubadours," *Semiotica*, 15 (1975), 63.

3. Marcabru, who wrote during the period 1130-1150, was an illegitimate son of peasants and, thus, the social, political and economic antithesis of Guilhem IX, the most powerful lord in Europe during the late 11th century. The juxtaposition of these two among the handful of founding poets reminds us of the cogency of Meylakh's observation that such oppositions as *cortés/vilans* ("courtly/peasant") lose their etymological value in this poetic universe: "In the sphere of the courtly universe the opposition of castle to town, feudal aristocrat to bourgeois, distinguished to lowborn, is removed" (p. 64).

4. *Biographies des troubadours: Textes provençaux des XIIIe et XIVe siècles*, ed. Jean Boutière and A.H. Schutz (Toulouse: Privat, 1950), p. 212.

5. Ibid., p. 80.

6. Ibid., p. 211. One manuscript even makes Marcabru the very first troubadour. Ibid., p. 398.

7. The *vida* of Guilhem IX, for example, stresses that he was "one of the greatest betrayers of women" and "went through the world for a long time ensnaring ladies." Ibid., p. 81.

8. See Claude Gilbert-Dubois, "Imitation différentielle et poétique maniériste," *Revue de Littérature Comparée*, 51 (1977), 142-51.

9. J.-M.-L. Dejeanne, Marcabru's editor in 1909, for example, asserts that the poem is "un chant de printemps et un sirventés. Marcabru est *laudator temporis acti*." *Poésies complètes de Marcabru* (Toulouse: Privat, 1909), p. 216.

10. See, for example, M.-M. Davy, *Initiation à la symbolique romane* (Paris: Flammarion, 1977); M.D. Chenu, *Nature, Man and Society in the Twelfth Century*, ed. Taylor and Little (Chicago: Univ. of Chicago Press, 1979); Bernard Cerquiliglini, *La Parole médiévale* (Paris: Editions de Minuit, 1981); Stephen G. Nichols, "Romanesque Imitation or Imitating the Romans?" in *Mimesis: From Mirror to Method, Augustine to Descartes*, ed. John D. Lyons and Stephen G. Nichols (Hanover, N.H.: University Press of New England, 1982), and *Romanesque Signs* (New Haven: Yale Univ. Press, 1983).

11. István Frank, *Répertoire métrique de la poésie des troubadours*, 2 vols. (Paris, 1953-1957), I, 476.

12. *The Reader's Handbook*, ed. E.C. Brenner (Philadelphia: Lippincott, 1899), I, 318. I am indebted to my colleague Marina Scordilis Brownlee for this reference.

13. C.G. Jung, *L'Homme et ses symboles* (Paris, 1964), p. 187.

14. *Initiation à la symbolique romane*, p. 36.

15. *Nature, Man and Society*, p. 115.

16. Ibid., p. 116.

17. Ibid., p. 103.

18. For a more complete exposition of this idea, see *Mimesis: From Mirror to Method*, pp. 36-59.

19. "The Structure of the Courtly Universe," p. 63.

20. Paul Zumthor, *Essai de poétique médiévale* (Paris: Seuil, 1972), pp. 189 ff.

Robert Garapon

Proust and Molière

The great French novelists and playwrights of the 20th century have been influenced—more than we often realize—by the masters of the French classical period. Fifteen years ago, in an article in the *Toronto Quarterly* (January 1967), I attempted to show how much Jean Giraudoux and Albert Camus owed to the 17th century. I would like to continue here by showing the links between Marcel Proust and Molière which may pass unobserved in the great mass of *A la recherche du temps perdu*.[1]

Proust often quotes Molière. Of course, he quotes as often, even more, other authors of the 17th century, beginning with Madame de Sévigné. But when he quotes Molière he does so with a particular insistence on integrating the quotation into the texture of his plot, using Molière to describe the character or scene that he presents us. It would be useful to begin by comparing the quotations Proust takes from Corneille and Racine to those he garners from Molière. Then we can sample some of the significant scenes and characters that are particularly Moliéresque and add clownish exaggeration of burlesque outrageousness to Proust's novel. But even more important than these surface manifestations is the profound resemblance between Proust's creative genius and Molière's. First of all, this resemblance appears in their sense of the organic development of character types. They further resemble one another in their resoluteness in maintaining the comic atmosphere and in refusing the tragic. This comparison will help us understand the comic inspiration that readers have sensed in Proust even without realizing its extent.[2]

I

A reader of *A la recherche du temps perdu* can easily call to mind the dinner at the Bloch home in *A l'ombre des jeunes filles en fleurs*. In that scene, the wealthy Nissim Bernard makes a fool out of himself with his boastful lies. He pretends to have known the Marquis of Saint-Loup very well: " 'Je me rappelle un dîner chez moi, à Nice, où il y avait Sardou, Labiche, Augier. . . . —Molière, Racine, Corneille, continua ironiquement M. Bloch le père, dont le fils acheva l'énumeration en ajoutant: Plaute, Ménandre, Kalidasa' " (I, 775). "Molière, Racine, Corneille . . .": the very order adopted by Bloch's father reveals a secret and subconscious preference on Proust's part, because the French usually name the famous triad of classical playwrights as Corneille, Racine, Molière.

Corneille is rarely mentioned in the novel—little more than a dozen times in the three volumes of the standard Pléiade edition. A verse of Corneille's tragedy *La Mort de Pompée* quoted from memory by Marcel's grandfather (I, 27), two verses of *Polyeucte* attributed to Voltaire by the younger Bloch (I, 880), Corneille preferred to Racine in a homework essay written by young Gisèle (I, 912), a remark on the emphatic sense of the word *ennui* in Corneille (II, 19) and on the political tirades he created a fashion for (II, 195)—these are all, except for a comparison between the early Victor Hugo and the Corneille of *Le Cid*, whose "romantisme intermittent, contenu" is praised by Proust (II, 549). Nowhere in the novel does Proust mention the Cornelian "heroic struggle," and this absence is very revealing, for Proust's heroes are anything but heroic!

Racine gets more attention: he is mentioned by name or quoted between 50 and 60 times in *A la recherche*, much more often than Molière or Madame de Sévigné. But, if we look closely, we soon see that the abundance of references is misleading. First of all, in almost a third of these instances Proust indulges in a kind of parlor game: he quotes verses from *Phèdre*, *Esther* and *Athalie* and applies them to his character's situation. By superimposing an exalted expression on everyday circumstances he gives his narration a subtly satirical savor. An example occurs in *Le Côté de Guermantes*, when the narrator has been invited by the Duke and Duchess of Guermantes for the first time:

. . . elle s'était dit de moi: "Un à qui nous demanderons de venir dîner." Mais d'autres pensées l'avaient distraite

> (De soins tumultueux un prince environné
> Vers de nouveaux objets est sans cesse entraîné)

jusqu'au moment où elle m'avait aperçu seul comme Mardochée à la porte du palais; et ma vue ayant rafraîchi sa mémoire, elle voulait, tel Assuérus, me combler de ses dons. (II, 378)

Elsewhere, Racine's name comes up in the ordinary course of the story, for instance, in connection with the little book that Bergotte wrote on the dramatist, or in reference to the actress Burma and her success in the role of Phèdre, or in the episode of Gisèle's homework assignment. In two passages Charlus cites Racine as a great poet of the passions (I, 783; II, 623), and still elsewhere the "Christian sweetness" of *Esther* is contrasted with the tone of *Andromaque* (III, 323). Racine is, thus, clearly not taken as a model, for the climate of Racinian tragedy is precisely the opposite of the repetitive pattern that dominates the Proustian plot, where each high-society function prefigures, recalls or forces a reinterpretation of all the others, right up to the reception at the Princess of Guermantes's which ends the last part of the novel.

The treatment of Molière is entirely different. There are, to be sure, several passages where Molière is mentioned only in an incidental way. But along with these unimportant instances there are so many others of great significance. Three times Molière is claimed to be the greatest author in French literature. In *A l'ombre des jeunes filles en fleurs* he is held forth as the champion of classicism in a contrast to Victor Hugo the Romantic (I, 532). In *Sodome et Gomorrhe*, Céleste Albaret is described as a strong, but ignorant woman, but she nonetheless uses Molière's name as a sort of witty reproach directed at Marcel, and Proust adds that it was the only writer's name she knew (II, 847). A little further, Monsieur de Charlus quotes Molière's *La Comtesse d'Escarbagnas* in front of Morel and, when the latter does not understand, Charlus scornfully adds, "Je vois, du reste, que vous ne savez rien. Si vous n'avez même pas lu Molière . . ." (II, 1010).

References to Molière are especially useful to the novelist when he wants to bring a character into sharper focus. Charlus had an old maidservant who spoke "un patois moliéresque" (II, 289). Charlus' own jealous hovering over Morel is compared to Molière's miser Harpagon: "Il est obligé, comme Harpagon, de veiller sur son trésor, et se relève la nuit pour voir si on ne le lui prend pas" (II, 921). Charlus is even compared, in a still more surprising image, to the farcical Scapin (II, 696).

Certain gestures—I almost wrote stage business—are made understandable by reference to the corresponding gestures in Molière. For example, when Marcel's grandmother meets Madame de Villeparisis at the Grand-Hôtel at Balbec:

. . . comme dans certaines scènes de Molière où deux acteurs monologuent depuis longtemps chacun de son côté à quelques pas l'un de l'autre, sont censés ne pas s'être

vus encore, et tout d'un coup s'aperçoivent, n'en peuvent croire leurs yeux, entre-
coupent leurs propos, finalement parlent ensemble, le chœur ayant suivi le dialogue,
et se jettent dans les bras l'un de l'autre. (I, 694)

Another amusing instance is the description of the dialogue between Charlus and the Duke of Sidonia, deaf to one another in their irrepressible and
impenitent babbling:

Ayant jugé tout de suite que le mal était sans remède, comme dit un célèbre sonnet,
ils avaient pris la détermination, non de se taire, mais de parler chacun sans s'occuper
de ce que dirait l'autre. Cela avait réalisé ce bruit confus, produit dans les comédies
de Molière par plusieurs personnes qui disent ensemble des choses différentes. (II,
638-39)

Some passages strike me as particularly interesting because Molière's
name appears suddenly and almost gratuitously in them. In the middle of
Robert de Saint-Loup's reflections on strategy erupts an allusion to the
way the actor Mounet-Sully understood *Le Misanthrope* (III, 981). In
the opening pages of the novel Proust describes the dreamer's perception
of a toothache as a ceaselessly repeated verse of Molière (I, 28). In these
instances Proust is curiously *haunted* by Molière, in the two senses of
haunting. The novelist is frequented by Molière's spirit and he is constantly
preoccupied by the playwright. It is hardly surprising, then, that a creator
capable of a sentence like the one containing the toothache comparison
can discover or reinvent spontaneously, in many a page in his own book,
the characters and scenes of Molière.

II

It would be impossible to catalogue all the characters in Proust who
resemble Molière's creations. There would be far too many! But we can
look at some of the more colorful and more characteristic ones.

There are, first of all, Marcel's two grand-aunts, Mademoiselle Cécile and
Mademoiselle Flora. These two spinsters, sisters of the narrator's grandmother, share "sa noble nature, mais non son esprit" (I, 21). When they
thank Swann for the "enormous" case of Asti that he has just sent them (I,
25), there is an evident resemblance between these two affectedly charming
women and Bélise of Molière's *Femmes savantes*. Just as Bélise imagines
that everyone who meets her falls in love with her, Flora and Cécile believe
that everyone around them passes his time working out an exegesis of their
least words and seizes their most subtle allusions.

In the same family as Cécile and Flora is Aunt Léonie, that *malade imaginaire* who ends up dying as a result of all her efforts to cure herself and
who fends off the fear of death by thinking constantly about her illness.

She resembles almost in every respect the hero of Molière's *Le Malade imaginaire* (I, 69-70).

The Duke of Guermantes is another Molière character in Proust. This powerful member of the upper aristocracy indiscriminately lavishes on everyone the empty favors of a rich man. Readers surely remember his entrance into the *salon* of his aunt, Madame de Villeparisis (II, 224). Here the resemblance is so clear-cut, *mutatis mutandis*, that we can simply cite the relevant passage from Molière's *L'Impromptu de Versailles*. The passage in question is the one where the Chevalier protests that Molière is not about to lack material for his comedies, and imitates those great flatterers in scene 4.

Both of these cases are caricature, but a caricature that is close to the reality of the period. I do not mean to imply that Proust consciously and deliberately imitated Molière. But I think that there are coincidences of style and inspiration. Proust clearly sees the Duke of Guermantes just as Molière sees his flatterer, and the novelist judges him in a similar way. In *Sodome et Gomorrhe*, the narrator, comparing the ceremonious reserve of the Prince of Guermantes with the Duke of Guermantes's "old boy" chumminess, concludes in favor of the Prince: "Des deux cousins, celui qui était vraiment simple, c'était le Prince" (II, 655).

In contrast to the aristocratic distinction of the Prince, the manager of the Grand-Hôtel at Balbec "émaillait ses propos commerciaux d'expressions choisies, mais à contre-sens" (I, 663). He "employait toujours des expressions qu'il croyait distinguées, sans s'apercevoir qu'elles étaient vicieuses" (I, 666), pretending, for instance, that he was "d'originalité roumaine" (ibid.). After several years, Marcel, with a mixture of melancholy and amusement, meets the manager again:

Il m'annonça qu'il m'avait logé tout en haut de l'hôtel. "J'espère, dit-il, que vous ne verrez pas là un manque d'impolitesse, j'étais ennuyé de vous donner une chambre dont vous êtes indigne, mais je l'ai fait rapport au bruit, parce que comme cela vous n'aurez personne au-dessus de vous pour vous fatiguer le trépan (pour tympan)." . . . Je pourrais faire faire du feu si cela me plaisait . . . , mais il craignait qu'il n'y eût des "fixtures" dans le plafond. (II, 751).

Proust uses here the Moliéresque technique of having an ignorant character mispronounce or misuse scientific or literary vocabulary. Molière's Marotte, the maidservant of the *Précieuses ridicules* says *filofie* for *philosophie* (scene 6), and Thibaut in *Le Médecin malgré lui* (III, 2) says *hypocrisie* for *hydropsie* and *syncoles* and *conversions* for *syncopes* and *convulsions*. Proust is obviously happy to exploit this comic vein as he multiplies the bloopers the manager makes in front of Marcel, who has just been overcome by the poignant recollection of his deceased grandmother in a passage marked by a curious counterpoint (II, 763-65).

The last of these Moliéresque portraits that I will recall is that of Professor Georges Dieulafoy, the doctor who comes to the grandmother's death-bed. In this case Proust has introduced an historical character, a famous professor of medicine and a colleague of Marcel's father, Professor Adrien Proust. As far as we can tell, Proust liked, admired and respected Professor Dieulafoy, but he could not resist creating an image of him in which the caricatural and Moliéresque traits are mixed in with elements of scrupulous realism (we know that Dieulafoy was devoted to the theater) (II, 342-43).

In trying to limit the examples of scenes in *A la recherche* that are reminiscent of Molière, I will choose only passages in which the egoism and thoughtlessness of Proust's characters make one think of Molière. For example, there is the celebrated "Sans dot!" with which Harpagon repeatedly justifies his choice of the old, but rich husband he insists his incredulous daughter marry. There is also Argan's ingenuous confession when he is thinking of marrying his daughter Angélique to the imbecile Thomas Diafoirus.

But even with this limitation on the choice of examples, I find an *embarras du choix*. There is first of all Professor E..., who has just told Marcel that his grandmother is about to die and who then has the effrontery to complain about his own heavy workload (II, 318). There is also the thoughtlessness that comes from the sense of caste. The Duke of Guermantes thus condemns Swann's pro-Dreyfus convictions (II, 678). Then there is Madame Verdurin, who has just managed to get her morning *croissants* in the middle of a world war and who reads in the newspaper details of the torpedoing of the *Lusitania* (III, 772-73).

Most of all there is the unforgettable scene that closes *Le Côté de Guermantes*. Just as they are going out to dinner and an evening in society, the Duke and Duchess learn from Swann himself that the doctors have told him that he does not have long to live. Madame de Guermantes is terribly embarrassed because a situation like this is not foreseen in her system of etiquette. She tries just the same to do something nice for Swann by inviting him to lunch to talk about his health. As for the Duke, he is ravenously hungry and does not want to arrive late for the meal at Madame de Saint-Euverte's, so he treats Swann's statement as a Jeremiad and he smoothly shows Swann and Marcel to the door. He literally thinks of no one but himself and simply denies the fact of Swann's illness for fear that he might spoil his evening (II, 597).

III

I realize, of course, that the incomplete nature of these comparisons means that they cannot be decisive. I have only given a few clues that will permit interested readers to find many more similar cases on their own. But I have a much more serious argument, for I believe that essential similarities link Proust's esthetic to Molière's poetics: the organic development of the characters and the constant refusal of the tragic.

First of all, Molière is devoted to clarity, and he makes of clarity one of the great principles of his dramatic psychology. At any given moment, the spectator must be able to understand clearly all the characters on the stage, however complex or simple those characters may be. This position implies that the poet must give us an initial idea of the character which will contain an embryonic notion of those aspects made explicit in the course of the play. In this way the initial figure will be enriched, deepened and brought into focus, but without betraying or contradicting itself—this is the concept of the organic development of characters. A good example is the opening of *Le Misanthrope* with Alceste's angry exclamation: "Moi, je veux me fâcher et ne veux point entendre." This is the fifth line of the play, the third spoken by the hero. It is a summary of Alceste's deliberate pessimism, naïve pride and choleric impulses that define the hero right up to the dénouement. Likewise, in *Les Femmes savantes* we meet Philaminte in the second act just when she has fired her unfortunate servant Martine and appears onstage in all her impetuous glory: "Je ne veux point d'obstacle aux désirs que je montre," "Sans doute. Me voit-on femme déraisonnable?" Later on we discover that this authoritarian woman, a fanatic about philosophy and crazy about "refined" language, is also a sincere feminist and a lady who has both great spirit and generosity. And all of this is promised by the first verses as she is chasing Martine out of the house.

Proust presents and develops his characters in the same way. Each time he introduces a new character he gives a strong and significant initial impression, an impression that the rest of the narrative enriches without rendering it obsolete. This feat is more admirable not only by reason of the sheer scope of the chronicle presented in *A la recherche*, which stretches over thousands of pages and not just over the 1800 verses of a Molière comedy, but also because Proustian characters undergo occasional and sometimes disconcerting mutations. However, even these alterations were mysteriously inscribed in the first encounter. There is the image of Madame Verdurin in the midst of her *salon*, perched on a high Swedish chair (I, 205). The whole character is given us in a nutshell: her determination to reign over this little court, her pretension to an intellectual culture liberated from all formality, but also her egoism and her acute sense of personal comfort. Just as she appears here, at the beginning of *Un Amour de Swann*, so she will reappear at the very end of the novel, at the reception she gives at the end of *Le Temps retrouvé*.

There is the Duke of Guermantes, whose first appearance I mentioned earlier, and also Charlus and his first contacts with Marcel, first at Tanson-ville, at the Swanns' (I, 141) and then in front of the casino at Balbec (I, 751). But I prefer, given the limits of space, to focus on the first descrip-tion of Robert de Saint-Loup, in the lobby of the Grand-Hôtel at Balbec (I, 728-29). The whole subsequent story of the character is latent in this passage: the brilliant horseman whom Marcel will visit at Doncières, the tumultuous love affair with Rachel, the marriage with Gilberte Swann and, finally, the surprising change in Robert's conduct, his liaison with Morel and Marcel's discovery of Robert coming out of Jupien's very special kind of house. Learning of his death on the battlefield, Marcel instinctively looks far back, and thus the circle closes:

Pendant plusieurs jours je restai enfermé dans ma chambre, pensant à lui. Je me rap-pelais son arrivée, la première fois, à Balbec, quand, en lainages blanchâtres, avec ses yeux verdâtres et bougeants comme la mer, il avait traversé le hall attenant à la grande salle à manger dont les vitrages donnaient sur la mer. Je me rappelais l'être si spécial qu'il m'avait paru être alors. (III, 847)

Finally, I would like to focus on the second profound resemblance between Proust's creative genius and Molière's: the very clear refusal of the tragic and the will to preserve the comic atmosphere, the only ambiance suitable for a real description of characters. First, some general reflections on these terms. What is the essential difference between comedy and trag-edy, or rather between the comic and the tragic? Is it necessary that we laugh in one case and weep in the other? Such a distinction is possible, but not sufficient, because not every comic passage of a work makes us laugh and not every tragic passage makes us weep. Taking as a basis some remarks in Bergson's book on laughter, one could say that the tragic climate is defined by the principle "Our acts follow us." The climate of comedy, on the contrary, depends on human acts being reduced to gestures without consequence. Molière thoroughly understood this principle. If Harpagon had taken Mariane as his wife and had married off his daughter to the rich old Anselme and his son Cléante to a wealthy widow, if Philaminte had sac-rificed the happiness of her daughter Henriette to her own obsession with being a learned lady and had made Henriette marry Trissotin, if Argan, in his panic at the thought of death, had gone through with his project of giving Angélique to the hateful simpleton Thomas Diafoirus, comedy would have been transformed into melodrama and the spectators would not pay attention to the character types, but instead to the fate of the sympathetic characters. The spectators would be preoccupied with resent-ment or with commiseration, with anger or with pity. But, of course, there is no need to worry; everything finishes happily in *L'Avare*, *Les Femmes savantes* and *Le Malade imaginaire*, for those whom we took for fearful

tyrants turn out to be only whimsical cranks who easily forget their reso-
lutions, or they are merely hot-heads who are brought to their senses just
in time. Harpagon, for example, upbraids his son Cléante sharply in the
second act of L'Avare and decides to watch his conduct very closely. But
Harpagon seems to have forgotten all about it at the beginning of the
following act, as Bergson noted. This shows that in comedy exaggerated
or unlikely actions do not detract from the truth of characters. Only the
motives of these actions need be true. The actions have no consequence;
they may be as exaggerated as the playwright wants. Such exaggeration is
even amusing and reassuring. Philaminte may indulge in parodic demonstrations of enthusiasm, Trissotin may be grotesquely ridiculous, Argan and
Harpagon may be extraordinarily caddish and credulous, but the truth of
their character does not suffer at all, for the very human motivations which
make them gesticulate appear all the more clearly, and their passions are
all the more spectacular.

Moreover, because comic actions are nothing but gestures without
consequence, they may be repeated indefinitely, and the characters that
accomplish them may remain unchanging. By definition, life teaches such
characters nothing and, so to speak, leaves them no scars. In the fifth
act, as in the first act of L'Avare or Les Femmes savantes, Harpagon is as
miserly and Philaminte just as much a blue stocking.

Three types of observations show that Proust approaches characters and
their comedy in the same way as Molière. First of all, the narrator of A la
recherche often reports the gestures, not the actual accomplishments, of his
characters—multiple and contradictory gestures that decorate the social cer-
emonies which he so tirelessly chronicles. Self-serving gestures or gestures
of indifference, as in the scene, just mentioned, which closes Le Côté de
Guermantes. Gestures revealing egoism, passion or character, but in no
way pledging a destiny or even changing a career. We just have to remember
the reception at the home of the Prince of Guermantes that opens Sodome
et Gomorrhe during which Marcel wonders desperately who can make the
gesture of introducing him to the Prince (III, 633-55).

Secondly, passion does not lead, in Proust's novel, to true actions, but
only to gestures without any effect or any weight. Saint-Loup breaks up
with his mistress Rachel—and then? Marcel nourishes a long idealistic love
for the Duchess of Guermantes, he follows her during her shopping and
her excursions—and then? On a deeper level, we must admire the immense
capacity for forgetfulness of almost all of Proust's characters: Swann forgets
his passion for Odette, Marcel forgets his grandmother (only to remember
her suddenly when he returns to Balbec), he forgets even Albertine, for
whom he had long been sick with yearning, Charlus himself forgets Morel

in spite of going so far as to think of killing him out of jealousy. Furthermore, some of the characters die in the course of the novel; none of them die of love or because of someone else's love for them, and they are all gradually forgotten.

The third and concluding observations concern the remarkable stability in the personalities of the characters. They grow old, of course, but they do not change substantially—not any more than the characters of Molière's comedies. They continue to maintain the mixed and enigmatic promises of their very first appearance. Clearly, then, Proust portrays characters much more than he follows destinies. Basically, the only destiny traced in his novel is the narrator's. He discovered his calling at that famous reception of the Duchess of Guermantes, and we know that that calling is precisely to portray characters! In doing so, Proust reveals his kinship with Molière, a kinship that makes of *A la recherche* not a tragic novel like *La Princesse de Clèves* or *Madame Bovary*, but rather a great comic masterpiece, one that underscores the vitality of the French literary tradition.

NOTES

1. All references to Proust's text indicate the volume and page number of *A la recherche du temps perdu*, ed. Pierre Clarac and André Ferré, Bibliothèque de la Pléiade, 3 vols. (Paris: Gallimard, 1954).

2. I think here of the chapter on Proust's comic aspect in Léon-Pierre Quint, *Marcel Proust, sa vie, son œuvre*, first published in 1925; of the lecture by André Maurois, "Le Comique et l'humour dans l'œuvre de Marcel Proust," *Conférencia* (May 15, 1948); of Lester Mansfield, *Le Comique de Marcel Proust* (Paris: Nizet, 1953); and of F.C. Green, "Le Rire dans l'œuvre de Proust," *Cahiers de l'Association Internationale des Etudes Françaises*, No. 12 (1960), 243-58. Further studies on this theme appear in R.A. Donzé, *Le Comique dans l'œuvre de Marcel Proust* (Neuchâtel and Paris: Attinger, 1955); Jean-Pierre Quint, "Le Comique dans l'œuvre de Marcel Proust," *Bulletin de la Société des Amis de Marcel Proust et des Amis de Combray* (1956); Michiko Susuki, "Le Comique chez Marcel Proust," *Bulletin de la Société des Amis de Marcel Proust et des Amis de Combray* (1961, 1962).

Mario Specchio

The Difficult Hope of Mario Luzi

Mario Luzi was 21 years old when his first book, *La Barca* (1935), appeared. It presented in the musical frailty of its forms a poet precociously lucid in his themes and in his stylistic means. Florence, his city of adoption, was then a nerve center of Italian culture, a culture defended only in islands of silent, but vigorous resistance to the gray depression of fascist conformity. The city of Dante and Machiavelli was continuing with less uproar, but certainly with no less energy, given the times, the work begun in the immediate pre-war period, the work of mediating the proposals and the pressures of the most noble voices of European culture. Magazines like *Solaria, Il Frontespizio* and *Campo di Marte* debated the boldest themes of 20th-century thought and poetics; they continued the project begun by, among others, *La Voce,* of making literary practice less provincial. In these pages the translations by Leone Traverso of Hölderlin, Novalis and Rilke came into the Italian limelight along with Carlo Bo's essays on Tolstoy. There Kafka and Eliot were translated; there the haunted verb of Rimbaud, as well as the agony of Mallarmé's impossible creation, were studied, or rather, breathed. The lesson of Montale, who with his harsh voice urged pitiless sincerity even to the point of the immobility of "Divine Indifference," and the lesson of Ungaretti, outstretched in elementary bareness towards memorial innocence, a bareness supported only by the courage of illusion ("Ungaretti / uomo di pena / ti basta un' illusione / per farti corraggio"), indicated to the new generations the coordinates—virtually the only possible ones—along which they might move.

Luzi's voice came forth with the security of youth, but above all with the intrinsic force of a discourse that had in itself, within itself, its own reasons and that compared itself, after having *lu tous les livres*, with the only book that irrevocably imposes its handwriting and its enigma—the world, nature:

> Lasciate il vostro peso alla terra
> il nome dentro il nostro cuore
> e volate via,
> quaggiù non è vostro l'amore.
> ("Canto notturno per le ragazze fiorentine," 1-4)

His is a "nocturnal song," a song that cherishes the images immersed in sleep and in expectation; it is a greeting to the fragility of adolescence locked in its destiny of unsteadiness. The perception of futility falls into line with the refraction of "sorrow," but at the same time links, with its medial attitude, the lament to love. Along with the fleeting and almost inconsistent nature of living creatures goes the change of the seasons, the burning of time; seasons trickle away like candle wax in a sorrowfully holy, but unarrestable flow. The will of God, accepted as law more than as promise of redemption, marks the dejected and reverent participation of the poet. The constant murmuring of time that lulls living creatures, suspended in the daily and unalterable actions of life, is the eloquent protagonist of this volume. The voice of mankind, of objects and of landscapes seem to be affectionately, but tenaciously attached to it; they have no way out. From here comes the invitation "leave your burden on earth." It appears that the profound religious sentiment that animates all of Luzi's early poetry is characterized by a painful note of loss and of vanishing, accepted with pitiful awareness, but exalted neither to consolation nor to explanation of the mysterious movement of the universe. The call to the "will of God" sounds, in fact, let us say, not like something external, but like a dimension in great part unrelated when compared with that which we could call the counter-song of loss. For that reason, it is "a hope without purpose" ("Lo sguardo," l. 17) that shines in the pensive eyes of the adolescents, the girls, the young women who populate the world of early Luzi and who move in an often enchanted breeze that recalls not only the Stil Nuovo, but also the sorrowful Leopardian nostalgia:

> Dagli alberi discendono le estati
> e dinanzi all'autunno
> pencolando le rose degli amati
> orti d'intorno, simili a quei volti
> cui la fatua beltà fugge ogni giorno.
> Ma il loro cuore aspetta il mattino.
> ("Le fanciulle di S. Niccolo," 14-17)

And if the young women live their fullness waiting for a future—promised, but already felt to be chimerical—the mother, the young woman of yesterday, expresses dismay at her own condition; she indicates the deluded and resigned stupor of long and patient faithfulness:

> Con amari sorrisi trascorrono
> le beltà conturbando i volti, il sole.
> Incredula la madre incanutita
> tocca i capelli della figlia
> odorosi di pioggia, il suo passato
> splendore, l'ombra, il vuoto
> di sé l'opprime come un' infeconda
> primavera i ruscelli.
>
> ("I fiumi," 9-15)

From this emerges Luzi's tendency to isolate the figurativeness of a gesture and charge it with all its individual meaning until it is exposed to be at the same time absolute and relative. Relative, that is, to a provisional, repeated order in time and space, and in its provisional nature; absolute because unique and symbolic of a world eternally being produced by and for that gesture. And yet one must note the pairs of opposites for which the smiles are bitter, the beauties troubled; the white-haired mother touches the daughter's hair as if to verify precisely with the gesture the continuity of life that manifests itself in the polyvalency of its contrasts and, in the final analysis, in its transforming and in its losing of itself.

But all this, mind you, is orchestrated not to diminish or even to deprive the world of its truth and stability. On the contrary, it is in the perception of the futility of existing that Luzi recognizes presence, his presence and that of other living creatures. From this preliminary awareness arise the will and necessity to comprehend in order once more to place the meaning of individual life within that of universal life: "Sulla terra accadono senza luogo, / senza perché le indelebili / verità . . ." ("L'immensità dell'attimo," 10-12). Truth, consequently, is "indelible," definitive and indisputable, be it considered on a cognitive or on a sentimental-religious basis, even if such truths are "without place," taken, that is, from our spatial-temporal perception, not confinable within the conventional order of abstract knowledge or even within that of formalized logic, "without a why," inexplicable perhaps, but perhaps precisely for that reason "indelible." And in that case we can understand the *point de vue* of *La Barca*:

> Amici dalla barca si vede il mondo
> e in lui una verità che procede
> intrepida, un sorriso profondo
> dalle foci alle sorgenti
> . . . .
>
> ("Alla vita," 13-16)

Montale in *Ossi di Seppia* had watched the sea from the shore, anchored to the physical and metaphysical prison of the "land-necessity," entrusting to marine creatures his nostalgia for the "impossible liberty" ("Falsetto"). Luzi observes the land from the boat, from the sea. *Ossi di Seppia* had opened with an invitation addressed to the beloved to escape, to search for a passage, for a saving ghost. Luzi begins his poetic discourse rejecting the hypothesis of escape as well as that of immobility. His poetry is born moving not in search of an impossible miracle or of a propitiatory action, but already immersed in a painful miracle that is the very force of life in its uninterrupted contraction of acceptance and denial. The result is the Luzian synthesis of which Zagarrio speaks: "The result is that the Montalian negative will is as much appeased as the Ungarettian insight; and a 'return to nature' suddenly emerges in which individual heroism no longer has a reason to be and is destined to translate itself into a heroism of the species."[1] One could hardly succeed in saying more than Luzi—an essayist exceptional for his breadth of perspectives and his conceptual and stylistic rigor—has said on this subject central to his meditation. In the essay entitled "On the Concept of Nature" (1947) we read:

Nature, it is important to insist, does not reside so much in the series of phenomena as in the man who is conscious of it. The figure of man introduced into the blind chase of physical or psychological causes, unrelated, is not less unnatural than that of artificial man, incorruptible in his physical being and his convictions. Between the antiphysis of Nietzsche and the physicality of Sartre, there is just that in common: they are both distant from nature. Beyond fatigue and resignation, on this side of pride and of Titanism, nature constitutes an active boundary within which man can act usefully, that is, in such a way that his acts effectively reflect on other men, united to him by certain properties inherent to nature.[2]

The possibility and the necessity of mediation that Luzi points out in the passage cited is the very one that his own poetry, from the first book, attempts with a lucid and precocious maturity. Luzi's greatness, which today appears at its height, still rests upon those distant premises, on the convinced originality of that humble voice. From there emerged Luzi's arduous struggle for a difficult hope, his tenacious confrontation with the impenetrable aspect of phenomena and of the *I* that is involved there, his struggle with time, relentless motor which from one side devastates us and from the other asks us to be redeemed by its very own modal-temporal connotations, because—again in Luzi's words—"the future is the same as the past if it is not enlightened by hope."[3]

Some poems from *Avvento notturno* (1940) lean towards the past, towards a space revitalized by memory—nostalgia for classicizing landscapes bathed by a smooth, ivory light that could remind one of Hölderlin. But the painful remembering and the anxious questioning of Luzi still address themselves, in these first lyrics of *Avvento*, to the "figures" that inhabited *La Barca*: the adolescent women. One of the most significant texts is precisely "Cimitero delle Fanciulle"

> Eravate:
> le taciturne selve aprono al piano
> e al sole il vasto seno:
> questo è il campo di fieno ove correste.
> E dai profondi borghi alta la torre
> suona ancora le feste
> onde animava ognunna alle finestre
> di gioia umana il volto inesistente.
>
> (II. 1-8)

The lyric opens with a dry, assertive imperfect tense, a tense arched in duration like the edge of a horizon which frames, fleeing, a Flemish interior. But Campana, too, in the *Canti orfici* had used, with quivering audacity, the imperfect of the auxiliary as an absolute ("Donna genovese"). The suspension of the imperfect, accentuated by the strophic isolation of the syntagm, first expands to the present which governs the two lines in which nature rests, spread out in a silent and unattainable vastness, and then leaps in the fourth line to a peremptory and irreparable remote past: *correste.* Leopardi had succeeded to such an extent: interweaving space and time in one voice and placing the living being at the crossroads, nailed to the bosom of pitiless nature and yet majestically alert. Indeed, the entire poem brings us back to Leopardi, to his impetuous voice subtly dissimulated in the internal music of the verse. In Luzi's poetry, all of the Silvias silent for more than a century found another voice, Silvia's, for whom youth had been but "amusing deceits," hopes deluded by the mockery of the future, beautiful in expectation and in memory, but never affirmable or enjoyable in the space of the true present that belongs to nature and not to living beings. And yet the Leopardian drama of determined youth and of deadened consciousness finds in Luzi a resonance more full, more profoundly matured from within and, hence, substantially modified. Leopardi resorted to the past, to "recollection," however "harsh," to take from it a minimum of consolation: he pursued hostile and indifferent Nature with painful questions:

> O natura, o natura,
> Perché non rendi poi
> Quel che prometti allor? perché di tanto
> Inganni i figli tuoi?
>
> ("A Silvia," 36-39)

Luzi responds to the questions of his own lyrics with his own inalienable presence: "But I am, I have nature and faith."

The hypothesis of Luzi's poetry was an "open" hypothesis—in this it is original with respect to other contemporary voices—open, that is, to "experimentation" with the possible and with the future, hence also with the opaqueness of the world and of the word. If we think, then, for a moment, that the years in question were the darkest years of pre-war fascism, it does not surprise us that Luzi found himself confronted with the possibility of an absolute word, or—although the term is loaded with risks and equivocations—with the hermetic word. It is certain that, with a lyric like "Già colgono i neri fiori dell'Ade," we find ourselves simultaneously before one of the greatest accomplishments of European poetry in the symbolist-Mallarmean tradition, and within a *Sackgasse* from which the poet should have emerged without docking at the moor of silence:

> Già colgono i neri fiori dell'Ade
> i fiori ghiacciati viscidi di brina
> le tue mani lente che l'ombra persuade
> e il silenzio trascina.
> Decade sui fiochi prati d'eliso
> sui prati appannati torpidi di bruma
> il colchico struggente più che il tuo sorriso
> che la febbre consuma.
>
> Nel vento il tuo corpo raggia infingardo
> tra vetri squillanti stella solitaria
> e il tuo passo roco non è più che il ritardo
> delle rose nell'aria.

It is useless to emphasize how this lyric is a *summa* of the most typical themes and images of 20th-century poetry: from the rose of Mallarmé to that of Rilke, to the *colchique* of Apollinaire, to the windows, again of Mallarmé ("que la vitre soit l'art, soit la misticité"), to the shadow of George and Trakl, to the Rimbaldian analogical syntheses, to the surrealist oneiric processes. Luzi roams here in a kingdom of nocturnal images, frozen by the very sound of the word that attempts the last *hasard*: does the dream of *Igitur* repeat itself? It would seem so if the heartfelt brotherhood that inspired the lines of *La Barca*—the natural flow that circulated in the "indelible truths" of life—has now frozen and obscured to the point of disfleshing, even dissolving the very presence of the poet. The book in which presence and faith were affirmed closes with the confession of a dubious, perhaps lost, identity, certainly put into question *ab imis*:

> Gelo, non più che gelo le tristi epifanie
> per le strade stillanti di silenzio
> e d'ambra e i riverberi lontani
> delle pietre tra i bianchi lampi delle fontane.

Ombra, non più che un' ombra è la mia vita
per le strade che ingombra il mio ricordo impassibile.
("Maturità," 7-12)

Neither life nor memory—a ghostly shadow that wanders in timeless streets
—settles in the indifference of aimless recollection. Absence, then. And how
can one not think of Mallarmean absence that attempts, with a throw of
the dice, to abolish the world in order to lead it back to the empty pure-
ness of the word and of the Absolute? But we know how much the wager
of the *maître* transformed itself in his own hands into a *tranquille désastre*,
and it is precisely Luzi who dedicated to the poet of Tournon one of his
most brilliant essays, demonstrating the sublime checkmate. Examining the
Coup de dés, Luzi writes:

It is in the first place, to the final act, a drama of poetic creation which, in spite of
all aspirations, declares itself necessarily subordinate to the impositions of life and
of the contingent: it is, in a broader sense, a drama of knowledge that notwithstanding the calculations, will never succeed in dominating fate and the future with its
rules, since in the very formulation of these rules re-enters the element of the uncertain. It is, in the end, the drama of existence that, while it seeks its own finality and
its supreme justification, must resign itself to a rash and necessary perpetuation. While
Igitur, be it still in a desperate extremism, denounces an inflexible and overstretched
purpose, the *Coup de dés* is a testament, a dramatic testament that bitterly concludes
the grandiose and stubborn reflection that occupies all of Mallarmé's life and sustains
all of his work. The themes of this reflection are immense and vertiginous and the
failure that concludes it is based on such immensity and such vertigo.[4]

In this extended passage it seems that Luzi, reliving through a subtle critical undertaking the moral and stylistic adventure of Mallarmé, has done
justice to a myth and a temptation of vast implications: the myth, that is,
of the Word engaged in the creation of an absolute world, autonomous and
closed to the breath of life in its intangible perfection. On the shores of this
adventurous sea, what Luzi calls "the proud romantic heresy" had ship-
wrecked in a blaze of light. It had been a heresy that attempted the recon-
quest of nature by resolving it in the space of the poetic *I* and—in the
boldest gestures of Symbolism—of the magic and demiurgic word. But at
the same time Luzi relived in these pages a *coup de dés* attempted by two
generations of 20th-century poetry and also, as we have seen, by his own.

The essay on Mallarmé is dated 1952, the year in which the collection
that constitutes the keystone of Luzian poetics appeared, *Primizie del
deserto*. But in the meantime war had devastated countries and consciences,
and Luzi's voice would rise again, this time driven by the convulsion of the
period, to leave the limbo of frozen words. The timbre of his new "convul-
sive and distressed" poetry—the adjectives are his—is manifest in *Un Brindisi*
(1946). The war established an indelible boundary beyond which every-

thing had to be put into question. It will be enough to think of books like *La Bufera* of Montale or Ungaretti's *Il Dolore* to recognize the about-face that poetic language had to accomplish in those years. Luzi, in the note that accompanied *Un Brindisi*, referring to the short poem that gives its name to the collection, wrote: "It is a prefiguration, between the delirious and the orgiastic, of the war that turned upside down the false Olympus or the garden of Armida in which many thought they lived upside down." The primal tremor of *Brindisi* grafted a personal event into the universal anguish of the war. If, as we have seen, *Avvento* had singled out and experimented with the immobility of being, the reified emptiness of ice and shade, the war came to upset every position and every hypothesis, taking from the poet the notion of existence and of nature that had come this far, shaping and forcing him to revoke his own voice threatened by the harsh, inexhaustible accent of a world unhinged from its physical and metaphysical assumptions. The disastrous spectacle of the world reflects itself, in this section, in the deformed face of a nature martyred by the Lucretian *tabes* and beaten by a suppressed howl, as in a picture by Edward Munch. Everything, though riddled with a shudder that recalls certain German expressionists, is blocked in a classical severity to which the Foscolian lesson of the *Sepolcro* is not alien:

> Silenzio della terra, bocche, bocche
> cucita dalle lagrime: e la morte
> chiusa e configurata nel silenzio
> della fronte dell'uomo sotto il cielo compatto;
> sulla terra concreta nell'attesa
> della pioggia e del sole, represso ogni respiro,
> l'uomo e il vuoto concentrico intorno alle sue spalle,
> il convolvolo eterno delle strade.
> Silenzio, solitudine dei gesti inadempiuti
> . . . .
> (II. 84-92)

The solitude of man, prisoner of his silence and of the fixity of "unfulfilled acts," makes us hear a Luzi more close than ever before to Mallarmé. It also tells us how much the Foscolian pity that observes with distress, but shares "human misfortunes" has shattered and enlivened the sublime and inhuman temptation of impassibility. And how could one not think, always on the same trajectory, of the "Divine Indifference" of Montale, there where the speaker's last hope is entrusted to the "erect calm of the statues," statues that recall "the statue in the sleepiness of midday" from "Spesso il male di vivere ho incontrato"? But also the object of indifferent immobility, of the reification of the *I*, is happily doubled by Luzi, who indeed entrusts to the statues the pledge of the speaker, of the witness of mankind, even if it be only a lament: "An everlasting ear perhaps will hear the lament." God is far from this *wasteland* committed to an anxious "perhaps," a land distinct and dubious like the lament that is lost in empty space. If the beginnings of Luzi had indicated the necessity and the possibility of a reintroduction of nature into the course of individual experience, and vice versa—but then how much sadness we had savored in the sweetness of the lines flowing like the passing of the seasons—the path is now that broader one of the magmatic history of the world, where good and evil, comedy and tragedy alternate and interpenetrate without the solution of continuity. Individual experience is, thus, constituted by the continuous modification of itself in its variable terms and in the persistence of irremediable individualization, never sutured or suturable. Luzi's Roman Catholicism, which has never been appeased by the evidence of dogma, but has always been nourished by an agonistic Christianity, in the sense given to the word by Mounier and Unamuno, is one that is still deepened and enriched. The young scholar of Mauriac (Luzi had dedicated his degree thesis to the French writer), of Bernanos and of Gide, perhaps always knew, as the country priest says, that all is Grace. But he also knows, now more than ever, how much this Grace is to be lost and regained every day.

If from the time of his collaboration on the magazine *Il Frontespizio* the poet had shown himself to be touched by the God of Augustine and of Pascal, now the implications of such a resonance make themselves more delicate and more suffered; in his poetry moves the spirit of the tortured and manly Gospel of the *Christus patiens*, of the Man who every day suffers his death in a confrontation with the obscure resistance of the world and of living creatures.[5] Only on the condition of a totally knowing wager on the world can poetry hope to reinsert itself in a trajectory that is not limited to the world's empirical characteristics:

> Riconosco la nostra patria desolata
> della nascita nostra senza origine
> e della nostra morte senza fine.
> E questa, l'avevo chiamata il caso,
> l'avevo chiamata l'avventura
> o la sorte o la notte o con quei nomi
> inquieti che mi dettava l'angoscia,
> non la pietà che penetra, che vede.
> ("Né il tempo," 29-36)

We are already at the heart of the book that bears the emblematic title *Primizie del deserto* (1952). The metaphoric space of the desert extends, indicating the paths of a journey that is simultaneously penitential and exaltant. Penitential because in the desert; time and the mobility of space

having been abolished, the poet recognizes the signs of abandon and forgetfulness. But also exaltant because a space open—thanks indeed to its ubi-
quity—to every end; a *tabula rasa* that is more than Eliot's "waste land,"
that can ready itself with every "first fruit":[6]

> Strane dove l'effimero ci porta
> si mettono radici, rami, foglie
> dove una lamentosa notte fruscia.
> E, la nostra foresta inestricabile,
> ascoltane le foglie vive, i brividi
> e la remota vibrazione, il timbro
> d'arpa di cui percuotano le corde.
>   ("Invocazione," 17-23)

Vortex of time and fixity of man. Fixed and, therefore, impotent, the living
creature does not recognize himself if not in the eternal future, in the cycli-
cal nature of the universe; yet he cannot impress direction on movement,
time or history. Nailed down and crucified by his own anxiety of knowledge and of consciousness, Luzi's man, like those of Bernanos, Mauriac,
Dostoevsky and Eliot, comsumes all the energies and all the poisons of the
"subsoil"; he struggles so as not to yield to the temptation of simplification
and discouragement; he is possessed by an indomitable tenacity that makes
him believe in that which he does not see, and doubt that which he does
see. The path that Luzi has marked out on the sand of the desert is that of
the *porte étroite*, that of an unconditional surrender that gives a mark of
the biblical to the pain, to the violence of all that in us generates itself
and regenerates us, destroying us. But the desert is slowly populated under
the gaze of one who has learned to recognize the shadows, to distinguish
their faces. The solitude in which each human being recovers his condem-
nation can open itself up to the solidarity of the species. From this point
the conversation with the dead, the disembarked, will be progressively more
intense; it is a hope and a wish for peace, for freedom from the whirling
motion of the "infernal storm that never ceases":

> Dà loro pace, pace eterna, portali
> in salvo, via da questo mulinare
> di cenere e di fiamme che s'accalca
> strozzato nelle gole, si disperde
> nelle viottole, vola incerto, spare;
> .   .   .   .
>   ("Las Animas," 12-16)

This, one of the most beautiful poems of *Onore del vero* (1957), is a song
and a sorrowful prayer that presupposes the hypothesis, or at least the fear,
that the whirling to which life is subordinate never completely ceases and

that not even the dead are spared the torment of perpetual breathlessness. But if this is true, so is its opposite, that is, that universal life is not formed only by facts concerning phenomena; the Orphic-religious reassumption of the dead into the community of the living implies a broadening of the very concepts of nature and of history. History, then, will not only be the recordable expression of the human journey; it will also take into account the third dimension, the hidden profundity wherein the intimate labors of individuals, as of events, find their secret reasons for being *per speculum* and *in ænigmate*. In a history in which every tear is worth the divine sacrifice, every creature serves, as best it can, the design of the universe:

Vivere vivo come può chi serve
fedele poi che non ha scelta. Tutto
anche la cupa eternità animale
che geme in noi può farsi santa. Basta
poco, quel poco taglia come spada.
("E il lupo," 21-25)

But in Luzi, it is not a given that the Manzonian faith in providential transcendence or in the *a priori* determination of dogmatic finalism be taken up. The poet's act of faith resolves itself in a desire to assent to the necessity of presence, of our own witness, though such witness is often inscrutable and enigmatic in its means and in its ends, sometimes mocking, always dramatic. And it is precisely this that renders so much more disquieting and disquieted the poet's religious tension, a tension that knows neither pause nor peace and can only hope and wish it for the dead:

Requie dai morti ai vivi, requie
di vivi e morti in una fiamma. Attizzala:
la notte è qui, la notte si propaga,
tende tra i morti il suo vibrio di ragna,
presto l'occhio non serve più, rimane
la conoscenza per ardore o il buio.
("Las Animas," 31-36)

United in the same fatigue and in the same hope, the living and the dead now populate a desert that has acquired the cosmic dimension of medieval paintings, paintings in which faces without names cross simple landscapes, immersed in an eternal present. The characters of this "comedy" seem to hide and protect their innermost truth in an anonymity that makes of them mere numbers in the pitiless book of official history. The simple figures of *La Barca* return, but no longer entrusted to an ambiguous fascination with fragility, rather isolated in the "realistic" gestures of a sacred chronicle that utilizes the lyric naturalness of acts to show all the painful force of the daily *epos*:

> La donna prende acqua alla fontana,
> risale su per il proferlio, guarda
> quella nave ancorata nel cielo che è Viterbo
> poi rientra, sparisce nell'interno
> della casa, della città, del tempo.
>   ("Richiesta d'asilo d'un pellegrino a Viterbo," 7-11)

And also the life of the poet, the poet's past, rediscovers in this humbly courageous confrontation the transparency that seemed lost. Above all, he regains, with the slow pace of one who knows that the road is long and the fatigue tremendous, the fullness of the voice and of the word that remain— in spite of all ingrained dangers of torpor and of aphasia—the only instruments with which a poet bears witness about himself and about others, the living and the dead who speak in a single chorus:

> Si sollevano gli anni alle mie spalle
> a sciami. Non fu vano, è questa l'opera
> che si compie ciascuno e tutti insieme
> i vivi i morti, penetrare il mondo
> opaco lungo vie chiare e cunicoli
> fitti d'incontri effimeri e di perdite
> o d'amore in amore in uno solo
> di padre in figlio fino a che sia limpido.
>   ("Nell'imminenza dei quarant' anni," 13-20)

Luzi's path continues to show unexpected vitality, or perhaps it is expectable in light of what I have tried to demonstrate. Works like *Su fondamenti invisibili* (1971) and *Al fuoco della controversia* (1978) have brought the parabola of the Luzian poetic adventure to a height without compare in the panorama of his generation. Certainly the song and the lament of life have not become lethargic; on the contrary, they echo with all their notes and cut with all their edges; but it is a life that recognizes itself—we know at what cost—in itself:

> vita fedele alla vita
> tutto questo che le è cresciuto in seno
> dove va, mi chiedo,
> discende o sale a sbalzi verso il suo principio . . .
>
> sebbene non importi, sebbene sia la nostra vita e basta
>   ("Vita fedele alla vita," 20-24)

Again, we find in these lines the fundamental nucleus of the questions that we have seen emerge and stand out in the Luzian *iter*, refracted on things and on faces, on cities and on the "humble tasks" of each day, the "sad rituals of life," always diverse and always similar to itself, like the sea.

The current that in *La Barca* was going "from the mouths of the rivers to the sources," here "goes down or up by leaps and bounds towards its beginning"; it reproposes the enigma of time, the physical and metaphysical insertion of man into the flow of nature, but what is by now clear, what counts is that this is *our* life to which we must never grow weary of asking questions, even if they will never be answered. And perhaps the task of poetry is not that of furnishing answers; the task of poetry is to give a sense to the why's. The torment is not futile: through it the eye becomes refined, the mind clear; in the meantime, the seeds bud and the fruits ripen: "Sofferenze che vanno / che vengono e ti sporcano. / E intanto ti maturano, ti portano al punto" ("Nel corpo oscuro della metamorfosi," 102-04).

Man will continue to combat, growing in knowledge and consciousness, to discover that all can be redeemed—the rivers can rise again—with "the pity that penetrates, that sees," with love. "This weariness will never end," the poet had said; it must not end; and the words are those of a mother:

> e una madre anche vinta tiene fede,
> sta salda o finge sulla terra
> che il figlio deve apprendere la vita
> e suggere dal campo anche sfiorito.
> Questa fatica non avrà mai fine.
> ("Incontro," 21-24)

And if it is true that, with the passing of the years, heritage and maternal example shine brighter in the eyes of a child, now more than ever Luzi honors memory, the truth of the mother, so many times cherished—and with so much intensity—in his lyrics. Now that the individual experience of the poet and that of his poetry seem dissolved and diffused into the blood of things, into the Virgilian *lacrimæ rerum*, the silent offering of a love, maternal love, that verifies itself in defeat and in darkness by holding lit a torch of difficult, but brave hope, invincible in every battle, seems to have become the deep and vast breath of the world, of the Mothers.

NOTES

1. G. Zagarrio, *Luzi* (Florence: La Nuova Italia, 1968), pp. 28-29.

2. M. Luzi, "Sul concetto di natura," in *L'Inferno e il limbo* (Milan: Saggiatore, 1964), pp. 36-37.

3. M. Luzi, "L'Uomo moderno e la noia," in ibid., p. 29.

4. M. Luzi, *Studio su Mallarmé* (Florence: Sansoni, 1952), pp. 127-28.

5. M. Luzi, "Gesù e la parola," in *L'Inferno e il limbo*, p. 66.

6. P. Bigongiari, "Primizie del deserto o il ritorno del padre," in *Poesia italiana del Novecento* (Florence: Vallecchi, 1965), pp. 291-301.

Judd D. Hubert

Hamlet: Student Prince and Actor

I. Words and Indirection

Quantitatively, *Hamlet* stands out as Skakespeare's longest play; and the Prince, both in the number of lines he speaks and in their ratio to the total length of the tragedy, verbalizes far more than any other Shakespearean protagonist.[1] No one has a better right to exclaim: "Words, words, words" (II, ii, 191), both as speaker and reader. Within the play, the garrulous Polonius comes in third, behind the enterprising villain Claudius, who has some 540 lines to his credit. Among major masterpieces of the stage, only Molière's hyperactive Scapin clearly exceeds the Prince's remarkable output.

Perhaps the profundity or skillful wording of Hamlet's speeches and soliloquies or, better still, their theatrical suitability preserve him from appearing verbose. We may indeed laugh at the Lord Chamberlain's windy moralizing, but we always take the Prince, who rarely hesitates to preach, most seriously, all the more so because, as spectators or readers, we remain steadfastly on his side while trying to sound the depths of his philosophy or complexes. Polonius, on the contrary, never departs from the wisdom of the ages and never expresses a sentiment that might shock his listeners. Despite his status and his political acumen, he appears to have at least a nodding acquaintance with the pedants of Italian comedy. Moreover, Hamlet, who always gives the impression of improvising and inventing, tends to react, rather than plan a course of action in the manner of King Claudius or young Fortinbras, who, having very little to say, reaps the rewards.

The unwonted wordiness of *Hamlet* has nothing surprising about it, granted the high quotient of scholars, in both senses of the term, among the dramatis personae: the Prince, Horatio, Laertes, Rosencrantz and Guildenstern, with Polonius preempting the part of archetypal alumnus. Hamlet, a far more dedicated intellectual than his fellow-students, experiences as great a difficulty in holding his tongue as the players in refraining from telling all. That he should have remained a student at the age of thirty may have seemed odd to an Elizabethan audience, aware that mostly teenagers attended and graduated from Oxford and Cambridge. A crown prince, once he had attained his majority, would have seemed dreadfully out of place, even in Wittenberg. However, apart from the First Clown's evidence concerning the hero's age, everything suggests that Hamlet may not have reached his twentieth birthday. As John W. Draper has suggested, the actor playing the part of Hamlet, and not the character, may have reached in 1604, the date of the Second Quarto, the age of thirty.[2] Shakespeare, in thus playing games with his audience, would have widened the initial cleavage between text and performance while adding still another example of displacement, so characteristic of the play. In any case, it takes a direct order from the King to prevent Hamlet from resuming his studies at Wittenberg, which, by means of a pun, becomes the prototype of all seats of learning, including Luther's alma mater.[3]

Unlike Shakespeare's sophisticated protagonist, the original Hamlet, or Amleth, a mere child who must play the fool to save his life, never has the chance or even the inclination to become a scholar. Indeed, he belongs to a rather barbaric society where only a few clerics know how to read and write. Obviously, Shakespeare has upgraded the legendary tale, both intellectually and politically—the Kingdom of Denmark replaces the principality of Jutland. And the term "upgrading" hardly does justice to Shakespeare's total transformation of a rudimentary society into a polished, but corrupt modern state or to the reversal of the situation described by Saxo Grammaticus and Belleforest. By greatly increasing Hamlet's age, the dramatist must also make Gertrude considerably older, thus putting her, as her son points out, at a season "When the hey-day of the blood is tame" (III, iv, 69). In short, Shakespeare has contrived, by modifying the legend, a displacement where he sacrifices obvious dramatic advantages in order to attain to a more sophisticated theatricality based more on indirection than on immediacy.

The predominance of intellectuality in the tragedy militates more than any other factor against the dramatic directness. Paradoxically, the author waxes more sententious and philosophical than in any of his other plays, even though he deals with a subject that would seem to preclude little else than overt action. We may perhaps explain this discrepancy between subject matter and treatment in light of the unusual spectators the Globe players had to entertain. *Hamlet* may indeed have received its earliest performances at Oxford and Cambridge. A typical revenge play, in the manner of Kyd, would scarcely have appealed to university audiences. Certainly, *Hamlet* owes more to Seneca than do the earlier *Romeo and Juliet* and even *Julius Caesar*, particularly in the Aeneas and Gonzago episodes. In addition to these two classical and already unfashionable inserts, the play features action-retarding soliloquies and moral lectures. Without Hamlet's genius for retarding the action, the entire drama could never have gone beyond the second act. Fortinbras, far from worrying about the honesty of the Ghost, would have quickly put an end to the King, who throughout the play leaves himself so open to attack that he very nearly succumbs to an uprising fomented, but hardly planned, by Laertes. With the exception of the murder, the villain's devious actions always take the form of indirection, an approach he shares with Polonius, who uses the term, and even Hamlet. Indirection, however, indicates far more than a course of action favored by various characters, for it coincides with a system of displacements and cleavages whereby the play repeatedly appears to take stock of itself.

Indirection provides the best method for discovering truth, or, as Polonius puts it, it helps those who "seek directions out." Far from resulting in the uncovering of some elusive verity capable of leading to direct and infallible action, indirection, as the word suggests, can create only a period of inaction. It results in a delay, in a suspension of time, and becomes synonymous with elusion, while fostering the illusion of an accomplishment. More important still, it coincides with the method of the dramatist and, thus, leads to no other truth than that of the theater in general and of the play *Hamlet* in particular. This interplay of elusion and illusion provides a chronological frame, removed from ordinary time, within which the performance can take place. And this frame repeats in another dimension the spatial framework of the stage. In any event, the performance occurring onstage remains one step removed from decisive action and, thus, generates a cleavage which in this highly intellectual tragedy magnifies the discrepancy inherent in all representation.

II. Lectures and Books

Inevitably, in a Renaissance play where the protagonist favors knowledge over power, lectures, lessons and books appear everywhere. Frequently, the moral lecture, reduced to a minimum, has the brevity of a maxim, notably in the Gonzago episode, where the Player King, parodying the outmoded formalism of 16th-century tragedy, expresses himself almost exclusively by means of moral sentences. And Polonius has a saw ready for every occasion. Whether or not they use maxims, the major characters, with the possible exception of Ophelia, love to lecture, usually on ethical or social behavior. Polonius unceasingly preaches to his children; and Laertes, the worthy son of a sententious father, almost misses the boat while telling his sister how a proper maiden should behave when pursued by a prince. The pursuing prince sermonizes more than all the other characters combined, e.g., when he chastises his mother in choice, if tactless rhetoric after having eluded his project of killing the King. Ironically, during his first appearance onstage, he finds himself on the receiving end of a lecture delivered by his hated uncle, who had just tried to justify his hasty marriage in terms of an aporic and unperformable cleavage: "With an auspicious and a dropping eye, / With mirth in funeral and with dirge in marriage" (I, ii, 11-12). Thus, it appears that the King can conceptualize as sophisticatedly as anyone in the play. Indeed, he shows remarkable skill in his lesson to his nephew in hypocritically developing a commonplace concerning the death of fathers.

Claudius' lecture sets in motion a procedure that will prevail in most of the lessons that follow, for in lecturing Hamlet he simultaneously reinforces his authority. Polonius will behave in a similar fashion towards his children, and Hamlet will do likewise in lecturing his mother and coaching the players. In any case, lessons and the assertion of authority coincide throughout the tragedy. But without such an assertion of power the lessons might degenerate into a sort of built-in Greek chorus capable of reducing the speaker to a minimally dramatic stasis. For this reason, lessons or lectures appear to occupy an intermediate position between non-hortatory philosophical discourse, such as the "To be or not to be" soliloquy, and simple commands, e.g., "Nay, answer me. Stand and unfold yourself," in the opening scene, and "Go, bid the soldiers shoot," which ends the play. Military commands reveal two indispensable aspects of the theater: strict obedience to cues and submission to stage directions, without which normal performance would become inconceivable. The play itself, with all its conceptual profundity, must willy-nilly fit into this performative scheme, which nonetheless remains inseparable from textuality. Ironically, the direct military commands that begin and end the tragedy frame a text based primarily on indirection and consisting more often than not of intellectual discourse. As a result, everything within this frame, or, in other words, the entire performance, originates in a mode of discourse quite opposed to it. We might also define military commands as a dress rehearsal for war, or rather for the enforcement of authority. The many moral lessons in the play relate in a similar way to the theater because of the intent to insure a proper performance on the part of the person who must suffer the lectures.

Practically all these lectures, while overtly dealing with moral and social behavior, depend on esthetic postulates and principles. Hamlet, even before he sees the Ghost, objects to Claudius as much for esthetic, not to say theatrical, reasons as for moral, psychological or political motives. His comparison between his father and Claudius as "Hyperion to a satyr" and "no more like my father / Than I to Hercules" (I, ii) recurs in the lesson he gives his mother in III, iv, where he contrasts the portrait of his majestic father to the unprepossessing likeness of his assassin. Here as elsewhere, the Prince must fall back on representation. His long, scholarly comparison ends most appropriately with a rhetorical question: "Have you eyes? / Could you on this fair mountain leave to feed, / And batten on this moor? Ha, have you eyes?" (III, iv, 66-68). The lesson concludes with Hamlet attempting to direct his mother's subsequent performances in her married life with Claudius.

The Prince's cruel and pointed lesson to his mother, as well as the less impassioned and triter lectures delivered by Claudius, Polonius and Laertes, derives essentially from books, classical or merely pedagogical; their number and length easily make *Hamlet* Shakespeare's most intertextual play, marked by an overdetermination of scholarly attitudes. The characters seem to have read a great deal, and many of the speeches and monologues in the play paraphrase or gloss previous texts. We could even claim that the various characters follow the order and procedure of actors: reading, memorization, rehearsal and performance. When speech and action do not originate in books, they tend to rely on learning and training. Hamlet's counterplot, to which his fellow-students Rosencrantz and Guildenstern fall victim, revolves around texts and learning. The Prince tells Horatio: "I once did hold it as our statists do, / A baseness to write fair, and laboured much / How to forget that learning . . ." (V, ii, 33-35). Training also plays an important part in Hamlet's fencing match with Laertes: "Since he went into France, I have been in continual practice" (V, ii, 199). Hamlet has, thus, carefully prepared and rehearsed for this encounter: everything pertains to a learning process, akin to the memorization and rehearsal of actors. The Prince succumbs in the end even though he has made himself ready for all eventualities, even though he states: "The readiness is all" (V, ii, 211), for he has prepared himself for death. In a sense, preparation and training bring about the downfall of the Prince, perhaps because they tend to become valuable in themselves and take the place of decisive action. As in the fencing match, they do lead to performance—to a performance destined to fall short of the performer's solemnly assigned mission. Thus, preparation by a strange reversal creates a displacement central to the play, for it corresponds to the protagonist's so-called tragic flaw. His esthetic

bias, based on years of schooling, provides a revealing instance of his fundamental flaw which critics, who insist on moral or psychological rather than
theatrical causes, attribute to indecisiveness. From a purely theatrical stand-
point, the Prince's insistence on preparation prevents him from functioning
as an effective dramatist and, hence, as a king.[4] A perfectionist in everything he undertakes, he dares not go beyond rehearsal.

The perfectly prepared Hamlet mirrors the texts to which he constantly
returns, and he knows how to transform a given situation into its bookish
equivalent. He behaves like a proper scholar at the very moment the Ghost
reveals Claudius' guilt:

> Yea, from the table of my memory
> I'll wipe away all trivial fond records,
> All saws of books, all forms, all pressures past
> That youth and observation copied there,
> And thy commandment all alone shall live
> Within the book and volume of my brain,
> Unmixed with baser matter.
>
> (I, v, 98-104)

In the very act of rejecting past experience and especially past readings,
the Prince willy-nilly reasserts his bookish nature. Instead of undergoing
a radical change, he remains faithful to a textual identity, and the intolerable event which he now consigns to memory will occupy a place, however
exalted, among other texts and, like them, will clamor for interpretation,
which will require a critic rather than a dramatist. This compelling textual
transformation of an event reflects and suggests a theory for the textuality
of the play itself—a script memorized, rehearsed and performed.[5] Moreover, the Prince's dependence on books repeats and comments on the
theater's own subordination to textuality. Shakespeare, in writing *Hamlet*,
probably rewrote texts by Saxo Grammaticus, Belleforest and Kyd, as well
as those of Seneca, Cicero, Virgil, Horace, Montaigne and countless others,
including, of course, his own plays. Hamlet traces back his origins less to
Danish legends than to the Bard's readings of the classics. As a result, the
play appears as a battlefield of conflicting origins in search of representation where the Prince's cultural background perpetually encroaches on his
legend. Cicero and other famous authors interfere with and misdirect the
hero's assigned role as avenger, thus providing indirections of their own. In
this respect, Shakespeare has contrived a thorough reduction of the original
Amleth for the greater benefit of intellectuality. He has indeed buried Amleth under an avalanche of quotations.

Hamlet's reliance on texts shines forth in the famous soliloquy where
he appears to comment on his wish "that the Everlasting had not fixed /

His canon 'gainst self-slaughter" (I, ii, 131-32). Apart from this obvious connection, the monologue on suicide has little to do with Hamlet's situation or character. Horatio, poor but noble, and undoubtedly subject to "the slings and arrows of outrageous fortune" as well as to "the proud man's contumely," might legitimately in a moment of weakness utter such discouraging thoughts. Coming from the Crown Prince of a warlike state, from a Prince Charming described by Ophelia as "The glass of fashion, and the mould of form, / Th' observed of all observers" (III, i, 153-54), they appear, from a rather superficial dramatic point of view, out of place. Only their beauty would seem to justify their presence. The ideas expressed in the soliloquy derive from Cicero's paraphrase of Plato.[6] As T.W. Baldwin has shown, Hamlet has paraphrased a classical text according to the procedures followed in Elizabethan grammar schools.[7] That the Prince has not invented these ideas does not in itself imply that he fails to express his own point of view and his own feelings. However, the First Quarto—the so-called "bad" quarto—sheds considerable light on the "sincerity" of the famous soliloquy. Claudius provides astonishing stage direction when he exclaims: "See where he comes poring upon a booke."[8] This would suggest that Hamlet does not really soliloquize, but either reads from a book, in all probability Cicero's *Tusculan Disputations*, or paraphrases what he has just read. Corambis—Polonius' name in the First Quarto—immediately gives directions to his daughter: "And here Ofelia, read you on this booke, / And walk aloofe, the King shall be unseene." Ophelia's book of orisons serves as nothing more than a stage prop, placed in her hands not for the good of her soul, but for deceit. Ophelia, in this instance a non-reader and a passive perpetrator of illusion, invites the treatment she will receive at the hands of her bookish lover. In the battle of texts she goes down to a humiliating defeat. Ironically, a nunnery would provide a suitable place for a respectful girl who, at her father's bidding, uses a prayerbook for a prop. Shakespeare's irony goes even further, for he has arranged a confrontation between a submissive heroine who must reluctantly play a prescribed part and a reluctant hero who reads, glosses, but hardly invents his own text. Indeed, he achieves his greatest success by merely changing around the names in the King's order to have him put to death upon his arrival in England. As he readily admits, he copies, but he does not rewrite. Even in this instance, he does not go beyond an existing script, but merely reverses or displaces its purpose. As author, he limits his creativity to the interpolation of a few lines in the Gonzago insert. Even here he does not actually invent, but merely rewrites the Ghost's narrative of Claudius' villainous plot. Unlike the legendary Amleth, he has learned and remembered too much.

Creative or not, Hamlet, the most fashionable man in all of Denmark, surpasses his rivals in all sorts of games, such as wordplay and swordsmanship, all of them part and parcel of his education. Like other dedicated students, he insists on remaining at the head of his class. For this reason, he cannot refuse the fencing match with Laertes, whom he had already bested during their ostentatious verbal confrontation at Ophelia's grave. Hamlet's juvenile propensity to emulate all rivals explains in part his contempt for Claudius, a prince incapable of matching in anything but carousing his warlike brother. Emulation, however, takes a rather special meaning in the theater, where the best way to surpass a rival consists quite simply in upstaging him. And Hamlet, the star of the show, leaves nothing to chance in upstaging all the characters who attempt to share the scene with him, including such seemingly unworthy opponents as the First Clown and Osric. He even, in the presence of Horatio and Marcellus, puts down the Ghost through the use of levity. This ghost has nothing to do with Danish legends, but owes its ultimate existence to the tragedies of Seneca, probably by way of Kyd's lost version of *Hamlet*. Thus, a stock character of tragedy assigns the learned Prince the unlikely part of avenger, where he sees himself as hopelessly miscast: "The time is out of joint. O cursed spite, / That ever I was born to set it right" (I, v, 188-89). Fate or the dramatist has given the leading man an unsuitable and, from a sophisticated point of view, the tritest of roles. That "the time is out of joint" not only indicates that things have suddenly gone awry in the continuum of history—in the natural deaths of fathers—but also reveals a gap between the hero's identity as scholar, courtier, man of fashion, and his forced assumption of a more rudimentary part, suitable no doubt to the single-minded Fortinbras or to the actor who had played the title role in Kyd's lost drama.

III. A Man of the Theater

A perplexing victim of his multiple origins, whether legendary and of limited scope or scholarly and universal, Hamlet can take refuge in the theater, to which he wholeheartedly belongs and which precedes and transcends all other possible sources.[9] Upon hearing that the players from the City have just set foot in Elsinore, for the first time he shows enthusiasm, even though he has not yet thought of using the stage to catch the "conscience of the King"; and he eagerly asks questions concerning the child actors who compete so successfully against seasoned professionals. He greets the players like old friends and with a warmth he had not shown his school fellows Rosencrantz, Guildenstern and Horatio.[10] In short, he behaves as though he had discovered his true home and his native land in a company of professional Thespians. He recites most commendably the first lines of the stilted Aeneas narrative, but leaves the most emotional part to the First Player, who even sheds tears while tearing passion to tatters and in the process makes the hero take stock of his own situation in purely theatrical terms. Hamlet asks himself a compounded rhetorical question: "What would he do, / Had he the motive and the cue for passion / That I have?" (II, ii, 535-37). According to the Prince, who has a very high opinion of the power of performance, strong and sincere acting "would make mad the guilty, and appal the free; / Confound the ignorant, and amaze indeed / The very faculties of eyes and ears" (II, ii, 544-46). Incidentally, he describes the effects of performance in intellectual terms, thus implying that he himself does not perform in this exaggerated manner. Indeed, he follows throughout the play a more sophisticated style of acting than the First Player; and closer to the stage behavior of those urbane gentlemen who grace Shakespeare's comedies. Unlike *A Midsummer Night's Dream*'s Bottom, Hamlet would carefully pick and choose his part. More important still, he implies that by performing according to a text he could solve all his problems and put an end to the state of corruption in Denmark. However, a text capable, if strongly performed, of insuring revenge would probably fall below Shakespeare's lofty standards. On the other hand, Hamlet's built-in failure as a player generates the success of the star actor playing the part. In any case, the Prince clearly places the solution to all his problems within the confines of the stage, just as he previously had cast his resolve to avenge his father in the frame of a printed text. We can surmise that his book of memory coincides with a script, performable only if he manages to push aside the type of role and style of acting in which he normally excels.

In his shocked acceptance of the role of avenger, Hamlet conforms to duty and hierarchy; but, apart from his public display of grief, costumed or not, at court, he does not really express filial sentiments. He greatly admires his father, whose name he bears, but essentially as a model and a spectacle: "'A was a man, take him for all in all, / I shall not look upon his like again" (I, ii, 187-88). In considering him the very paragon of men, the Prince transforms him into an unrepeatable spectacle, gone forever from the stage.

Despite this esthetic attitude towards the murdered king, Hamlet by no means shows a lack of filial sentiments, but it so happens that he directs them to a less worthy and competitive person, to Yorick the jester, who had died not two months, but 23 years earlier. In his remarks on this professional performer, the Prince uncovers still another among his multiplicity of origins: ". . . he hath borne me on his back a thousand times . . . . Here hung those lips that I have kissed I know not how oft" (V, i, 171-74). Hamlet as man of the theater descends from Yorick, in whom we can see the lowest common denominator of theatrical performance, insofar as a jester normally operates without a plot or a prepared text. As origin, Yorick stands at the farthest remove both from Hamlet's scholarly background and from his legendary or aristocratic antecedents, but right at the center of performance. To complicate matters, the Prince has two mothers: Gertrude and his Alma Mater, rivals for his attendance.

The multiple filiation of the hero may help us define more precisely his performative presence within the tragedy. He appears as a student prince who must avenge his father, but also as the actor entrusted with the star part. As a result, he conforms to and at the same time criticizes the plot and, hence, the play where he must function willy-nilly as protagonist, asserting himself all the while both as matinée idol and drama critic capable of theorizing about the theater in general and his own part and performance in particular. In a sense, he contemplates suicide in the manner in which a prominent actor would consider forsaking a star role—both of them would eagerly bear the burden of textuality as long as they had breath to speak their lines.

Hamlet's theatrical situation, based on a fundamental ambiguity—the character's awareness of belonging both to the fable and to the stage—affects in varying degrees the other participants. Even the dead king, in order to prompt his son towards revenge, dresses for the part by conforming to the warlike image that had so impressed his people. His performance leads to a discrepancy, for he appears in middle age, yet tries to look like the young warrior who some thirty years earlier had conquered the king of Norway in single combat! Perhaps, like Hamlet, the Ghost must conform to the approximate age of the actor representing him. In any case, this martial image may correspond to his official portrait the very one Hamlet compares to the unprepossessing likeness of Claudius. The latter not only puts on a false front and uses "painted words" (III, i, 53), but, in order to rule Denmark and marry Gertrude, he also had composed and presently performs in a play unworthy of a king. Laertes' behavior smacks of ostentation, an ostentation that would have served Hamlet well if only he could have sunk to so low a performative level; the gravediggers double as clowns; Ophelia supinely accepts a role in her father's banal plot. Polonius alone, but on a lower level, rivals Hamlet's mastery of the theater, for he, too, functions as director, player, critic. He, too, had become enamored of the stage in his student days, playing, no doubt to great applause, the star role of Julius Caesar, killed somewhere in the course of the play by Brutus. His erstwhile fate on the stage programs his destiny in the present tragedy, where he must die as a stand-in for the King while playing the part of hidden spectator. Shakespeare may very well have added a revealing "in joke" far more humorous than the Prince's pun on "Capitol" (III, ii,100), for the two Globe players performing the parts of Hamlet and Polonius may have recently enacted Brutus and Caesar. It would dawn on Shakespeare's audience that the habitual fate of the performer has theatrically overdetermined the destiny of the character he represents. We see that, like everything else in the theater, Polonius' death becomes just another repetition leading from one performance and one play to the next.[11]

IV. Theatricality and Truth

The search for Truth, in theme no less than in plot, pervades the entire tragedy.[12] The King and with him the entire court need to know the truth about the strange behavior of the Prince, who in turn must verify the authenticity of the Ghost. And, of course, they use theatrical means in order to apprehend an elusive truth. The Prince, the King, Polonius function not only as dramatists, directors and actors, but also as critics who must step back and interpret correctly, on the pain of death and damnation, the performances of others, thus generating a continuous series of *mises en abyme*, including, of course, the play within the play, ably discussed by many scholars. Shakespeare, in the very act of stressing truth —a paradoxical achievement in a pure game of elusion and illusion—has admirably succeeded in rendering his chief characters puzzling. Should we consider Claudius an unmitigated villain with no attenuating circumstances? Did the Queen commit adultery and, worse still, condone assassination? The Prince stands out as by far the most enigmatic character, so much so that some scholars, holding too strong a belief in his "reality," regard his insanity as more genuine than feigned, perhaps as a result of an Oedipus complex. But critics have merely continued, with endless elaborations, the exegesis initiated by Claudius, Gertrude and Polonius. They have all, down to the last scholar and courtier, beaten a path to the author's superlative mousetrap, for the play *Hamlet* can hardly contain truth in the ordinary sense, either for the characters, even when they double as spectators, or the general audience. Indeed, the enigma of the characters refers, in the final analysis, to the paradox of performance with its attendant overdetermination of theatricality.

Knowledge for—and of—the Prince consists in the appreciation of a performance; and the truth about Hamlet, about Claudius, about the Ghost comes down to an awareness of the performative functions of the text as revealed mainly by verbal relationships. For Hamlet, knowing the truth consists essentially in uncovering and verifying an event that had preceded the play: the assassination of his father. But this crime, in order to come into being as representation, must take on the imprint of a performance: thanks to the Ghost it becomes a dramatic narrative, and thanks to the Prince it becomes first a dumb show and then, by means of textual interpolation, a dialogue. Moreover, this crime, as represented both by the Ghost and by the players, relates by implication to speech—to the very substance of theatricality—for Claudius has poured a deadly poison into his brother's ear.[13] The resulting rottenness in Denmark may, thus, have a textual origin. The King's antecedent play, which he never intended to represent, has provided him not only with a crown and queen, but also with an indelible, if at first unwritten, text capable of blasting and curtailing his career. His deed has deprived him of the creative freedom necessary to a successful ruler. He has lost that mastery over time, indispensable to a king and a dramatist. He has become a prisoner of his own drama, a drama to which *The Tragedy of Hamlet Prince of Denmark* owes its existence; and it serves simultaneously as cause and aftermath. From this evil drama, whose existence can come into performative being only through *The Tragedy of Hamlet*, we could derive a theory concerning the preconditions of all drama—concerning origins.

The King's criminal deed, inseparable, in the text of the play, from moral and esthetic coherence, has broken historical continuity and made a mockery of the lesson he gives his nephew concerning the death of fathers. His poison has "curded" more than the blood of his brother; it has corrupted the whole of nature. Not surprisingly, numerous metaphors associate Claudius with weeds, infesting the entire space of the play, whereas Ophelia, the most vulnerable and natural character, remains inseparable from flower imagery.[14] His short reign, like that of Macbeth, appears as an interregnum which can last no longer than the play itself and which generates its own peculiar time. Claudius indeed has put not only "the time," but also "time," out of joint, initiating by his deed the delayed or suspended time of *Hamlet*, while introducing "something rotten in the state of Denmark" and corrupting language. His many-tiered displacement has provided, no less than the multiple stage set, a frame for the performance of *Hamlet*. He alone has made performance necessary. He seems to regret more than anything else the corruption of language, of the King's Danish, for it has reduced him to "painted words" which he must use forever. He approaches language in they way an artist approaches his medium. Like Shakespeare himself, he uses words artfully at the expense of truth and reality by performing with words and making words perform. We can consider him, even more than Hamlet, an extension of the dramatist, for his own falsity serves as a matrix for and a mirror of the fraudulence of theatricality.

All the other characters follow his example—the example of Shakespeare. Nor can we consider the Prince an exception in this respect. Even when, as in the soliloquy, he paraphrases the writings of others, he does little more than expand the cleavage in words and action initiated by his hated uncle. This cleavage or displacement, which simultaneously constrains and enables Hamlet to function as a complete man of the theater, substitutes illusion as well as the elusion of truth for reality and makes staging not only possible, but compulsory. Throughout the tragedy, a reversal repeatedly takes place, for the King's initial crime has brought about the falsity of all representations and reduced morality to esthetics. Shakespeare has indeed built the ultimate mousetrap, where all systems of knowledge and value, our own as well as those of the Renaissance, come to grief. The myopic Fortinbras remains together with the Globe Theater.

NOTES

1. Information derived from *The Pelican Shakespeare* (New York: Viking Press, 1979), p. 31.

2. John W. Draper, *The Hamlet of Shakespeare's Audience* (New York: Octagon Books, 1966), p. 195.

3. Cf. Yves Bonnefoy's note to this effect in his remarkable translation of *Hamlet* (Paris: Mercure, 1962), pp. 217-18.

4. For a discussion of kings as dramatists, cf. James Claderwood, *Shakespearean Metadrama* (Minneapolis: Univ. of Minnesota Press, 1971).

5. Cf. Nigel Alexander, *Poison, Play and Duel* (Lincoln: Univ. of Nebraska Press, 1971). The author shows how Hamlet uses "Remember me" as a trigger word in applying Quintilian's art of memory to his situation, pp. 47 ff.

6. T.W. Baldwin, *Small Latine and Lesse Greeke* (Urbaba: Univ. of Illinois Press, 1944), II, 603 ff.

7. Ibid., II, 69 ff.

8. William Shakespeare, *The Tragicall Historie of Hamlet Prince of Denmarke* (London, 1603), in *Elizabethan and Jacobean Quartos*, ed. G.B. Harrison (New York: E.P. Dutton, 1966).

9. Alexander, p. 14.

10. Cf. Draper, pp. 17 ff., for Hamlet's relationships with his fellow students.

11. For the "in joke," see *Hamlet*, in *The Players' Shakespeare* (London: Heinemann, 1978), p. 188.

12. Cf. Timothy J. Reiss, *Tragedy and Truth* (New Haven: Yale Univ. Press, 1980), pp. 162-82.

13. Alexander, p. 19.

14. Cf. Harold Fisch, *Hamlet and the Word* (New York: Ungar, 1971), pp. 37 ff.

Richard Regosin

The Text of Memory: Experience as Narration in Montaigne's *Essais*

Historically the relationship of subject and memory has been cast positively as a project of forceful recollection which affirms cultural tradition and asserts personal identity. In this light, Montaigne's insistence on his weak and ineffective memory appears especially paradoxical. Evidently he could not expect his readers to accept his claim at face value. In part, the evidence of his writing, the fact that the essayist clearly and vividly recollects past events in his own experience and that he draws confidently from the storehouse of memory myriad aspects of his reading, belies his contention. In part, Montaigne's seeming delight in the idea of his unreliable memory, his satisfaction in its hyperbolic depreciation—"Il n'est homme à qui il siese si mal de se mesler de parler de memoire. Car je n'en reconnoy quasi trasse en moy, et ne pense qu'il y en aye au monde une autre si monstreuse en defaillance" (I, 9, 34)[1]—undermine the literalness of his protestation and suggest that perhaps more than the simple desire to be sincere informs his presentation.

This discrepancy poses the issue of the nature and function of memory in the *Essais* and of its relation to the persona of the essayist and to his essaying. At the same time it forces broader, philosophical questions concerning the nature of the subject itself. If Montaigne's exaggerated negation were to be taken literally, time would fragment irretrievably into an infinity of isolated moments, history would no longer be conceivable, and the subject itself would disappear. But the view of memory which Montaigne inherited guaranteed duration and the integrity of the subject. In the concept of the book of memory resided notions of continuity, of tradition, of authority which, while privileging the past, situated the subject by defining him in relation to it, locating him in a present seen as prolongation. The art of memory guaranteed access to human history and knowledge; it made of the mind an encyclopedia, a reflection of the universe and its order; it substantialized the image of man the microcosm. Whatever the causes, however—unsettling religious and political issues, contemporary interest in skepticism, revulsion with medieval practices, the invention of printing—Montaigne turned against a traditional view of memory and traditional reliance on it to pose (with Erasmus and other humanists) new relationships to books, to knowledge, to the past. And in the process he also began to delineate a different sense of self, a different sense of the subject.

I

Readers of the *Essais* have long appreciated the problematical nature of Montaigne's presentation of memory. Interpretations have ranged from the early accusations of Malbranche and Rousseau that Montaigne embellished his portrait through false modesty to a modern view which appeals to the complexity of relations which operate in self-presentation, as the process of writing necessarily transforms historical reality.[2] In general, recent scholarship has tended to rehabilitate Montaigne's forlorn memory both by insisting on its negative value and by emphasizing its positive contributions to the quality of experience the essayist seeks to articulate. Deficient memory emerges from the first perspective as a virtue, a hedge against the stultifying effects of traditional education, the bombast of rhetorical eloquence, the arrogance of acquired erudition and the pitfalls of insincerity. In his essays on pedantry and education (I, 25; 26), Montaigne rejects traditional pedagogy based on memorization and recitation—and the implication that memory stands metonymically for mind—in order to liberate understanding and judgment as major intellectual faculties. Depicting the mind in spatial terms, he imagines it not to be filled (*remplir*) or furnished (*meubler*), but formed (*faire*). Rather than the space of inert storage, it becomes the locus of process, of tasting (*gouster*), choosing and discerning, above all of transforming things to make them one's own. Evidence of weak memory, then, testifies to the development of judgment and conscience on the essayist's part, to his practice of virtue rather than of mere knowledge (*science*). And, when the student becomes essayist, defective memory serves him to repudiate rhetoric with its demand for a predetermined and fixed form based on traditional and memorized standards. Instead, Montaigne affirms his freedom as writer, choosing the open form by which he expresses the flux and inconstancy of the world and his own experience of it.[3]

If more than a pedagogical issue appears at stake, the essays can also be conceived entirely in pedagogical terms as Montaigne's efforts to realize through his writing the educational aims he sets forth. Unlike his ideal student, however, Montaigne does not exist as a *tabula rasa*, as pristine matter to be molded. He is in a sense already formed, already filled with remembered book learning and knowledge, with a range of attitudes and dispositions which shape his perception and understanding. Montaigne's initial task—and one from which he can never entirely free himself—comprises his unmaking, that is, his shedding of what he comes to consider the traditional trappings which must inevitably obscure his sense of that natural and particular self he desires to uncover through his writing. Weak memory, or perhaps, more precisely, selective memory, allows him to pretend to that ignorance which "saves" him from both the influence of the outside world and his own inclinations. By "forgetting" a certain intellectual past—both broadly and personally historical—Montaigne seeks to avoid the pride and arrogance which accompany the assurance of knowledge and to recapture the innocence and humility which characterize the learned ignorance of that Socrates he so vividly recalls. With the bookish tradition put aside, the essayist can set his own book of the self in its place and seek through it all that he need know of the world and himself.[4]

Alongside memory valued as weakness and lack, Montaigne allows for another memory, one which functions implicitly as presence or wholeness. From that operative faculty he selects aspects of his social, political and familial life, and, most strikingly, of his intellectual life—his reading—to serve both as the matter on which he exercises his judgment and as illustration and commentary in that process. The essays are, thus, in part the product of memory, but, because judgment is exercised in and as the text, they become its surrogate as well: "A faute de memoire naturelle," he says, "j'en forge de papier" (III, 13, 1092). Writing originates Montaigne's history and comprises its record.[5] On a personal level, the essays allow his experiences to be more than a mere succession of discrete instants in a never-ending present. If the writer appears to exercise his judgment in the moments of actuality, his experience is also that of a life lived over time.[6] And in the process of quoting, referring and alluding to the texts of classical antiquity, in the incorporation of elements from a broad cultural tradition, Montaigne recreates an historical past in terms of which he attempts both to locate and to define himself. The essays "remember" the historical past, they serve as its memory and the affirmation of its duration. Whether Montaigne inserts himself as an element in its continuity—as the spiritual child of Socrates, for example—or situates himself in opposition as absolute originality—as when he insists on the singularity of his undertaking (II, 6, 377-78)—he cannot begin to delineate himself without reference to this "memory."

II

Montaigne opens the essay on liars (I, 9) with the exaggerated claim of almost totally lacking memory, or at the very least of having the worst memory in the world. While this lack spares him the pitfalls of lying—of no small importance, since human intercourse depends on the integrity of one's word—it plays a more significant personal role in ensuring the growth and development of judgment. Though Plato calls memory "a great and powerful goddess" and current wisdom equates it with understanding, Montaigne's own experience demonstrates that "les memoires excellentes se joignent volontiers aux jugemens debiles" (p. 34). The vigorous memory debilitates by assuming preeminence: "et irois facilement couchant et allanguissant mon esprit et mon jugement sur les traces d'autruy, comme faict le monde, sans exercer leurs propres forces, si les inventions et opinions estrangieres m'estoient presentes par le benefice de la memoire" (p. 35). Everything is at stake here, for to follow these traces subsumes one in otherness and alienates oneself from the potential of selfhood. To inhibit the flowering of *esprit* and *jugement* denies the means to realize that potential, for the development of judgment *is* the development of self. Montaigne often posits this tension between self and other as the opposition of inside and outside, and he speaks repeatedly of coverings, mantles, robes and barks which have either to be stripped away or appropriated as an aspect of the inside, transformed so as to be made one's own.[7] Memory takes in that which cannot be *of* the inside until recuperated in an act of judgment. As inert storehouse, memory substitutes other for self, outside for inside, nothingness for being.

In the case of lying, the coin of memory has two sides, for, if the inability to remember what one has said likely brings the lie to light, memory's strength, ensuring the possession of what it takes to be true, also trips up the liar. Montaigne endows memory with the capacity to register faithfully and depicts it as affected differently by truth and by falsehood, deeply impressed by the substantiality of the one and untouched by the emptiness of the other: "par ce que la chose, comme elle est, s'estant logée la premiere dans la memoire, et s'y estant empreincte, par la voye de la connoissance, et de la science, il est malaisé qu'elle ne se représente à l'imagination, délogeant la fauceté, qui n'y peut avoir le pied si ferme" (p. 36). The implications of this passage appear, however, to exceed the limited focus on lying to touch on aspects of his central concerns. What Montaigne takes in comes by way of those essential modes (or products) of apprehension—*connois-sance* and *science*—with which the exercise of his judgment is so directly engaged. In memory's presentation of its contents to imagination, as it brings things to mind, resides a basic means of initiating the process of mak-ing those things one's own. If things "as they are" are lodged in the mind, the potential for the discovery of truth would appear to be significantly enhanced. At the same time, Montaigne's use of the vocabulary of represen-tation, of imprints, images and re-presentations, could undermine certainty by introducing the factors of mediation, imitation and resemblance. While the description in this passage essentially reiterates the contemporary under-standing of memory's operation, the associations it suggests and the consid-erations to which its particular cast gives rise compellingly invite further examination in the larger context of the essays.

Montaigne's remark in the essay on presumption (II, 17, 649) that "c'est un outil de merveilleux service que la memoire," without which "le juge-ment faict bien à peine son office," makes a pivotal connection explicit by situating memory centrally in his concern with the exercise of judgment. His immediate disclaimer—"elle me manque du tout"—affirms the modesty and lack of presumption called for in this context, but, if taken at face value, would deny him any chance at all of engaging meaningfully in that introspective activity which is his writing: "et, y regardant de pres, je crains que ce defaut, s'il est parfaict, perde toutes les functions de l'ame" (p. 651). And Montaigne supports this observation with the weight of ancient wis-dom, quoting from Cicero: "It is certain that the memory is the only recep-tacle, not only of philosophy, but of all that concerns the conduct of life, and of all the arts." Yet in a manner which appears playful and facetious, Montaigne draws a line from Terence to depict himself: "I'm full of cracks, and leak out on all sides."[8]

The memory to which Montaigne refers in this context, which he lacks and can afford wholly to lack, is the memory of rhetorical practice, of oratory and verbal eloquence: he claims that to memorize a speech lies almost beyond his power and to demand recall only ensures forgetfulness. To quote Cicero, then, betrays a touch of irony, but what it rejects is not the connection between memory and the conduct of life, but a partic-ular classical conception of memory as storehouse, which would make the retention of learning as knowledge a prolegomenon to the practice of virtue. Montaigne's memory becomes emblematic of his aversion to com-mand, obligation and constraint, and representative of his emphasis on ease and naturalness in living as well as writing. What leaks from the vessel of recollection is the thread of his conversations with others, the names of his servants and the authors, places and words of the books he has read; these are items which the mind bent on virtue, wisdom and self-knowledge can readily spare. Montaigne does indeed recall his reading, but he retains, as he says, what he no longer recognizes as anyone else:s: "c'est cela seulement dequoy mon jugement a faict son profict, les discours et les imaginations dequoy il s'est imbu" (p. 651).

We return in a way to the larger pedagogical concerns of the essays, to the question of knowledge. Montaigne apparently sets aside the exclusive concern with a fixed cultural tradition, contained in books by revered authors (as *auctores*, authorities), to be taken in whole, stored, recalled as learning and applied of a piece. Weak memory neutralizes that privileged tradition by making it anonymous, so much reading matter for the exercise of judgment. The essayist engages the tradition as only one element of his experience, tries it and his mind on it; and, in the process of transformation by which exterior things are taken in and personalized, judgment becomes imbued with those thoughts and ideas which benefit it. These, Montaigne claims, are what remains with him; nothing need be pressed into the storehouse of memory, for the mind retains naturally what is now of it, what has penetrated and become one with it, permeated as if by stain or dye (Latin *imbuere*). Rather than existing *a priori*, knowledge is self-generated, the result of judgment working through experience.

Ever the student, Montaigne understands that he does not have to look beyond his own life, to the outside, to learn all that he need know: "De l'experience que j'ay de moy, je trouve assez dequoy me faire sage, si j'estoy bon escholier. . . . La vie de Caesar n'a poinct plus d'exemple que la nostre . . . . Escoutons y seulement: nous nous disons tout ce de quoy nous avons principalement besoing" (II, 13, 1073-74). If memory seems to be subordinated, even to disappear as an independent (and primary) faculty, subsumed in the proper operations of the mind, its functional links to the learning process remain intact. Ideally, the mind retains what has profited it not as lifeless register of the past, but to reintroduce it appropriately to judgment; it records experience to exercise the rational and critical faculties. Montaigne may forget a name, a title, a fact or a speech he has memorized—and particularly if he tries hard to remember—but there is little indication in the essays that he loses sight of what is central to his project of self-discovery.

Personal emotional experience also serves as the raw material of judgment and, if recalled to mind, figures as a basis for learning:

Qui remet en sa memoire l'excez de sa cholere passée . . . voit la laideur de cette passion . . . . Qui se souvient des maux qu'il a couru . . . se prepare par là aux mutations futures et à la recognoissance de sa condition. . . . Qui se souvient de s'estre tant et tant de fois mesconté de son propre jugement . . . . (pp. 1073-74)

To remember, in this context, allows the possibility of seeing, of gaining that "recognoissance de sa condition" which is both the essential recognition and the knowledge of self Montaigne seeks. The good scholar reminds judgment of its own past mistakes so that it may judge itself, affirm its weakness and what the essayist calls "la trahison de [son] entendement." By thus engaging his own experience, Montaigne learns his most important lesson: "c'est par mon experience que j'accuse l'humaine ignorance, qui est, à mon advis, le plus seur party de l'escole du monde" (pp. 1075-76).[9]

Paradoxically, the learning process concludes with ignorance. Essentially an act of denial or negation (denial of judgment's capacity to judge, of memory's ability to remember, of the mind's power to know, that is, of each faculty to fulfill itself), the very act, however, originates affirmation. When judgment condemns its own lack of judgment, it judges correctly and thus certifies its integrity just as memory redeems itself by the recall of its own forgetfulness. When Montaigne admits that he does not know, he affirms that he knows something. The reduction to nullity is at the same time reconstruction; the self never entirely disappears, for it restores itself at the moment of negation, through the very process of denial. Montaigne apparently allows himself the possibility of being the good student whose vigorous memory provides that recall and review of the past which lead to reformation (p. 1073). But more centrally, he reiterates the weakness of memory and makes negativity and absence themselves its subject. Montaigne thus endows himself with a past (of forgetfulness), one which directly informs the present and his experience of it, that is, his ignorance.

III

In terms of memory, then, Montaigne would appear to have it both ways: he benefits on multiple levels from his lack of memory (or its weakness), as we have seen, and he leaves ample room for profit from recollection as well. The most developed presentation of recall occurs in De l'exercitation (II, 6), where the essayist recounts his near brush with death and draws conclusions intended for his instruction. The purpose of practice, Montaigne states at the outset, is to exceed the limits of reasoning and education and to form the soul by experience to the way we want it to go. Instead of abstract and impersonal study based, one suspects, on the lessons of books commented on and memorized by the student, the essayist poses direct engagement with and experience of the subject in question, suggesting through a range of military metaphors the manner of the soldier who both tests himself out (essayer and experimenter) and trains himself (exercer) in action.

On the face of things, Montaigne recounts a simple episode, however dramatic or disturbing, which he claims has reconciled him somewhat to his eventual passing. Out one day on horseback with his men, he is ridden down accidentally, knocked unconscious from his horse and taken for dead. From the slow process of returning fully to his senses, as he apparently languishes at the edge of life, he gains an awareness of the sensation of dying and so, in a way, exercises himself in it. Both narrator and narration complicate our understanding considerably by raising fundamental questions of the essayist's relationship to his own experience. While Montaigne lived through the event in its actuality, both he and we are here engaged with a text, with experience which can be said to originate through recollection, or, to draw a richly ambiguous term from the text, through *recordation*, suggesting in this context both recalling and recording.

Montaigne situates himself both inside and outside of his account, as victim unconscious, as self-conscious victim, as observer-narrator: "un de mes gens . . . vint à . . . pousser [le cheval] à toute bride droict dans ma route, et fondre comme un colosse sur le petit homme et petit cheval, et le foudroier . . . nous envoyant l'un et l'autre les pieds contremont" (p. 373). The narrator distances himself by a third-person perspective, referring to "le petit homme et petit cheval" as if another. At the same time, his use of "colosse" to magnify the size of the horseman and the repetition of "petit" to diminish that of the victim express from within ("us" and "me") the point of view of the man about to be run down. To the recollection of the participant the narrator apparently adds a dimension from without by telling the story, but is the simple opposition of inside-outside a valid one? Montaigne's sentence draws the narrator into the first-person account, juxtaposes the two perspectives, and so implies the inescapable compass of narration. Beyond the inarticulated immediacy of sensation, the attempt to account must narrate, that is, recount: to relate is always *re-latus*, carried back, out of memory, recalled both in and through language, which gives it shape and meaning. Poulet depicts Montaigne's judgment acting in the moment of actuality, "in the very moment in which consciousness operates, and in operating, possesses."[10] But to the extent that Montaigne engages his experience in an act of judgment articulated as his text, one is obliged to say that judgment in the essays occurs in a moment of *deferred* actuality, which is the writing of the book. To speak of judging as if uncoupled from writing reduces the text to a mere record of what is supposedly accomplished elsewhere. The route Montaigne chooses to follow involves him irresistibly with recounting and recollecting: knowledge and narration, as the etymology implies (*narrare*, from *gnarus*, to know), cannot be separated.

Montaigne does not purposefully undermine memory in *De l'exercitation*. In fact, the more vigorously and resolutely it operates, the closer he apparently comes to recapturing his experience as a meaningful exercise. Yet memory here does reflect in its gaps and imprecision the larger sense of its unreliability, its propensity for reporting falsely or for not responding to the demand for recall. At the level of narration, there are bound to be pieces missing from the first-person account because the rider is unconscious part of the time and semi-conscious for much of the rest. Montaigne must fill in the lacunae either by inferring from what he claims to remember or by relying on the testimony of other witnesses. His description of events immediately after the accident derives implicitly from what he has been told: "Ceux qui estoient avec moy, apres avoir essayé par tous les moyens qu'ils peurent, de me faire revenir, me tenans pour mort, me prindrent entre leurs bras . . ." (p. 373). When Montaigne moves and gestures in a state of unconsciousness, he can learn of this movement only from others after the fact: "car, premierement, estant tout esvanouy, je me travaillois d'entr'ouvrir mon pourpoinct à belles ongles . . ." (p. 375). And there are parts of the story which he explicitly attributes to members of his family present: "non seulement je respondois quelque mot à ce qu'on me demandoit, mais encore ils disent que je m'advisay de commander qu'on donnast un cheval à ma femme . . ." (p. 376). The fact is, he adds, that he was not there at all ("Je n'y estois aucunement"). The event cannot be recorded when the soul is not conscious of itself (pp. 374-75), when consciousness itself is not (physically or spatially) there (y).

Without reducing this extended presentation to a simple-minded allegory, we can draw inferences about memory's function. Although this essay represents a particularly striking instance, every act of remembrance is an act of reconstruction, for every experience records as fragments to be pieced together through recollection (*re-com-legere*, "to gather together again," what are obviously units or fragments into a larger whole). Montaigne understands profoundly that life is not engraved on the soul like a lesson learned by heart and reproduced on demand. There are always already gaps to be filled in, connections to be made, so that experience gains the shape and sequence that endow it with meaning. In the hiatus between observer and observed (Montaigne observing himself or/as another), between the imprint of immediate sensation or thought and its recollection, recounting inserts itself as the narrative act, as *recordation*.

Recollecting emerges clearly as reconstruction from Montaigne's observations at the end of his account. With a touch of irony, he adds that he does not want to forget this: "que la derniere chose en quoy je me peus remettre, ce fut la souvenance de cet accident; et me fis redire plusieurs fois où j'aloy, d'où je venoy, à quelle heure cela m'estoit advenu, avant que de le pouvoir concevoir" (p. 377). How does he recover the memory of the accident? In part, he implies, the passage of time allows the shock—both physical and emotional—to wear off, as if the mind settles down, regains its composure so that memory can issue forth to consciousness the images imprinted upon it: "Mais long temps apres, et le lendemain," he says, "quand ma memoire vint à s'entr'ouvrir et me representer l'estat où je m'estoy trouvé . . ." (p. 377). But, more significantly, the recollections of others are appropriated as his own. Montaigne needs help in situating the accident. The context must be re-created, reconstituted—mediated—before he can see himself in it; it must be narrated before he can identify himself and identify with himself. This "taking in" (concevoir) is also conception as birth, creation, of the image of self in Montaigne's mind.

After the mediation of the witnesses (does a fundamental distinction exist between this and the mediation of one's "original" memories?) and the re-inscribing of himself into the context, Montaigne comes, significantly, a second time to take up his description of the moment of impact. In the first instance, he had needed a third-person narration, a view from outside the event, in order to frame the view from inside, the first-person dimension. At that early point in his development of the essay, Montaigne's use of the dual perspective implies that the rider does not have that possession or comprehension of the episode which would allow him to tell it by himself. The physical and emotional shock of the incident dominates its initial unfolding; the first person's limitations coincide with his stunned mind and memory. The second account occurs after the process of reconstitution which gives rise to logical and meaningful sequence. The two points of view collapse in a single account of the recollections of the first person. Where earlier the narrator introduced the image of the thunderbolt to depict the colossus coming down on the little man and little horse, on "them" ("fondre comme un colosse sur le petit homme et petit cheval, et le foudroier"), the later version draws on the same vocabulary, but makes it entirely a function of the inside: "en l'instant que j'avoy aperçeu ce cheval fondant sur moy . . . il me sembla que c'estoit un esclair qui me frapoit l'ame de secousse . . ." (p. 377). What had been a rhetorical device of narration, introduced both for its expressive impact on the reader and as an element of a certain high style, functions in the second instance as the very language in which (remembered) experience is cast, indeed as the only language in which it can be cast. Metaphor exceeds its merely rhetorical function to express resemblance and analogy itself in recollection.

The death which Montaigne seeks to engage cannot be met directly, as his quote from Lucretius affirms: no one (nemo) awakens once he has felt the icy end of death (p. 371). He resolves the impass in part by shifting the focus from death itself to its approaches, but most significantly by affirming the validity and usefulness of resemblance and by proceeding by correspondence. Casting the functioning of his memory as his text, originating its operation in and as the written word, Montaigne draws on the resources of language—most centrally on those which derive from similitude and which both generate and confirm it: analogy and metaphor—to confront the paradox of experiencing what cannot be experienced. In the con-text of *De l'exercitation*, the essayist (the tester as writer) can then die without dying, become that *nemo* which elsewhere is accessible to no one. And in the process the language of (literary) representation reveals itself as the re-presenting language of recollection.

The critical analogy of the essay affirms the correspondence between sleep and death: "Ce n'est pas sans raison qu'on nous fait regarder à nostre sommeil mesme, pour la ressemblance qu'il a de la mort" (p. 372). Even though Montaigne shifts to focus on the effects of his violent accident, sleep itself provides the analogical language, so that fainting is like sleep is like death. When he illustrates the return of his senses, he does so with a quote from Tasso depicting the state of one who is half awake: "come quel ch'or apre or chiude / gli occhi, mezzo tra 'l sonno è l'esser desto" (p. 374). As he imagines himself dying, he recalls a sensation not only free from distress, but "meslée à cette douceur que sentent ceux qui se laissent glisser au sommeil" (p. 374). Those lying comatose near death are not conscious, Montaigne believes, in spite of any utterances or movement they may make: "j'ay tousjours pensé . . . qu'ils avoient et l'ame et le corps enseveli et endormy" (p. 374). The incoherent words of the dying do not testify to life: "Il nous advient ainsi sur le beguayement du sommeil, avant qu'il nous ait du tout saisis, de sentir comme en songe ce qui se faict autour de nous . . ." (p. 375). Montaigne associates sleep with night and darkness and most dramatically with the loss of consciousness, "de la lumiere," he says, "et de nous." Using a vocabulary which implies the movement of consciousness as if in space away from the body, he juxtaposes the fading or disappearance of consciousness in his swoon (*esvanouissement*, from *evanescere*) with the passage of death (*trépas*), the flight of the soul.

Montaigne represents a metaphorical death and return to life, but the rhetorical cast of his prose seeks to transcend mere analogy. I refer again to the first description of the moment of impact: "voilà le cheval abbatu et couché . . . moy dix ou douze pas au delà, mort, estendu à la renverse . . ." (p. 373). He is dead to those who witnessed the accident (twice he repeats that they thought him dead), but can he be dead to himself except upon return and in retrospect, when through recollection and writing he, too, becomes witness? Montaigne elaborates on this death by comparing himself to an inert, unfeeling stump or log as he remains without movement or breath (?) for over two hours ("n'ayant ny movement ny sentiment, non plus qu'une souche"). Even his gestures and words could not be taken as signs of life: these do not bear sufficient witness (*tesmoignage*) that one is alive. When he begins to regain his senses, the essayist portrays himself as coming back to life ("reprendre un peu de vie"), although he maintains that his vision was still dead (*morte*). Montaigne implies that he has returned from death to life ("quand je vins à revivre") and experiences so much pain that he believes he will die a second time: "j'en cuiday remourir encore un coup . . ." (p. 377).

If Montaigne cannot engage death as immediate experience, he can claim to engage it as mediated experience, analogically, through recollection articulated as a literary text. What makes death like sleep is the creation of analogy, the act of juxtaposition which lends the qualities of each to the other. Resemblance is a product of the mind, an affirmation of likeness over difference expressed as reasoning or argument, established by such rhetorical devices as comparison (*comparatio*), metaphor, simile, by juxtaposition itself: "Toutes choses se tiennent par quelque similitude, tout exemple cloche, et la relation qui se tire de l'experience est toujours defaillante et imparfaicte; on joinct toutesfois les comparaisons par quelque coin" (III, 13, 1070). Montaigne does not invent the comparison of sleep and death; it may be as old as language and writing. But he engages in (rhetorical) invention, choosing and elaborating his argument so that in a real sense we can say that his text originates the analogy as it employs it. His language, as we have seen, draws death and sleep together; it even attempts to transcend its own limitations to posit the impossible, so that the first-person subject can die and come back to life to write of his experience. Montaigne's most profound experience of death, and the lesson from which he draws his most significant instruction, derives from the functioning as a text of judgment upon memory.

However unique death may appear (since it can be known only obliquely), the experience of *De l'exercitation* bears a fundamental relationship to all other subjects of the essays: to friendship, glory, coaches, books, etc. Montaigne's writing mediates his every experience, including that of writing itself. If experience is by definition the actual observation of facts or events, or the fact of being consciously the subject of a state or condition, or of being consciously affected by an event, it is also by its etymology the action of putting to the test, the essay as trial and written text. Montaigne becomes most consciously the subject and is most consciously affected when judgment operates in the deferred actuality of his essays. Within this vast rhetorical complex, both through and by it, the essayist defines and delineates his experience by affirming resemblance or establishing difference, by drawing examples and posing paradoxes, by situating himself as persona and narrator (as he who accounts). The book is most profoundly the locus of *connaissance*, the place where Montaigne gains both consciousness and knowledge of self.

Paradoxically, death becomes an emblematic experience. Montaigne comes near to it, grasps it through judgment and makes it his own by writing about it, by making it a written experience. He recalls and recounts, draws upon memory and creates it as his text. But if the text becomes his (paper) memory, his memory has always been a text. Montaigne uses a vocabulary of representation which exceeds mere re-presentation to describe memory and its function.[11] Printed on its surface (*empreint*) as on a page or canvas, the face and image of death (*visage, idée*) are represented (*representer*) to the mind's eye to be judged, interpreted, understood. But the face of death is a metaphor; like literature itself, memory represents through figures (of speech); and, like those other faces in *De la phisionomie* (those of war, of experience), the signs which comprise it must also be "read." In the narrator's language, as we have seen, the moment of impact translates as a metaphor—the thunderbolt; and memory as well articulates itself in the same idiom as the flash of lightening which strikes Montaigne's soul. The signs of recollection present the same difficulties to the reader as those of the written text. Problems of interpretation and comprehension caused by halting remembrance, unreliable recall, gaps in logic and sequence reflect those experienced by the reader in the face of language which obfuscates meaning, gives rise to ambiguity, cloaks truth, defies logical penetration.

We picture Montaigne situated within a circle of textuality, drawing experience from the text of memory, engaging it as the experience of judgment in the text of its exercise, the essays. Within this space which serves as the arena of his instruction, Montaigne claims knowledge of death's "vray et naturel visage" (II, 6, 372, 373). By itself the event is trivial, the essayist admits; its significance lies in its account: "ce n'est pas ici ma doctrine, c'est mon estude" (p. 377). More important even than what he learns of death is the lesson of the process itself. As he draws from this exercise the imperative to study himself (*s'espier*), Montaigne commits himself to the very self-reflexive separation of observer and observed, subject and object, which underlies narration itself. At the same time, he weds himself to language as the idiom of self-expression: "Je peins principalement mes cogitations, subject informe, qui ne peut tomber en production ouvragere. A toute peine le puis je coucher en ce corps aërée de la voix" (p. 379). The consequences of these choices are paradoxical indeed, for, if narration allows Montaigne to recognize death's true face, it is also true that faces in this context remain figures. And if narration implies knowledge, it also implies mediation and distance, a gap filled by what he calls the "corps aërée de la voix." This tension lies at the very heart of the essays, as we have seen, and it characterizes as well the paradoxical text of memory, which speaks the same language.

NOTES

1. Quotations are from *Les Essais de Michel de Montaigne*, ed. Pierre Villey (Paris: Presses Universitaires de France, 1924; rpt. 1965).

2. Richard Sayce, *The Essays of Montaigne* (London: Weidenfeld and Nicolson, 1972), pp. 100-01, 179-80.

3. Hugo Friedrich, *Montaigne*, trans. Robert Rovini (Paris: Gallimard, 1968), p. 351.

4. Richard L. Regosin, *The Matter of My Book: Montaigne's Essais as the Book of the Self* (Berkeley: Univ. of California Press, 1977), pp. 67-227.

5. Georges Poulet, *Studies in Human Time*, trans. Elliott Coleman (New York: Harper Torchbooks, 1979), pp. 39-40.

6. Sayce, p. 180. See also Françoise Joukovsky-Micha, *Montaigne et le problème du temps* (Paris: Nizet, 1972), pp. 175-76.

7. Poulet makes this a pivotal activity by which Montaigne obtains communication with being and overcomes the fragmented experience of temporality.

8. English translations of the Latin are from Donald Frame, trans., *The Complete Essays of Montaigne* (Stanford: Stanford Univ. Press, 1958), p. 494.

9. In spite of Montaigne's careful avoidance of affirmation through his use of the interrogative "Que sais-je" as his motto, there are in the essays innumerable declarative statements such as this one of his ignorance.

10. Poulet, p. 47.

11. To a certain extent, the art of memory could always be conceived as an art of representation, an art which functioned through the use of images, analogies, similitudes of various kinds meant to stand for or signify the things to be remembered and, upon recall, produced to be "read" by the mind's eye. See Frances Yates, *The Art of Memory* (Chicago: Univ. of Chicago Press, 1966); however, Yates does not take up the status of memory as a text.

James M. Cox

Richard Henry Dana's *Two Years Before the Mast*: Autobiography Completing Life

Whoever looks at the bibliographies of articles and essays written since 1950 on American literature will find it difficult to believe that *Two Years Before the Mast* could ever have been chosen by D.H. Lawrence to appear in his extremely select list of *classic* American literary works. Of the thousands and thousands of items on American writers and writings, only four or five are devoted to Dana—and here it is well to note that there are significantly *fewer* articles devoted to him after 1950 than before. To be sure, there is Robert Weinstein's extremely helpful 1964 edition published by the Ward Ritchie Press; there is Robert Lucid's excellent edition of Dana's journals (1968); there are two books—Samuel Shapiro's *Richard Henry Dana, Jr.* (1961) and Robert Gale's *Richard Henry Dana* (1969); and there is William Spengemann's intelligent emphasis on the book in his *The Adventurous Muse* (1977). Yet, aside from Spengemann, there is a perfunctoriness about the attention—a perfunctoriness that in itself tells us that the book is slipping from academic consciousness. Whatever struck Lawrence about it in his arresting chapter—and his treatment of Dana, like his treatment of every writer in his remarkable book, is arresting—no longer strikes anthologists. The leading American literature anthologies now run towards 5,000 pages, but not a page is Dana's.

It would be possible to attribute Dana's slippage to the academic institutionalization of the New Criticism, which has in turn caused the decline of non-fiction prose (as it is now called) in the face of ever-increased emphasis on poetry, drama and fiction. Yet the rise of women's studies, black studies and native American studies has been attended by renewed interest in discursive prose. Even more important, the social and theoretical interest in autobiography in the last ten years has brought that form very much into the foreground. And *Two Years Before the Mast*, as I shall try to show, is in a profound way an autobiography. Yet in this very period the book has, if anything, lost ground.

So we have to find better reasons, a primary one of which is that, for all of Dana's attempt to be before the mast, he has come to be associated with the genteel tradition. He was, after all, a Harvard man at the very time he made the trip, a Harvard law student at the time he wrote the book, and a Boston lawyer at the threshold of a Brahmin career at the time the book was published. Though his defense of fugitive slaves in the early cases around 1850 made him feel estranged from proper Boston society, it came to constitute a new basis for respectability as New England, finding itself more and more against the South, provided much of the moral spearhead in the war for the Union. It was precisely that respectability that came under attack in the 20th century. Thus, Lowell and Whittier came to be classed with Holmes and Longfellow as the Schoolroom Poets. Insofar as they were poets, they could and can still be anthologized as representatives of "literary" New England's effort to equal at best or to imitate the culture of old England. But, insofar as they were prose writers, who reads them? Lowell's only claim to attention is that he wrote a negative essay on Thoreau. And where is the American literature class exposed to *The Autocrat at the Breakfast Table*? Now, put Richard Henry Dana, with his one book, and that a long one, into such a context, and his disappearance into obscurity becomes much clearer.

But there is a second and much more important reason for Dana's decline: the rediscovery of Herman Melville. It is a matter of no small importance that Melville had been fully discovered in 1922 when Lawrence wrote *Studies in Classic American Literature*. Indeed, I think the rediscovered presence and immediacy of Melville—Lawrence devoted two chapters of his book to Melville's work—are very much culturally related to Lawrence's whole enterprise. For there is a Melvillian quality in Lawrence's style—an insistent Ahabic intensity coupled with a bluff Ishmalean exuberance. The subsequent rise and all but enthronement of Melville in American literature seems to me exactly paralleled by Dana's slide into obscurity. The tolling of Dana's bell might have been unknowingly struck by Bliss Perry's essay "Dana's Magical Chance" in *The Praise of Folly* (1923). Perry wrote much in praise of Dana and in the confident manner of the late genteel tradition (members of which were for the most part by that time quartered in the academy); he was himself literary and judicious, realizing that Dana's book was somehow his essential life in that it liberated him from the proper Bostonianism of his time—Perry was precisely genteel enough to be critical of the old-fashioned proper Bostonians—and provided the magical moment which would convert Dana's literary romanticism into the romance of the real. Yet Perry did no more than intelligently approve the book, just as he intelligently approved some of Dana's later writing. When all is said and done, Perry views Dana as part of the fabric of the post-Civil War New England civilization that forgot Herman Melville and led more or less in a straight line to . . . Bliss Perry.

Be all that as it may, the rise of Melville has without question cast Dana into shadow. Thus, the most likely way a graduate student today encounters Dana is through Melville's letter to him praising *Two Years Before the Mast*. Dana's readers will remember his remarks on meeting the whaleship *Wilmington & Liverpool Packet* of New Bedford: "A spouter we knew her to be, as soon as we saw her, by her cranes and boats, and by her stump topgallant masts, and a certain slovenly look to the sails, rigging, spars, and hull; and when we got on board, we found everything to correspond, spouter fashion." When we think of *Moby Dick* and the grandeur Melville brought to whaling, it is, of course, difficult not to direct a condescending literary judgment upon Dana's critical scrutiny of the dirty whaler which he views with scarcely less aversion than the greasy Russian brig he encounters in San Francisco harbor. And when we think of the long, lonely, forlorn and yet incredibly lofty struggle of Melville's creative life, then Dana's retreat from his one book into a Boston law office seems downright pathetic.

But Dana's life is not his work—or perhaps it would be better to say that his work, *this* work, is his intenser life. And it is much too easy to use Melville to devalue Dana. Anyone who knows Dana's book knows that it is a match for anything Melville wrote before *Moby Dick*. Melville himself knew that best of all and never tired of praising Dana's work. Nor is there in his praise the slightest note of condescension. It was in a letter to Dana, after all, that Melville first mentioned his writing of *Moby Dick*. And so a sustained look at Dana's book seems to me an effort well worth taking. Such a look is perforce introductory in nature, but I shall try to provide a measure of analysis along the way.

Everyone knows or should know the dimensions of the book—this account of a nineteen-year-old Harvard student going to sea in a two-year voyage around Cape Horn to California. The title of the book makes clear both the novelty and achievement of the journey, for it was life before the mast and not aft that Dana lived and wrote about. His motive in taking ship had been to give his strained eyes a rest—and so there was, or is, a particular resonance in that common phrase, going to sea, as if the element into which Dana went were sounding the very sense he sought to strengthen.

Returned from his trip with healed vision, Dana graduated from Harvard in 1837, attended law school and emerged with his narrative at the same time as he was ready to set up as a lawyer. His announced aim in his narrative was to bring to the world the experience of the common sailor; his unannounced purpose was to gain public identity in such a way as to strengthen his possibilities as a maritime lawyer. Thus, his original concluding chapter was devoted to the possible reforms that might be considered regarding the relation between ship captains and crew—or, we might say, between masters and men.

Even to make such an equation is to gain a much fuller perspective on the book in its own time. For *Two Years Before the Mast* is devoted to two paramount subjects: the relations between captain and crew aboard an American merchant ship and the possibilities of life in California in the mid 1830s. Published in 1840, the book was in its way a profound expression of the culture. First of all, it was adventurous—written by a young man, an Easterner, who was finding his manhood in going west. Second, it was informative, giving a detailed and intelligent account of the customs and culture of California—that Catholic, Spanish-Mexican space towards which the Protestant-ethic United States was expanding more rapidly than it could quite know. Dana saw the economic, if not the manifest, destiny of that expansion in the very facts of voyaging around Cape Horn for California hides and returning to Boston to manufacture shoes which in turn would be shipped back around the Horn to California to be sold to Mexicans and Spaniards. In fact, Dana, remarking on how little holiday the Yankee captains gave their crew in relation to that granted by Italian ships, could compute the number of extra work days Americans got from their workers per year. He saw even further that, but for religious observances on Sunday, the crew would have no leisure at all if matters were left to shipping companies and their captains. At the same time, he saw the readiness with which secular Americans were beginning to settle in a Catholic country, and he recorded the beautiful phrase they had for the removal: to leave one's conscience at Cape Horn. The very resonance of the phrase, coupled with the polar plunge and resurrection that stood behind it, presaged the world to come. If settlers could brave Cape Horn on hermaphrodite brigs, how much more readily they would move once a true overland trail were secured that would cut the distance from 18,000 to 3,000 miles.

But there was more than the adventurous outreach so expressive of American expansion and eventual war with Mexico that lay ahead in the decade after the book was published. There was also the matter of the Captain's absolute authority aboard ship—authority that could either express or indulge itself by means of corporal punishment, which is to say flogging.

The dramatic high point in Dana's narrative comes when, shortly after arriving in California, two members of the crew are flogged by Captain Francis Thompson. The first man flogged was Samuel Sparks, hesitant of speech and hailing from the Middle States (actually Westmoreland County, Virginia). Somehow exasperated by Sam's behavior, Thompson increasingly badgers him until a response is drawn:

> "I'm no Negro slave," said Sam.
> "Then I'll make you one," said the Captain; and he came to the hatchway, and sprang on deck, threw off his coat and rolled up his sleeves, called out to the mate, "Seize that man up, Mr. Amerzene! Seize him up! I'll teach you all who is master aboard."

Seeing the full fury of the Captain, a second sailor, John the Swede (whom Dana calls the best sailor on board) objects and is seized up, too:

> When he was made fast, he turned to the captain, who stood rolling up his sleeves and getting ready for the blow, and asked him what he was to be flogged for. "Have I ever refused my duty, sir? Have you ever known me to hang back, or to be insolent, or not to know my work?"
> "No," said the captain, "it is not that that I flog you for; I flog you for your interference, for asking questions."
> "Can't a man ask a question here without being flogged?"
> "No," shouted the captain. "Nobody shall open his mouth aboard this vessel but myself," and began laying the blows upon his back . . . .
> The man writhed under the pain until he could endure it no longer, when he called out, with an exclamation more common among foreigners than with us: "O Jesus Christ! O Jesus Christ!"
> "Don't call on Jesus Christ," shouted the captain. *"He can't help you. Call on Frank Thompson!* He's the man! He can help you! Jesus Christ can't help you now!"
> At these words, which I never shall forget, my blood ran cold. I could look on no longer. Disgusted, sick, I turned away, and leaned over the rail, and looked down into the water. A few rapid thoughts, I don't know what—our situation, a resolution to see the captain punished when we got home—crossed my mind; but the falling of the blows and the cries of the man called me back once more. . . . Everyone else stood still at his post, while the captain, swelling with rage, and with the importance of his achievement, walked the quarterdeck, and at each turn, as he came forward, calling out to us: "You see your condition! . . . You've got a driver over you! Yes, a slave driver—a nigger driver! I'll see who'll tell me he isn't a nigger slave!"

I quote the passage at such length because it vividly dramatizes as well as summarizes the issue of tyranny in the book—and summarizes it upon lines of slavery at the very moment the anti-slavery movement was becoming the country's major concern. Moreover, in the very act of becoming the flogging master, Thompson also becomes a blasphemer, as if he were fitting himself for the very role of plantation tyrant that anti-slavery pamphleteers and slave narratives were going to depict. It is not an immeasurable step from this factual Frank Thompson to the fictional Simon Legree twelve years later.

Yet if these aspects of the book—the youthful adventurousness, the western "matter" and the issue of absolute tyranny—give a hint of the book's expression of and relation to the cultural and political issues of 19th-century America, they are but the beginning of the book's power. There are other aspects of the book which are equally important in measuring Dana's strength and depth. But the flogging scene remains the dramatic high point of the narrative—and remains so, I contend, because it *precedes* in Dana's own mind the anti-slavery cause he himself was later to become involved in. The scene's great power, in other words, derives not from the subsequent stereotype, but from the profound priority it had in Dana's mind and narrative. It is just here that D.H. Lawrence is very helpful—because he goes against the grain of so much that has been and still may be written about the book. For Lawrence, it is not the flogging, but the idealism of both Dana and John the Swede that is offensive. The idealism mucks up what would have been a simple and swift punishment, and so John's interference results in making Sam ashamed when he should have been simply hurt. Forced to see the sacrifice his shipmate has made, Sam finds his pain becoming misery, and the couple comes to humiliation and confusion, rather than to the clarity of a master-man relationship. But let Lawrence speak in his inimitable way:

As a matter of fact, it was John who ought to have been ashamed for bringing confusion and false feeling into a clear issue. . . . The case was one of passional readjustment, nothing abnormal. And who was the sententious Johannus, that he should interfere in this? And if Mr. Dana had a weak stomach as well as weak eyes, let him have it. But let this pair of idealists abstain from making all the other men feel uncomfortable and fuzzy about a thing they would have left to its natural course, if they had been allowed. No, your Johannuses and your Danas have to be creating "public opinion," and mugging up the life-issues with their sententiousness. O, idealism!

The great strength of Lawrence's vision is that it arrests us at the verge of our usual academic mistake of subjecting ourselves to the anti-slavery conscience. For Dana, that ideal is primarily rooted in experience; for us, it is primarily imposed by history. Surely there are few readers who can agree with Lawrence, *really* agree with him on this matter; yet surely also there are few who, however intensely they might disagree with him, would refuse to acknowledge that *Studies in Classic American Literature* is one of the greatest books—perhaps the greatest—ever written on the subject. It is great enough to deserve a real criticism. And if we have provided a beginning to placing Dana in his time, it is well to remember that Lawrence's book, appearing in 1922, opened with the unforgettable attack on (and appreciation of) Benjamin Franklin. That attack concluded with these lines:

> Now is your chance, Europe. Now let Hell loose and get your own back, and paddle your own canoe on a new sea, while clever America lies on her muck-heaps of gold, strangled in her own barbed-wire of shalt-not ideals and shalt-not moralisms. While she goes out to work like millions of squirrels in millions of cages. Production!
> Let Hell loose, and get your own back, Europe!

To feel the genuine force of Lawrence's assault is to know that Hitler at that moment was waiting in the wings of history. Is it too much to imagine him, upon hearing Lawrence's apostrophic plea, saying, "Would you repeat that just one time so I can be sure I heard you right?" Do not mistake me. I do not indulge such fancy in order to smear Lawrence with an association to Nazism, but to suggest both the burden and consequences of his vision. For if we cite the implications of that sentence, we also have to remember that Lawrence also said, in reference to Cooper's Natty Bumppo, "The essential American soul is hard, isolate, stoic, and a killer," at just the moment Hemingway was waiting in the wings of American literature.

To see just how good Lawrence is on Dana, one merely has to see how the very people who would most deeply disagree with his praise of flogging nonetheless wind up complaining of Dana's idealism on other counts. There is a long tradition of lamentation about Dana's bowdlerizing primness. There are hints that, for all his polite presentation of himself in the book, Dana actually drank, swore and even womanized in his western sojourn. And much can be made of Dana's Americanized Victorian disposition (which he exercised in later life) to go to cities, frequent red-light districts and find himself engaging prostitutes in conversation, most likely to urge them to go and reform. Whereas Lawrence upbraids Dana for vomiting over the side rather than look at the flogging, these high-minded opponents of Lawrence's blood vision lecture Dana on being squeamish about sex and the true hurly-burly of maritime life. It is just here that Lawrence shines. He never complains, because he realizes that Dana's idealism gives him what we might call the mysticism of the factual. It is no fuzzy or foggy mysticism, but a special kind of clarity. Lawrence puts it in this way: "It is in the dispassionate statement of plain material facts that Dana achieves his greatness. Dana writes from the remoter, non-emotional centers of being—not from the passional emotional self." And at another point, after quoting Dana's description of a thunderstorm at sea, Lawrence observes, "Dana is wonderful at relating these mechanical, or dynamic-physical events. He could not tell about the being of men, only about the forces."

Because Lawrence has the daring to affirm master over man against Dana's idealism, he sees the strength of that idealism itself, sees how it is determined to master facts and culture and hides and trade and even the elemental ocean itself. Put another way, Dana's decision to avoid or censor sexual matters is precisely what liberates him to write the narrative he does. That sense of self strong in moral idealism keeps him distant from the crew, enables him to take pleasure in reading Sir Walter Scott's *Woodstock* to them, lets him see with assured detachment that they respect his education, and frees him to see, describe and confront the forces of sea and sky and land. No wonder that Henry Adams memorably sketched Dana in *The Education*:

Dana . . . affected to be still before the mast, a direct, rather bluff, vigorous seaman, and only as one got to know him better one found the man of rather excessive refinement trying with success to work like a day-laborer, deliberately hardening his skin to the burden, as though he were still carrying hides at Monterey. . . . Dana's ideal of life was to be a great Englishman, with a seat on the front benches of the House of Commons until he should be promoted to the woolsack; beyond all, with a social status that should place him above the scuffle of provincial and unprofessional annoyances, but he forced himself to take life as it came, and he suffered his longings with grim self-discipline, by mere force of will.

Adams' characterization catches the contradiction that has come to work against Dana in the minds of the very people who, inheritors and even progenitors of gentility—as the whole academic establishment perforce must be—come down hardest on him. I am not thinking merely of scholars, but of students. They seem to resent Dana's ultimate retreat from the sea; they resent his literariness, his refinement, his decorum and his return to genteel Boston society. Part of that resentment is, of course, the luxury which 140 years of historical perspective affords. The strong vernacular tradition was only beginning in American literature at the time Dana wrote, and even then only in the comic mode of Jack Downing and the early Southwest humorists. But the deeper clue to the resentment lies in the students' recognition that Dana's betrayal of his experience is their own future betrayal writ large—writ large because at least Dana left behind him on the trail of retreat a written testimony of his resistant experience. This whole response is related to the emotional alienation on which American middle-class society thrives. Give a person a leg up the cultural ladder of social mobility, and he either apes high culture or consciously plunges into the muck, as if the very law of the middle-class mind lay in displacing the present space with an acquisitive grasp of future possibility (there is the idealist aspiration) or a nostalgia for the "experience" from which the aspiration has averted itself.

There is no need to complain about this state of affairs, other than to know that the complaint is but one more example of middle-class displacement. The point is that, whatever his refinement censors, Dana is aware of the true middle-class drama of his life. He does not repress that drama in order to show off his experience. There is no point in upbraiding him for returning to Harvard and Boston society any more than there is a point in scolding him for not revealing the "true" chaos and vulgarity of life at sea. Dana knows that all these identities lie like reefs and icebergs and squalls on every hand, just as he knows in the profoundest way that his very language of seeing and charting his course is that of a straightforward description that betrays his refined identity even as it adheres sufficiently to objects to require both fidelity and lucidity of exposition. It is not that Dana is committed to experience or facts, but that he is apart from them, that gives him his very particular objectivity. The facts—whether they be the sails of the ship, the men on board, the storms at sea, the coast of California or the hide-curing process—are narratively thrown forward to displace the true chaos Dana felt at the heart of the romantic adventure that had drawn him out of Boston society. This narrative displacement, converting the submissive fear that had caused Dana to withdraw from the experience, becomes the very authority that seals his identity as a writer. For Dana the writer, the facts are themselves the forces. Thus, men and ships and coasts and hides are facts sufficiently stripped of moral idealism or informational inertia to seem accelerating into naked action.

At the heart of this action is the writer Dana, not in any way functioning as rememberer or celebrant or confessor (though the book is an act of memory, a tribute to the experience and a harbinger of loss and guilt), but as a recorder—and himself almost a record, as if he were marooned between his text and context. No wonder Dana later called the experience a parenthesis in his life, as if he recognized that his life was a sentence in the sad full meaning of the term and his book was somehow at once interpolated into, yet exempt from, it. The action of the book, therefore, does not happen to Dana so much as it happens. He is part of the happening in the sense that the narrative recounts his presence in the field of forces and, in the sequence of events, lets the presence take shape as part of the ship.

To see the force of the book and how it takes shape to reveal Dana, it is necessary to go back to the relation between him and Captain Thompson, for Thompson, of all the figures in the book, is the one most recurrently present. He is the down-east johnny cake who makes thing happen—the master of the ship and perforce the figure of authority who assumes in the flogging scene the character of tyranny. The fact that Thompson has died between the time of Dana's experience and the time of the writing frees Dana to expose his tyranny. Dana's narrative discloses, almost immediately after the flogging scene, Thompson losing control of his ship just as, in the flogging, he had lost control of himself. Thus, in San Diego the *Pilgrim* gets out of control and drifts into the *Lagoda*. Once freed, it drifts down upon

the *Ayacucho*, whose captain has to come and assist Thompson in maneu-
vering his vessel. Later, when Thompson is announced on board the *Lagoda*,
her salty old skipper inquires whether he has brought his brig with him, a
remark which elicits enormous amusement from Dana's tyrannized shipmates.

Yet, clearly, as Dana's sequence exposes Thompson, his account of
the action always takes precedence over the psychology of the characters.
Indeed, the men in this book, even Thompson himself, cannot become
characters; the action of the book *includes* them; they belong to it as units
of force and presence. Of those units of force, Thompson is, of course, the
one who most threatens to become a dramatic character, only to have the
full encounter with California force him into the background. To be sure,
he does not disappear. He shows his hard-bitten lack of sympathy by refusing to give medicines from the ship's stores to Dana's sick Kanaka friend,
Hope—and Dana at this point rather piously remarks almost outside the
narration: "This man died afterward of a fever on the deadly coast of
Sumatra; and God grant he had better care taken of him in his sufferings
than he ever gave to anyone else."

Yet the Captain is never again released into the dramatic identity of the
flogging scene; rather, he remains as resistant fact and force. Thus, when
the ship *Alert* is about to return home with Dana on board and Thompson
commanding, Thompson calls Dana aft and requires him to get one of his
shipmates to take his place on the *Pilgrim* in exchange for his chance to
go home. Dana here reveals to Thompson that he has connections back in
Boston and that he also has information that Thompson has orders to bring
him home and so stands his ground: "But it would have all availed nothing
had I been 'some poor body' before this absolute, domineering tribunal.
But they saw I would not go, unless 'vi et armis,' and they knew that I had
friends and interest enough at home to make them suffer for any injustice
they might do me."

At first a sailor, English Ben, is brought forward in great dejection to
take Dana's place:

Ben was a poor English boy, a stranger in Boston, without friends or money; and
being an active and willing lad and a good sailor for his years, was a general favorite.
"Oh Yes!" said the crew. "The Captain has let you off because you are a gentleman's
son, and taken Ben because he is poor, and has got no body to say a word for him." I
knew that this was too true to be answered but I excused myself from any blame and
told them I had a right to go home at all events . . . yet . . . the notion that I was not
"one of them" which, by participation in all their labor and hardships, and having no
favor shown me and never asserting myself among them had been laid asleep, was
beginning to revive. But far stronger than any feeling for myself was the pity I felt for
the poor lad.

There is so much value in that brief sequence. There is, first of all, the resistance of the Captain. We never see his mind at work because his interior space is never opened, but we can imagine him. He has figured out Richard Henry Dana and has forced him into the truth of his identity: that he is privileged, is separate, is a gentleman's son with influential connections; and Thompson is determined that Dana's return to society—despite all his fine sentiments—is going to be at the expense of a poor sailor. How good that Dana does not repress this detail of his life, and how good that the Captain's character must be *inferred* here. That is at once an example and a revelation of Dana's economy.

The only way Dana can extricate himself from these toils is to publish an offer giving "an order upon the owners in Boston for six months wages, and also the clothes, books and other matters which I should not want upon the voyage home." Harry May, a Boston boy, accepts the offer, and Dana is let off the hook, though not without full exposure. Moreover, in Dana's concluding chapter, he notes that Harry May went to ruin as fast as ever he could. It is not that Dana is merely to blame; rather, it is a sequence in which he is implicated, and the implication is both articulated and reinforced in the sequence itself.

To begin to see this relation between Thompson and Dana is to see that Thompson has indeed measured his idealistic, subversive crewman and drawn him out of the berth he had made for himself among the crew. But the figure of Thompson, though ever at the threshold of independent dramatic identity, nonetheless remains submerged in the force of authority. It is law itself, from which there is no appeal, and Thompson is merely the agent. Seeing the relation is also to see how the other figures in the book function. They emerge in Dana's field of vision as revelations of relation to, yet separateness from, Dana. Thus, George Marsh, a sailor from apparently good English family, is about to ship into the infinite Pacific, where Dana will never see him more; and there is Bill Jackson, the most handsome figure Dana has ever laid eyes on, yet who is unaccountably not an officer; and there is Tom Harris, possessed of the finest mind Dana has ever encountered, yet a man who has been to the bottom of every sin and every experience; and there is the Kanaka Hope, Dana's friend who all but perishes to venereal disease. These are all modes of being which constitute the disasters of experience awaiting or threatening Dana should he remain before the mast; at the same time, they are the possibilities of existence because he is returning to the civility of civilization. Here Dana never asserts the relationship; the figures appear, asserted prominently into the record. But for this assertion, they would be unrecorded points of consciousness. The full relationship they bear to Dana must be inferred from their essential depersonalization into presences in the space of Dana's factual account.

To see Dana's presentation of these figures is to begin to grasp fully the purity of Dana's narrative. They remain in the record as evidences of humanity in the element of relatively unconscious nature. To imagine them further into being would be to pursue them into a more novelistic structure; or to imagine them beyond a certain point in relation to Dana would be to convert the book into a confessional form and to evade the very direction of the writer's consciousness to get out of or stay out of the inner space. It is, after all, the looming presence of the external journey itself that comes between the literary intelligence that is writing, shaping and valuing the experience, and the very tendency of such shaping to reduce and *plot* the sequence.

All of which brings us to what we can call the travel matter in the book. This matter—the matter of California—occupies the middle portion of the account and is itself a presence of fact, information and escape for Dana. As source of fact, it provides him with assurance that he is conveying useful information to his audience; and it also possesses the kind of referential reassurance that he is not merely recounting his emotional life or the "excitement" of his adventure at sea. Just as it provided a space into which Dana the sailor could escape onto ground ungoverned by the tyranny of the master, the presence of California is the expository space by means of which Dana can elude the dramatic and novelistic closures that constantly threaten him. The flogging scene seems to me to represent those forces in their purest and most powerful form. Readers remember it because its very vividness arises out of its purely dramatic form as the dialogue between Captain and men thrusts aside the recorder. It is of great interest, I think, that the next chapter of the book describes a liberty day in California. In that chapter Dana recounts the particular joys he and his friend Stimson had in getting away from the ship and even the crew. But the point is that California actually exists as a landed space—a place of horses and customs which Dana the writer can occupy, thereby freeing himself and his narrative from being overrun by the tyranny of plot that the flogging scene so powerfully generates. It is just this value of freedom—for both Dana the sailor and Dana the writer—that gives both energy and economy to Dana's descriptions of California and makes those descriptions a strong part of the narrative rather than a mere segmented portion of information filler in his account. Dana can feel in the particular grace of Spanish culture, as it almost idly and lazily presents itself before the fierce aggression of Protestant energy, something of the pure civilization he cannot quite be sure of even in Brahmin Boston, underpinned as it is by the relentless and almost vulgar capitalistic energy that eventuates in a hide-hunting ship captained by the Yankee Thompson. It is not surprising that Dana somehow finds a wistful sympathy for George Ballmer, the English sailor who falls overboard

and is lost, and for George Marsh, who is very possibly an aristocrat abandoned into the Pacific infinite. Moreover, both Tom Harris and Bill Jackson,
whom Dana idealizes, are Englishmen. To be sure, these are implications
more than they are explications of the text, yet they are inevitable implications that buttress Dana's determination to return to civilization.

California is, after all, the place where European civilization, which has
already conquered a primitive civilization, is about to be defeated once
again by aggressive Yankee capitalism, and in this book the matter of California and the adventure of the journey meet in the action of getting hides
for the return to Boston. California is thus the connection between an agri-
cultural and an industrial civilization, and the journey itself is an expression
of the relation between the two. Though the California civilization seems
sleepy and lazy to Dana, it is nonetheless furnishing the raw material that
the ship has come in search of. Dana's account of the hide gathering is
thus not merely a part of his account of the "nature" of California; it is
really the essence of the place. And at the very end of his California stay
there is a passage on the subject which seems to me to represent the very
essence of Dana's factual matter. It at once describes and defines the process of loading hides for the homeward journey. First, the lower hold is
filled with hides laid one atop the other to within four feet of the beams,
and then

... all hands were called aboard to commence steeving. As this is a peculiar operation,
it will require a minute description.

Before stowing the hides, as I have said, the ballast is levelled off, just above the
keelson, and then loose dunnage placed upon it, on which the hides rest. ...

Having filled the ship up, in this way, to within four feet of her beams, the process
of steeving commenced, by which an hundred hides are got into a place where one
could not be forced by hand, and which presses the hides to the uttermost, sometimes
starting the beams of the ship, resembling in its effect the jack-screws which are used
in stowing cotton. Each morning we went ashore, and beat and brought off as many
hides as we could steeve in the course of the day, and, after breakfast, went down
into the hold, where we remained at work until night. The whole length of the hold,
from stem to stern, was floored off level, and we began with raising a pile in the after
part, hard against the bulkhead of the run, and filling it up to the beams, crowding
in as many as we could by hand and pushing in with oars; when a large "book" was
made of from twenty-five to fifty hides, doubled at the backs, and put into one
another, like the leaves of a book. The opening was then made between two hides in
the pile, and the back of the outside hide of the book inserted. Two long, heavy spars,
called steeves, made of the strongest wood, and sharpened off like a wedge at one end,
were placed with their wedge ends into the inside of the hide which was the centre of
the book, and to the other end of each, straps were fitted, into which large tackles
were hooked, composed each of two huge purchase blocks, one hooked to the strap
on the end of the steeve, and the other into a dog, fastened into one of the beams as
far aft as it could be got. When this was arranged, and the ways greased upon which

the book was to slide, the falls of the tackle were stretched forward, and all hands tallied on, and bowsed away until the book was well entered; when these tackles were nippered, straps and toggles clapped upon the falls, and two more luff tackles hooked on, with dogs, in the same manner; and thus, by luff upon luff, the power was multi-plied, until a pile in which one hide more could not be crowded by hand, an hundred or an hundred and fifty were often driven in by this complication of purchases. When the last luff was hooked on, all hands were called to the rope—cook, steward, and all—and ranging ourselves at the falls, one behind the other, sitting down on the hides with our heads just even with the beams, we set taut upon the tackles, and striking up a song, and all lying back at the chorus, we bowsed the tackles home, and drove the large books in chock out of sight.

This passage might well stand for the very form of the book—and it is surely no accident that the metaphor applied to the hides also applies to Dana's narrative. I do not mean that Dana is always so minute in his description of process, but that this passage, like the flogging scene, repre-sents the essence as well as the extremity of Dana's factual prose. More-over, we might well say that Dana's own book has about it the charged compactness of the stowed hides, as if the matter of the journey were being driven home.

The manner in which the book of hides is made and then driven into and between the piled hides as if it were a wedge seems to me an apt description of Dana's composition. Instead of seeing expansion or compression as his dynamic principle, Dana here discloses it to be *insertion* which at once pro-duces both expansion and compression. That act could very well express the nature of the book. Surely the chapter on liberty following the flogging is in a real sense inserted, which is to say wedged in, in such a way that the discontinuity of the process is largely concealed by the increased compact-ness. The result is a swiftness of sequence that greatly reinforces the *active* element of the factual descriptions. The matter and culture of California are, in effect, invaded with process.

Here again we can see how this form at once invites and resists whatever logic of direction we might wish to put on it. There is, of course, the master trope and master fact of departure and return. And there is the archetype of the *Bildungsroman* much present, so that we might well see Dana grow-ing up or passing through crises. There is, for example, the fierce and lengthy passage of Cape Horn on the return voyage, the terrible storms of which could be seen psychologically to represent Dana recovering the con-science he had left at Cape Horn. The outward voyage around the Cape had been a relatively easy summer passage, but the midwinter return passage near the 4th of July is perilous in every respect. There Captain Thompson seems to lose his courage, but then Dana comes down with a paralyzing toothache, leaving him no way to be smug about the Captain, if indeed the Captain is afraid. Such psychologizing of the narrative is too easy, too dramatic, too novelistic for the current of Dana's prose. Dana *is* sick, so sick he cannot stand watches and is sentenced to lie miserably in his bunk at the very height of the crisis—he who had all his life a superb constitution. Yet this inner space is never really allowed to open because of Dana's interest in the ship, the waters and the weather. An object like an iceberg thus displaces whatever interior logic we might wish to impose:

And there lay, floating in the ocean, several miles off, an immense, irregular mass, its top and points covered with snow, and its centre of a deep indigo color. This was an iceberg, and of the largest size, as one of our men said who had been in the Northern ocean. As far as the eye could reach, the sea in every direction was of a deep blue color, the waves running high and fresh, and sparkling in the light, and in the midst lay this immense mountain-island, its cavities and valleys thrown into deep shade, and its points and pinnacles glittering in the sun. . . . But no description can give any idea of the strangeness, splendor, and, really, the sublimity of the sight. Its immense size— for it must have been from two to three miles in circumference, and several hundred feet in height; its slow motion, as its base rose and sank in the water, and its high points nodded against the clouds; the dashing of the waves upon it, which, breaking high with foam, lined its base with a white crust; and the thundering sound of the cracking of the mass, and the breaking and tumbling down of huge pieces; together with its nearness and approach, which added a slight element of fear,—all combined to give to it the character of true sublimity.

This passage, filled as it is with active verbs, gives a clue to how much motion means in this narrative of travel. In this instance, it is the slow motion that Dana's description is at once catching and arresting, but there are times when the currents and clouds seem to rush towards the ship until it careens like a race horse. In this narrative all things seem in motion, the sun running low in the heavens, the great storms bearing down upon the frail ship, the wind lashing the rigging, the sea running astern, a dark cloud looming up on the horizon. If we wanted to choose a passage where this movement is captured in its muted purity, it might be this one:

When all sail had been set, and the decks cleared up, the *California* was a speck on the horizon, and the coast lay like a low cloud along the northeast. At sunset they were both out of sight, and we were once more upon the ocean, where the sky and water meet.

Here the verb, which is held to the end, embraces the inertial might of moving forces that all but exclude the ship.

But, of course, there is the ship itself which figures so prominently in the book. If Dana's passages on the factual matter tend to pervade description with active process, his passages on ships pervade the act of sailing with description. Full of technical terminology which he never really explains, these passages become expositions of rife activity. Dana knows—and even happily knows—that most of his readers are landsmen and can scarcely know half the verbs and nouns he uses to describe the elaborate activity of rigging and reefing and furling in the face of ever-shifting winds; he even observes in his preface that this ignorance has never seemed a hindrance to novel readers of Cooper and Marryat because, as he says, he "has found from my own experience, and from what I have heard from others that plain matters of fact in relation to customs and habits new to us, and description of life under new aspects, act upon the inexperienced through the imagination."

Dana is no doubt right in his contention, but the imagination to which he refers is not novelistic. For in his world, as we have seen, men appear almost like sketches lacking both causal force and vivid portraiture of characters. They are given only an outline and a bare life history either inferred or reported by Dana. And so in this narrative the activity of sailing is the very process of movement. This entire matter, which constitutes so great a portion of the book, like the matter of California, lies between the expert sailor (who presumably could explain and verify every movement) and the ignorant reader, who feels the mysterious terminology as *facts in action*.

Here, at this moment in 1840, Dana instinctively grasped a matter of great importance. Any reader today at once feels the "romance" of this movement—a romance which all but depends on his own ignorance—and senses the elaborate technology of a sailing ship. The ignorance functions as the great *unconscious* power of movement, just as the actual sails and the terminology attending them are the highly conscious technology of dealing with the true unconscious forces of nature which propel the ship. The ship itself, as described by Dana, is thus a displacement of all the human unconsciousness into which Dana does not voyage. His own voyage chronicles his mastery—a highly conscious mastery of every line and sail on the vessel—yet his narrative converts that conscious mastery into descriptions clearly designed to evoke vague comprehension (except to the most privileged insiders who have actually spent years at sea). There is a fine passage on the homeward voyage—after the *Alert* has rounded the Horn and is rushing north towards home—that both represents and sums up the large narrative component of a ship at sea:

One night, while we were in these tropics, I went out to the end of the flying-jib boom, upon some duty, and, having finished it, turned round and lay over the boom for a long time, admiring the beauty of the sight before me. Being so far out from the deck, I could look at the ship as at a separate vessel; and there rose up from the water, supported only by the small black hull, and towering up almost, as it seemed in the indistinct night air, to the clouds. The sea was as still as an inland lake; the light trade wind was gently and steadily breathing from astern; the dark-blue sky was studded with the tropical stars; there was no sound but the rippling of the water under the stem; and the sails were spread out, wide and high, the two lower studding sails stretching on each side far beyond the deck; the topmast studding sails like wings to the topsails; the topgallant studding sails spreading fearlessly out above them; still higher, the two royal studding sails, looking like two kites flying from the same string; and, highest of all, the little skysail, the apex of the pyramid, seeming actually to touch the stars, and to be out of reach of the human hand. So quiet, too, was the sea, and so steady the breeze that if these sails had been a sculptured marble they could not have been more motionless. Not a ripple upon the surface of the canvas; not even a quivering of the extreme edges of the sail, so perfectly were they distended by the breeze.

Here, as the ship approaches home, Dana finds it at last motionless upon a silent ocean, and so almost consciously he produces a piece of set description, as if he were painting or sculpting the ship. Yet the passage is much more than a set piece of description, for Dana literally builds the ship before our eyes, moving from the water to the stars. And Dana at such a moment is characteristically separate from his scene, located as he is on the prow of the ship, looking aft upon the image of the fact that is literally sending him home backwards.

To see and sense such a passage is to understand the particular apathy Dana felt in actually arriving in Boston. He had had the anticipation of home as if it were to be the climactic ending of a novel. Yet the movement and arrival leave ship, shore and ocean somehow behind him like an iceberg of attraction. In building this image of the ship, Dana brings to rest all the furious action of making and reefing sail. And in a deeper way he is, I think, completing the life of the great sailing age. He is much aware of steamships; indeed, he has had to confess to his readers how inept he was in explaining to the Kanaka sailors the technology of steam power.

Be that as it may, the image of the completed ship at full sail might well stand as the ending of the book. As an ending, it would give the lie to any interpretation which put the flogging as the central action of the book. We might conclude instead that, unlike the Californians who had left their conscience at Cape Horn, Dana had actually found his conscience upon the western passage, only to lose it on the difficult return voyage. It is well to remember in this connection that, in the course of the wonderfully smooth voyage north towards Boston, there is another flogging. This time it is the black cook who receives the Captain's blows for having become involved in a vocal and physical altercation with the mate. In this instance, Dana treats the matter as if D.H. Lawrence himself had instructed him, which is to say that he treats it as a matter of passional readjustment. Since the cook is black, it would, of course, be possible to see Dana's treatment of the incident as a manifestation of the barely submerged racism running just beneath the surface of liberal Boston gentility. The possibility is certainly there (it is remarkable how little critical attention has been devoted to this second flogging), yet Dana's writing cannot be reduced to such a strait. Rather, Dana, in the moment of at once constructing and arresting the image of the ship—and in that action literally turning his back on Boston even as the ship drives him home—is affirming the imaginative dominion of the external journey as his true life and subject.

There remains, however, the fact that the imagined ship is not the ending of the book. Instead, Dana, like the Dickens of *Great Expectations*, had two endings. The first was a concluding chapter focusing on the possible legal and moral reforms that might be effected between captain and crew. That ending, rooted in Dana's socially reasoned fear of the passionate drama of elemental human conflict—the fear that enabled him to concentrate objectively on the much more elemental and unconscious forces of nature—led him directly out of the book into the life of law that lay before him. But nineteen years later, Dana returned to California on a steamship; and, 29 years after writing, he got the copyright of his book and then displaced the original concluding chapter with an account of his return visit. And so Dana actually ended his book by returning to it, as if the book itself had attracted him back into it and literally annihilated the link he had originally wrought to connect his experience to his professional life. The book *was* his life and had fatally identified him. Thus, as if he were in a Victorian novel, he told what had happened both to California and to the sailors and captains he had sailed with or met upon his voyage.

Dana's return to his book discloses how completely he had actually completed his life in his early voyage. He had thought, when he finished the book, that he was ready for his life in law—and indeed he was. Yet, even as he began his legal career, he also began in 1842, married and living in Boston, to keep a journal. His first act in his journal "life" was a brief narrative account of his life up to the time of taking ship to California, as if he were, in the manner of *Two Years Before the Mast*, completing the early portion of his life. Significantly for our purposes, Dana saw his early life at school much as he had written of his life at sea. The chief event is a flogging he received from a schoolmaster—and a fine problem for anyone writing about his life would be to decide how much his writing of *Two Years Before the Mast* actually *shaped* his whole prior life.

However much his written narrative may have thrown his early life into focus and form, it left his later life to the mercy of the law. Thus, having narratively accounted for his early life at the outset of his journal, Dana drops into a discontinuous (and conventional) record of his thoughts and activities. As his years at law wore on, so did the journal; Dana could not give up the law, or at least he did not; he even achieved distinction in it through meticulous labor and attention to detail. But years of the most conscientious labor told on his constitution, and in 1859 his doctor advised a long vacation. The opportunity afforded Dana a chance to fulfill a life-long dream of making a voyage around the world. And around the world he went, as if he were at last going into the infinite expanse of the Pacific that he had somehow fled from when he made the deal with Frank Thompson to return to Boston. It was on that trip that he returned to California and got the material with which to complete the book of his life. From California he went on to Japan and China—and to Penang in Sumatra, where he visited the grave of his cousin, George Edward Channing, who had shipped with Francis Thompson. When Thompson caught the fever which killed him, Channing—who, according to Dana, had not "consulted me as to the captain"—in nursing the dying Thompson also contracted the disease and lost his life.

If this cousin lived out the destructive life at sea that Dana had retreated from, it was another cousin, Francis Dana, who lost all but a small portion of the journal Dana had entrusted to him upon his arrival in Boston on the *Alert*, forcing Dana to reconstruct largely from memory the book of his life.

These two "losses" left Dana with his two "lives"—the life of the book he was to write and the life of the law he was to live. The addition of his final chapter had the practical value of providing a distinctly new edition of the book of his life, as he at last secured the copyright from Harpers, who had never given him a penny of royalty beyond the flat fee of $250 they paid him for his manuscript (Dana estimated that the publishing company had made $50,000 from the sales of the book in their 28 years of possession). More important, it brought him back into the book that had completed his life more than he could know.

All that remained for Dana was to practice law in a more leisurely style, enjoy the High Church Episcopalianism to which he was more and more devoted, and finally go to Rome, where he died in 1882. He is buried there —in the Protestant Cemetery.

Elizabeth D. Harvey

Speaking Without Bounds:
The Extra-vagant Impulse in Thoreau's "Walking"*

Walden could be characterized as obsessed with defining, delineating, surveying and otherwise rendering the unknown known and bounding the unbounded. However, this impulse is balanced by an equally powerful but opposite urge to dissolve the very limits and distinctions Thoreau describes. He announces his successful attempt to plumb the depths of Walden Pond with smug satisfaction, as if science had at last managed to silence the superstitious fantasy that the pond might be, in fact, bottomless:

There have been many stories told about the bottom, or rather no bottom, of this pond, which certainly had no foundation for themselves. It is remarkable how long men will believe in the bottomlessness of a pond without taking the trouble to sound it. . . . Many have believed that Walden reached quite through to the other side of the globe.[1]

Thoreau reassures the holders of these superstitions that he has sounded the pond and can safely report (can give a "foundation" to the bottomless fictions) that it "has a reasonably tight bottom at a not unreasonable, though at an unusual, depth" (p. 189). But no sooner has he provided his readers with the assurance that boundaries and bottoms will prevail against unfounded fears, that reason will cushion the mind against the terrors of the unknown, than he remarks on the deleterious effects the shallowness of ponds may have on the minds of men. Indeed, he professes gratitude that Walden Pond was discovered to be deep and pure, since as long as "men believe in the infinite some ponds will be thought to be bottomless" (p. 189).[2]

Towards the end of *Walden*, these double and ostensibly antithetical impulses—the wish for defined boundaries and the urge for immeasurability—alternate with increasing frequency and intensity. In one characteristic passage, for example, Thoreau claims that, if one "advances confidently in the direction of his dreams," he will

> ... meet with a success unexpected in common hours. He will put some things behind, will pass an invisible boundary; new, universal, and more liberal laws will begin to establish themselves around and within him; or the old laws be expanded and interpreted in his favor in a more liberal sense, and he will live with the license of a higher order of beings. . . . If you have built castles in the air, your work need not be lost; that is where they should be. Now put the foundations under them. (p. 214)

Thoreau does not here advocate annihilating boundaries; rather, he is concerned with pushing them back and constantly enlarging the territory they encompass. As the careful balance of his prose acknowledges, the desire for expansion depends upon the prior existence of boundaries; each attempt to describe an unfettered state inevitably refers, whether implicitly or explicitly, to an earlier, circumscribed state. To advance in the direction of dreams is to follow an unarticulated, unrestrained urge, to pass an invisible boundary. However, once the dreamer has broken away from his bounded existence, he finds himself not in a universe free of law, but in one governed by a new law, or perhaps simply by an old law that has been more leniently interpreted. Even the gesture towards "castles in the air" is immediately modified to include the earth-bound foundations they so urgently require. As if Thoreau recognizes the conservative qualifications he constantly introduces into the articulation of his radical vision, he asserts a moment later: "I fear chiefly lest my expression may not be *extra-vagant* enough, may not wander far enough beyond the narrow limits of my daily experience, so as to be adequate to the truth of which I have been convinced. *Extra vagance!* it depends on how you are yarded" (p. 214). Even "extra" implies an inside of which it is the outside, just as "how you are yarded" presupposes limits, no matter how relative. Chafing against the restraints of language, Thoreau cries impatiently, "I desire to speak somewhere *without* bounds; like a man in a waking moment, to men in their waking moments" (p. 214), as if that liminal moment between sleeping and waking could give him the freedom he desired: the control of waking expression still informed by the boundless power of dreams and not yet subject to the constraints of the waking mind. In *Walden*, however, the extra-vagant— whether in movement or language—is always checked by the surveyor; while the two contradictory impulses exist in harmony, each vigilantly modifying the other, the extra-vagant is never allowed unqualified expression.

To "speak somewhere *without* bounds" became for Thoreau a life-long project, an occupation that found its most sustained expression in the shifting, shapeless form of the *Journal*, and its most perfectly distilled treatment in the essay "Walking." Speaking without bounds required the creation of a form that scrupulously mimicked the very formlessness Thoreau sought to portray, so that he might simultaneously employ language while denying the restraints it necessarily imposed on him, might convert nature directly into words without recognizing what he considered to be the mediatory step in the transmutation. He demands in *Walden* that the "volatile truth of our words should continually betray the inadequacy of the residual statement. Their truth is instantly *translated*; its literal monument alone remains. The words which express our faith and piety are not definite; yet they are significant and fragrant like frankincense to superior natures" (p. 215). The task of "Walking" could be described as an attempt to bring the "volatile" nature of truth, its changing (or flying, as the root sense of "volatile" implies) character, into correspondence with the "residual" element, its abiding (Thoreau again invokes the etymological sense: Latin *residere*, to stay), static remnant. The project involved translating "truth" into "monument," that is, instilling immediacy and energy into what Thoreau considered to be the relatively lifeless permanence of the written word. To do this required the transgression of linguistic boundaries, a disruption that is mirrored in the transgression of geographic limits. The subject of the essay is walking, a durative activity that finds its linguistic reflection in the gerundial title, a form that makes the process of the essay at once permanent and transcendent, at once verb and substantive. The atemporality of the gerund contrasts with the other essays which describe walks, for in these ("A Walk to Wachusett" and "A Winter Walk"), the activity has already become past, something memorialized in description.[3] As the title promises, the structure of "Walking" is meandering, almost desultory. Its origins—composed, as it is, largely of passages extracted from the *Journal*[4]—attest less to the polishing of a final form than to an overall effect of fragmentation. Although the finite form of the essay seems to set itself in opposition to the boundlessness of the *Journal*, in fact "Walking" both invokes and continues the disjointed quality of its source. The strategy of the essay is to unsettle expectations by providing, instead of a walk between specified locations, a directionless meditation on the activity in its abstract form. As a result, the essay is not an excursion that its readers can enjoy from the safe remove of time and space, but an aimless collection of philosophical remarks, a labyrinth in which Thoreau's readers lose themselves and, in losing themselves, are implicated in the "volatile" truth of the essay.

In offering a model of a literature "which gives expression to Nature," Thoreau describes the ideal poet as one "who nailed words to their primitive senses, as farmers drive down stakes in the spring, which the frost has

heaved."[5] True to that model, the essay begins by advancing two specu-
lative etymologies for walking or "sauntering": in the first, sauntering is
derived from *Sainte Terre*, after the wandering crusaders of the Middle
Ages who became known as "Sainte Terrers," or saunterers. The second
derivation has *sans terre* as its root: as Thoreau understands it, "in the
good sense, [it] will mean, having no particular home, but equally at home
everywhere" ("Walking," p. 205). This second meaning, the sense of being
at once rootless and having roots everywhere, is the secret of successful
sauntering. It is also, as Thoreau tries to show, the secret of successful
writing: breaking with traditional form results in "homelessness," but the
pervasive attention to etymology provides "homes," or roots, linguistic
stability in an otherwise unsettling experiment. Although the first etymology seems initially less important, the essay proceeds from both definitions
and manages to arrive at the first—with its attendant edenic connotations—
by means of the second.[6]

The essential quality of walking, according to Thoreau, is the ability to
lose oneself. He never makes explicit how one goes about losing oneself,
however, for although the experience must be a willed one, it must also be
inadvertent, one not subject to the bounds of prescription. What Thoreau
does—all he can do and still adhere to his own philosophy—is to offer a
paradigm in the form of his essay. Thoreau confides his own difficulty in
achieving the desired state, for sometimes when he is walking "the thought
of some work will run in my head and I am not where my body is,—I am
out of my senses" ("Walking," p. 211). But losing oneself, for Thoreau,
does *not* imply a division within the self or a transcendence of the self—
that way lies madness, as the pun on the colloquial phrase "out of one's
senses" registers—but a state in which the self communicates with nature
through the instruments of the body. "In my walks," Thoreau says, "I
would fain return to my senses" ("Walking," p. 211). The most crucial
organ of sense for this process of unification is the skin, the mediating
membrane that bounds and contains the self and yet is also sensible and
responsive to the world outside it. Tanned skin presents unmistakable phys-
iological evidence of its communication with the natural, external world,
since, while it remains bonded to and obedient to the self, it also expresses
its contact with outside phenomena through its alteration in color. Thoreau
praises tanned skin as more natural than pale skin: "A tanned skin is something more than respectable, and perhaps olive is a fitter color than white
for a man,—a denizen of the woods" ("Walking," p. 226). Not only color,
but also the smells of the surroundings imbed themselves in the skin:

The African hunter Cumming tells us that the skin of the eland . . . emits the most
delicious perfume of trees and grass. I would have every man so much like a wild ante-
lope, so much a part and parcel of nature, that his very person should thus sweetly

advertise our senses of his presence, and remind us of those parts of nature which he most haunts. ("Walking," pp. 225-26)

Skin has become a slate upon which nature inscribes herself through the signs of smell and color; it is a receptive transparency that does not require mediation, since it represents its outside and its inside simultaneously. It is itself an act of translation, of translating nature onto (and, therefore, into) the self. Thoreau offers a cautionary example of this translation gone awry in quoting Darwin, who likens white skin to a plant "bleached by the gardener's art" ("Walking," p. 226). Cultivation—or civilization—produces a being whose appearance has been artificially determined, leaving it a prisoner within its own boundaries. The naturally reciprocal membrane has become exclusively one-way, reflecting an interior that can no longer respond and draw vigor from outside itself.

The concept of the skin as the organ of translation between the self and the external world, radical though it already is, insinuates itself into Thoreau's prose, making the original terms of the idea interchangeable, and confusing the margins of the distinction. This transmutation of terms begins in an ostensibly simple act of metaphorization:

Living much out of doors, in the sun and wind, will no doubt produce a certain roughness of character,—will cause a thicker cuticle to grow over some of the finer qualities of our nature, as on the face and hands, or as severe manual labor robs the hands of some of their delicacy of touch. ("Walking," p. 210)

What serves in this passage as a striking simile—a "thicker cuticle" grows over some of the "finer qualities of our nature," just as it would over skin exposed to sun and wind—becomes in a subsequent passage disconcertingly intertwined, disorienting our sense of where metaphor begins and more "literal" language leaves off:

The callous palms of the laborer are conversant with finer tissues of self-respect and heroism, whose touch thrills the heart, than the languid fingers of idleness. That is mere sentimentality that lies abed by day and thinks itself white, far from the tan and callus of experience. ("Walking," p. 210)

In an astonishing series of conversions, so rapid in their transformations that they almost beguile the mind into unhesitating acceptance, Thoreau moves from the "callous palms of the laborer" to the "tan and callus of experience," having severed "tan" and "callus" from the hand that earned them and grafted both qualities onto "experience." The transformation is set into motion by the inversion of "conversant" and "touch": the laborer's calloused hands are endowed with the ability to communicate, so that the callus, far from being a barrier, becomes the instrument of access to the "finer tissues." The "touch" that "thrills the heart" may be applied by either the laborer's palms or the finer tissues; they have become inter-changeable and synonymous in "touch," each bestowing its respective qual-ities on the other and each becoming a viable antecedent for "whose." The blurring of syntactical boundaries is mirrored in the confusion of "literal" and allegorical language, so that the spiritual characteristics of the heart become accessible to the external touch of a hand, just as "heroism" and "self-respect" become qualities that reside in "tissue," a "finer" version of flesh. By disturbing the boundaries of language, Thoreau attempts to detach conventional social values from the language that represents and embodies them. The synecdochic excision of "tan" and "callus" from the bodily organ that produced them (and from which they are physiologically inseparable) also severs these words from their previous association of man-ual labor and sets them in a new context of heroism and experience.

Thoreau's desire for a new order requires less the destruction of an old order than a trick of vision, an "intention of the eye,"[7] that would take the world in its ordinary ways of being known and reshape it. He illustrates this faculty of vision in a parable:

I saw the fences half consumed, their ends lost in the middle of the prairie, and some worldly miser with a surveyor looking after his bounds, while heaven had taken place around him, and he did not see the angels going to and fro, but was looking for an old post-hole in the midst of paradise. I looked again, and saw him standing in the middle of a boggy Stygian fen, surrounded by devils, and he had found his bounds without a doubt, three little stones, where a stake had been driven, and looking nearer, I saw that the Prince of Darkness was his surveyor. ("Walking," p. 212)

The parable makes heaven and hell coterminous; which realm one occupies depends upon a way of seeing. For the man determined to quantify, meas-ure, and possess, heaven becomes hell, and the instrument of transformation is the devil in the guise of surveyor. There is, of course, an intentional irony in representing the devil as surveyor, since it was a profession Thoreau prac-ticed; but, irony aside, the surveyor also stands more generally for every man's impulse to measure and own. The parable fragments and externalizes the self, allegorizing the constraining impulse in the act of overcoming the desire to expand and destroy limits. Reconstructing an old fence according to pre-existing and pre-determined boundaries is an activity analogous to that of a walker who incessantly retraces his steps in a familiar geography: both activities reinforce worn-out patterns of vision. Finding one's bounds "without a doubt" may temporarily alleviate anxiety, but the property obtained shrinks to the proportions of the owner's mind or to the size of the instrument through which it is obtained. In this case, it is the surveyor's stake ("three small stones, where a stake had been driven"), but in *Walden* Thoreau makes language the instrument of a more positive form of appro-priation: "The owner [of a farm] does not know it for many years when a poet has put his farm in rhyme, the most admirable kind of invisible fence, has fairly impounded it, milked it, skimmed it, and got all the cream, and left the farmer only the skimmed milk" (p. 56).

Even though Thoreau condones poetic ownership—the appropriation of a landscape by converting it into poetry—he is wary of any relationship that produces familiarity or habit. It is not so much the occupation of surveyor that he objects to, then, but the internalized surveyor in each of us, a devil who insists on boundaries as static and absolute entities. He describes and enacts the desired dissolution of boundaries in these terms:

The walker in the familiar fields which stretch around my native town sometimes finds himself in another land than is described in their owners' deeds, as it were in some faraway field on the confines of the actual Concord, where her jurisdiction ceases, and the idea which the word Concord suggests ceases to be suggested. These farms which I have myself surveyed, these bounds which I have set up, appear dimly as through a mist; but they have no chemistry to fix them; they fade from the surface of the glass, and the picture which the painter painted stands out dimly from beneath. The world with which we are commonly acquainted leaves no trace, and it will have no anniversary. ("Walking," p. 242)

The familiar limits and divisions have been obliterated and have given way to a new and unknown landscape; deeds of possession have become void, and jurisdiction by the actual Concord has lost its force. Even the chain of cognition that connects the name "Concord" to the idea of place has been broken. Once the unilateral correspondence that links a name with a place is dislodged, the word itself is left, in this case evoking a sense of harmony (concord) between man and his surroundings, a complacent pact that Thoreau wishes to dissolve in favor of a resurrected wilderness. The passage effects a kind of progressive erasing; gradually the familiar landscape, in its previous ways of being seen, grows dimmer until its outlines are visible "as through a mist." It is the same mist that had obliterated the civilized world in *A Week on the Concord and Merrimack Rivers* and had restored the Maine landscape to its primitive grandeur in *Ktaadn*.[8] The obliteration is not complete here, for Thoreau recognizes familiar territory, but only indistinctly. It is a quality that allows the eye to disregard (in the etymological sense of "not look") the surface in order to concentrate more fully on the background. The image he employs is that of a painted landscape extending backward into an infinite horizon; in order to see this, the conventions of surface and paint—the bounded things that tether us to shallow surfaces—must dissolve. The passage seems to contain deliberate echoes of I Corinthians 13:12 ("For now we see through a glass, darkly: but then face to face"), except that Thoreau would emphasize seeing through a glass darkly as an essential prelude to being able to see "face to face." The edenic connotations are also apt, and they appear over and over (albeit in different forms) in "Walking," always in the context of the new kind of vision Thoreau espouses. In order to insure that the reconstruction of the ordinary world will not occur again, he extends his erasing rhetoric into the future with the phrase "it will have no anniversary." The prolepsis guarantees the integrity of the dissolution, since not even the vanishing of the old world will be celebrated. That celebration would require a turning back each year (*anni-versare*) and, in so doing, would inevitably preserve the memory of what is familiar.

Just as losing oneself has positive and desirable effects, forgetting—the act of losing memory—is essential to the recreation of a new world. Thoreau describes America as bounded on each side by a river of forgetfulness:

> We go eastward to realize history and study the works of art and literature, retracing the steps of the race; we go westward as into the future, with a spirit of enterprise and adventure. The Atlantic is a Lethean stream, in our passage over which we have had an opportunity to forget the Old World and its institutions. If we do not succeed this time, there is perhaps one more chance for the race left before it arrives on the banks of the Styx; and that is in the Lethe of the Pacific, which is three times as wide.
>
> ("Walking," p. 218)

The process of constructing identity, particularly a literary identity, depends upon our forgetting our English and continental heritage in favor of a new American tradition. Thoreau conflates geographic and temporal designations so that a westward movement comes to have the spiritual triumph associated with overcoming the past. But instead of having the westward and future impulse be a repudiation of the past as, say, it is for Emerson or for the more didactic Thoreau of *A Week*, it is simply a forgetting. There is in "Walking" a pervasive awareness of the ineluctable nature of history: it will always exist, since the shape of the past determines the outline of the present, but the form in which it exists can be altered through the alchemy of oblivion. Thoreau's new use of history would have the past act as a fertile ground which nourishes the future without intruding in any recognizable form into it. "To use an obsolete Latin word," says Thoreau, characteristically invoking the authority of an ancient language while simultaneously denying it a corresponding vitality, "*Ex Oriente lux; ex Occidente FRUX*. From the East light, from the West fruit" ("Walking," p. 221). From the east comes the ineffable source of inspiration; from the west, the tangible, living product. But Thoreau pushes the equation a step further. Although light from the east is essential, the inspiration must never become more than a sustaining source, must never have its own coherent identity, lest it threaten the very life it nourishes. Therefore, to pass successfully through the Lethe renders negligible the fatal power of the Styx; that is, to forget or decompose our European literary and historical sources is to insure the survival and health of a new American identity.[9]

In his discussion of national and literary identity, the swamp figures prominently as Thoreau's metaphor for the mnemonic digestion that will bring about the assimilation of European culture. The essence of his fascination focuses on the swamp that was once a forest, for, although the constituent elements have lost their respective identities, they have not, nevertheless, been obliterated, only re-formed. "A township where one primitive forest waves above while another primitive forest rots below,— such a town is fitted to raise not only corn and potatoes, but poets and philosophers for the coming ages" ("Walking," p. 229). It is precisely this dark, forgotten place, where the specific boundaries of time and shape have fused together, that provides the richest soil for subsequent growth. The nourishment which this decaying host produces is made evident in the vigor of its offspring: "The civilized nations—Greece, Rome, England—have been sustained by the primitive forests which anciently rotted where they stand. They survive as long as the soil is not exhausted. Alas for human culture! little is to be expected of a nation, when the vegetable mould is exhausted ..." ("Walking," p. 229). Just as the greatness of a civilization stands in direct proportion to the richness of the decay which nourishes it, so does each poet's stature depend on the decomposed sustenance of his poetic ancestors, "for the decay of other literatures makes the soil in which [the new literature] thrives" ("Walking," p. 233). Not content with merely observing this phenomenon, Thoreau proceeds to enact it, making his own prose the vehicle and the embodiment of the transformation. He says of himself:

When I would recreate myself, I seek the darkest wood, the thickest and most interminable and, to the citizen, most dismal, swamp. I enter a swamp as a sacred place, a *sanctum sanctorum*. There is the strength, the marrow, of Nature. . . . In such a soil grew Homer and Confucius and the rest, and out of such a wilderness comes the Reformer eating locusts and wild honey. ("Walking," pp. 228-29).

In other words, he enters the swamp as Thoreau in search of re-creation; what emerges from the swamp at the end of the passage is the Reformer, or Thoreau re-formed into the prophet of Nature. He links himself implicitly with the greatness of Homer and Confucius, but he *becomes* John the Baptist, first by divesting the biblical prophet of his name and then by himself assuming the identifying attributes of the prophet. The shift from past to present tense in "comes" signals both the process of re-creation and the immediacy of the prophetic presence.

We have already seen that Thoreau regarded the suppression of a name as a step towards disturbing the configuration of convention, of severing the ties of the familiar in order that nature might reclaim the over-civilized. In becoming the prophet and poet of this decomposing process, Thoreau converts his writing into a swamp that in turn digests the writings of his poetic predecessors. In "Walking" it is as if fragments of Chaucer, Dante and Milton had undergone an organic disintegration that had erased their identic shapes and subordinated their respective voices to the larger authority of Thoreau's prose. The names of the authors are systematically divorced from their poetry, as if Thoreau wished to sever the identifying tag from the words in order that he might reform them in his own image. A name for Thoreau functions as a boundary of possession, but, once the name has been eradicated, the quotation is weaned from its context of origin. Its meaning will subsequently depend upon each new context, although each later meaning will inevitably draw on an earlier, decomposed significance. A meditation on westward exploration and the discovery of America, for example, becomes a context for the concluding lines of *Lycidas*:

Columbus felt the westward tendency more strongly than any before. He obeyed it, and found a New World . . . . The herd of men in those days scented fresh pastures from afar.

> "And now the sun had stretched out all the hills,
> And now was dropped into the western bay;
> At last *he* rose, and twitched his mantle blue;
> To-morrow to fresh woods and pastures new."

Where on the globe can there be found an area of equal extent, with that occupied by the bulk of our States, so fertile and so rich and varied in its productions, and at the same time so habitable by the European, as this is? ("Walking, pp. 219-20)

The quotation seems apposite because it locates a sense of optimistic possibility within a westward and future movement, and because that westward expansion suggests the acquisition of new land. But instead of having the "he" refer to the "uncouth swain" of Milton's poem, Thoreau converts the antecedent to Columbus (or the generalized westward explorer), a substitution he makes explicit by italicizing the "he." Although the lines contribute a poetic and pastoral resonance to Thoreau's argument, the psychic consolation of Milton's elegy has been subordinated to the triumphant sense of physical, geographical expansion. The elegiac tone is not inappropriate, however, for, just as bereavement gives way to consolation in the elegiac tradition, so for Thoreau does the decay of one civilization nourish the life of the succeeding one. In one sense, then, Milton and European literature are the mourned dead and the subjects of the residual elegiac tone, while Thoreau is the embodiment of its consolation. Or, put in even more physical terms, Thoreau's prose becomes the rich and varied "States," a domain which can comfortably contain a European or a Milton within its boundaries, a land with space enough to absorb another tradition.

One method by which Thoreau decomposes his poetic ancestry, then, is by severing an author's name from his poetry—making all poetry in "Walking" of implicitly equal stature—and unmooring the quotation from an original context.[10] In other cases he acknowledges an author only to super-impose his own signature immediately. For example, he quotes Ben Jon-son's phrase "How near to good is what is fair!" in order that he might rewrite it in the next line to read, "How near to good is what is *wild*" ("Walking," p. 226). Again, his substituted word is italicized. Repetition becomes a vehicle for inspiration, and through repetition the boundaries of ownership are blurred. Thoreau's insight is parasitic on Jonson's in the same way that new vegetable life is sustained by the swamp. It is not sur-prising to discover that translation is the most common form of quotation in "Walking," for it offers the built-in possibility for appropriation. Since the selection of suitable words in a translation always requires an act of interpretation, the resulting words will take on the stamp of the transla-tor's mind. A similar kind of appropriation is effected through paraphrase, Thoreau's translation of one author's poetry into his prose. In these cases he does not even acknowledge his borrowing by the customary typograph-ical signs, for the matter is so decomposed that it has lost integrity of its own. "I am reminded once more that there is nothing in a name" ("Walk-ing," p. 236), he says, mimetically illustrating that assertion by his appro-priation of Shakespearean language. On another occasion he paraphrases Shakespeare as an introduction to a quotation from Confucius, making Shakespearean poetry the unacknowledged stepping-stone to an observa-tion on the uniqueness of Confucius: "Any man can stop a hole to keep the wind away, but no other man [except Confucius] could serve so rare a use as the author of this illustration did" ("Walking," pp. 235-36). The Shakespearean paraphrase is, of course, from the graveyard scene in *Ham-let*, an appropriately deathly original context. Thoreau laments the tame-ness of English poetry:

> I do not know of any poetry to quote which adequately expresses this yearning for the Wild. Approached from this side, the best poetry is tame. I do not know where to find in any literature, ancient or modern, any account which contents me of that Nature with which even I am acquainted. You will perceive that I demand something which no Augustan nor Elizabethan age, which no *culture*, in short, can give. ("Walking," p. 232)

In order to convert the tameness of past poetry into an instrument that could express Nature, Thoreau must dispossess that poetry of its civilized origins, dissolve its boundaries, and use that decay to nourish the new American literature.

At the end of "Walking" Thoreau returns to his earlier use of the inclu-sive "we," as if his readers had accompanied him throughout the essay and, having absorbed the new philosophy of walking and reading, now walk beside Thoreau in his entry into Elysium:

We walked in so pure and bright a light, gilding the withered grass and leaves, so softly and serenely bright, I thought I had never bathed in such a golden flood, without a ripple or a murmur to it. The west side of every wood and rising ground gleamed like the boundary of Elysium, and the sun on our backs seemed like a gentle herdsman driving us home at evening.

So we saunter toward the Holy Land, till one day the sun shall shine more brightly than ever he has done, shall perchance shine into our minds and hearts, and light up our whole lives with a great awakening light, as warm and serene and golden as on a bankside in autumn. ("Walking," pp. 247-48)

The journey described in "Walking" is the reverse of the account of birth in Book X of Plato's *Republic*, where the souls pass from Elysium through the River of Forgetfulness to birth. Thoreau's essay is an inverted version that passes from earthly, bounded existence, through forgetting, back into Elysium. In accordance with his model of west as future, the new paradise is located in the afternoon light, and it has no prescribed boundaries, but moves as we walk. It is a home, or it is like a home, for those who have learned to be both homeless and at home everywhere. In order to arrive at the Holy Land and earn the right to be called a saunterer, one must pass through the *sanctum sanctorum* of the swamp, dissolving the boundaries as static limits, and emerge in a new identity that draws vigor from the past, but has a unique new form of its own.

NOTES

*I wish to thank Sharon Cameron for her generous critical guidance throughout the various incarnations of this essay.

1. Henry David Thoreau, *Walden* and *Civil Disobedience*, ed. Owen Thomas (New York: W.W. Norton, 1966), p. 189. All subsequent quotations from *Walden* are from this edition and are followed in the text by the page number.

2. See Walter Benn Michaels, "*Walden*'s False Bottoms," *Glyph*, 1 (1977), 132-49, for a discussion of the same subject in the context of *Walden*'s contradictions. It is an essay to which my own comments on *Walden* are indebted.

3. As early as the publication of "A Winter Walk" (1843), Thoreau is experimenting with the immediacy of language. "A Winter Walk" is couched entirely in the present tense, and it includes its readers in the observations of the essay through the pronoun "we."

4. See in particular Vol. II of the *Journal* (1850-September 15, 1851), in *Thoreau's Writings*, ed. Bradford Torrey (Boston and New York: Houghton Mifflin, 1906), VIII, 18-231.

5. "Walking," in *Thoreau's Writings*, V, 232. All subsequent references are to this edition.

6. Thoreau's ideal paradox—being homeless and at home everywhere—recalls the traditional double sense of utopia: an ideal community that is nowhere (Greek, no place).

7. Henry David Thoreau, *A Week on the Concord and Merrimack Rivers* (New York: Thomas Y. Crowell, 1961), p. 53.

8. Cf. ibid., pp. 231-34; and *The Maine Woods* (New York: Thomas Y. Crowell, 1961), pp. 82-85.

9. This is, of course, a version of *translatio imperii*, the notion that empire can be transferred or translated geographically. See Ernst Robert Curtius, *European Literature and the Latin Middle Ages* (London and Henley: Routledge and Kegan Paul, 1953), p. 29. See also Frank Kermode, *The Classic* (London: Faber and Faber, 1975) for a discussion of the connection between *translatio imperii* and *translatio studii*.

10. All of the poetic quotations in "Walking" are introduced with silence, including Thoreau's own poetry. It is also significant that botanists, geographers and other scientists are quoted throughout "Walking" and are always acknowledged as the authors of their writings.

CONTRIBUTORS

James M. Cox is Professor of English and Avalon Professor of the Humanities at Dartmouth College. He has written many articles on such American authors as Emerson, Hawthorne and Frost. His books include *Mark Tawin: The Fate of Humor.*

Hugh M. Davidson, formerly chairman of the Department of Romance Languages and Literatures at Dartmouth College, is Commonwealth Professor of French Literature at the University of Virginia. He is the author of numerous studies on French 17th-century literature, including *Audience, Words and Art* and *The Origins of Certainty.*

Robert Garapon, now professor at the Sorbonne, helped Lawrence Harvey establish the Dartmouth Foreign Study Program at Caen. He has made many scholarly contributions to the study of French theater from the Middle Ages through the 17th century.

Colette Gaudin is Professor of French at Dartmouth College and former chair of the Department of French and Italian. She has published studies on Gaston Bachelard's poetics and on several French novelists of the 20th century.

Elizabeth D. Harvey is completing her Ph.D. in English and American literature at Johns Hopkins University. She is Lawrence Harvey's daughter.

Judd D. Hubert is Professor of French at the University of California, Irvine. Lawrence Harvey was one of his earliest graduate students. Among his broad-ranging works on French literature are books on Racine and on Baudelaire.

John D. Lyons is Professor of French and Italian and chairman of the Comparative Literature Program at Dartmouth College. His latest book is *The Listening Voice: An Essay on the Rhetoric of Saint-Amant.*

Stephen G. Nichols, Jr., who was a student of Lawrence Harvey, is chair of the Department of French and Italian at Dartmouth College and Professor of Comparative Literature. His most recent books are *Romanesque Signs: Early Medieval Narrative and Iconography* and *Mimesis: From Mirror to Method, Augustine to Descartes,* which he co-edited with John D. Lyons.

Glyn P. Norton, Associate Professor of French at The Pennsylvania State University, taught for several years at Dartmouth College. He is the author of numerous studies of Renaissance literature, especially on Montaigne and on the theory of Humanist translation. He has recently completed a book entitled *The Ideology and Language of Translation in Renaissance France.*

Neal Oxenhandler is Professor of French and Comparative Literature at Dartmouth College. His many books and articles are devoted to theory of criticism, film and modern French literature. In his most recent work he attempts to restore the affective roots of literary criticism.

Richard Regosin, Professor of French at the University of California, Irvine, was both a student of Lawrence Harvey and his colleague at Dartmouth for six years. He is the author of articles and books on French Renaissance literature, including *The Matter of My Book*, a study of Montaigne's essays.

Elias L. Rivers, from South Carolina, taught for ten years at Dartmouth College and is now Professor of Spanish at the State University of New York at Stony Brook. His latest book on aspects of Spanish literature, entitled *Quixotic Scriptures*, is being published by Indiana University Press.

Mario Specchio, Professor of Literature at the University of Urbino, has translated two novels of Hesse and published articles on modern German and Italian literature as well as a book of poems, *A piene mani*. He taught with Lawrence Harvey in Siena and has been Visiting Associate Professor of Italian at Dartmouth College.

Nancy J. Vickers is Associate Professor of French and Italian at Dartmouth College. She is author of articles on Dante, Petrarch and Claudel and the editor of several volumes of literary criticism. She has recently completed a book on woman's body in the poetry and art of the Renaissance.

FRENCH FORUM MONOGRAPHS

1. Karolyn Waterson. *Molière et l'autorité: structures sociales, structures comiques.* 1976.
2. Donna Kuizenga. *Narrative Strategies in* La Princesse de Clèves. 1976.
3. Ian J. Winter. *Montaigne's Self-Portrait and Its Influence in France, 1580-1630.* 1976.
4. Judith G. Miller. *Theater and Revolution in France since 1968.* 1977.
5. Raymond C. La Charité, ed. *O un amy! Essays on Montaigne in Honor of Donald M. Frame.* 1977.
6. Rupert T. Pickens. *The Welsh Knight: Paradoxicality in Chrétien's* Conte del Graal. 1977.
7. Carol Clark. *The Web of Metaphor: Studies in the Imagery of Montaigne's* Essais. 1978.
8. Donald Maddox. *Structure and Sacring: The Systematic Kingdom in Chrétien's* Erec et Enide. 1978.
9. Betty J. Davis. *The Storytellers in Marguerite de Navarre's* Heptaméron. 1978.
10. Laurence M. Porter. *The Renaissance of the Lyric in French Romanticism: Elegy, "Poëme" and Ode.* 1978.
11. Bruce R. Leslie. *Ronsard's Successful Epic Venture: The Epyllion.* 1979.
12. Michelle A. Freeman. *The Poetics of* Translatio Studii *and* Conjointure: *Chrétien de Troyes's* Cligés. 1979.
13. Robert T. Corum, Jr. *Other Worlds and Other Seas: Art and Vision in Saint-Amant's Nature Poetry.* 1979.
14. Marcel Muller. *Préfiguration et structure romanesque dans* A la recherche du temps perdu *(avec un inédit de Marcel Proust).* 1979.
15. Ross Chambers. *Meaning and Meaningfulness: Studies in the Analysis and Interpretation of Texts.* 1979.
16. Lois Oppenheim. *Intentionality and Intersubjectivity: A Phenomenological Study of Butor's* La Modification. 1980.
17. Matilda T. Bruckner. *Narrative Invention in Twelfth-Century French Romance: The Convention of Hospitality (1160-1200).* 1980.
18. Gérard Defaux. *Molière, ou les métamorphoses du comique: de la comédie morale au triomphe de la folie.* 1980.
19. Raymond C. La Charité. *Recreation, Reflection and Re-Creation: Perspectives on Rabelais's* Pantagruel. 1980.
20. Jules Brody. *Du style à la pensée: trois études sur les* Caractères *de La Bruyère.* 1980.
21. Lawrence D. Kritzman. *Destruction/Découverte: le fonctionnement de la rhétorique dans les* Essais *de Montaigne.* 1980.
22. Minnette Grunmann-Gaudet and Robin F. Jones, eds. *The Nature of Medieval Narrative.* 1980.
23. J.A. Hiddleston. *Essai sur Laforgue et les* Derniers Vers *suivi de Laforgue et Baudelaire.* 1980.
24. Michael S. Koppisch. *The Dissolution of Character: Changing Perspectives in La Bruyère's* Caractères. 1981.
25. Hope H. Glidden. *The Storyteller as Humanist: The* Serées *of Guillaume Bouchet.* 1981.
26. Mary B. McKinley. *Words in a Corner: Studies in Montaigne's Latin Quotations.* 1981.

27. Donald M. Frame and Mary B. McKinley, eds. *Columbia Montaigne Conference Papers*. 1981.
28. Jean-Pierre Dens. *L'Honnête Homme et la critique du goût: Esthétique et société au XVIIe siècle*. 1981.
29. Vivian Kogan. *The Flowers of Fiction: Time and Space in Raymond Queneau's Les Fleurs bleues*. 1982.
30. Michael Issacharoff et Jean-Claude Vilquin, éds. *Sartre et la mise en signe*. 1982.
31. James W. Mileham. *The Conspiracy Novel: Structure and Metaphor in Balzac's Comédie humaine*. 1982.
32. Andrew G. Suozzo, Jr. *The Comic Novels of Charles Sorel: A Study of Structure, Characterization and Disguise*. 1982.
33. Margaret Whitford. *Merleau-Ponty's Critique of Sartre's Philosophy*. 1982.
34. Gérard Defaux. *Le Curieux, le glorieux et la sagesse du monde dans la première moitié du XVIe siècle: L'exemple de Panurge (Ulysse, Démosthène, Empédocle)*. 1982.
35. Doranne Fenoaltea. *"Si haulte Architecture." The Design of Scève's Délie*. 1982.
36. Peter Bayley and Dorothy Gabe Coleman, eds. *The Equilibrium of Wit: Essays for Odette de Mourgues*. 1982.
37. Carol J. Murphy. *Alienation and Absence in the Novels of Marguerite Duras*. 1982.
38. Mary Ellen Birkett. *Lamartine and the Poetics of Landscape*. 1982.
39. Jules Brody. *Lectures de Montaigne*. 1982.
40. John D. Lyons. *The Listening Voice: An Essay on the Rhetoric of Saint-Amant*. 1982.
41. Edward C. Knox. *Patterns of Person: Studies in Style and Form from Corneille to Laclos*. 1983.
42. Marshall C. Olds. *Desire Seeking Expression: Mallarmé's "Prose pour des Esseintes."* 1983.
43. Ceri Crossley. *Edgar Quinet (1803-1875): A Study in Romantic Thought*. 1983.
44. Rupert T. Pickens, ed. *The Sower and His Seed: Essays on Chrétien de Troyes*. 1983.
45. Barbara C. Bowen. *Words and the Man in French Renaissance Literature*. 1983.
46. Clifton Cherpack. *Logos in Mythos. Ideas and Early French Narrative*. 1983.
47. Donald Stone, Jr. *Mellin de Saint-Gelais and Literary History*. 1983.
48. Louisa E. Jones. *Sad Clowns and Pale Pierrots: Literature and the Popular Comic Arts In 19th-Century France*. 1984.
49. JoAnn DellaNeva. *Song and Counter-Song: Scève's Délie and Petrarch's Rime*. 1983.
50. John D. Lyons and Nancy J. Vickers, eds. *The Dialectic of Discovery: Essays on the Teaching and Interpretation of Literature Presented to Lawrence E. Harvey*. 1984.

French Forum, Publishers, Inc.
P.O. Box 5108, Lexington, Kentucky 40505

Publishers of *French Forum*, a journal of literary criticism